The **AA** Best Drives
New England

www.theAA.com/travel

Written by Kathy Arnold and Paul Wade
Additional research: Lans Christensen, Gael May McKibben, Tom Arnold and Harlan Levy

Published by AA Publishing, a trading name of Automobile Association Developments
Limited, whose registered office is Fanum House, Basing View, Basingstoke, Hampshire
RG21 4EA. Registered number 1878835.

ISBN-10: 0-7495-5079-1
ISBN-13: 978-0-7495-5079-0

The contents of this publication are believed correct at the time of printing. Nevertheless,
AA Publishing accept no responsibility for errors, omissions or changes in the details
given, or for the consequences of readers' reliance on this information. This does not
affect your statutory rights. Assessments of the attractions, hotels and restaurants
are based upon the authors' own experiences, and contain subjective opinions that may not
reflect the publisher's opinion or a reader's experience. We have tried to ensure accuracy,
but things do change, so please let us know if you have any comments or corrections.

A CIP catalogue record for this book is available from the British Library.

Colour separation: MRM Graphics Ltd
Printed and bound by G. Canale & C. S.P.A., Torino, Italy

Find out more about AA Publishing and the wide range of travel publications and services
the AA provides by visiting our website at www.theAA.com/travel

First published 1997
Reprinted and updated 1999; Reprinted 1999
Revised second edition 2001
Reprinted 2003. Information verified and updated
Reprinted December 2003
Revised fourth edition 2005
Revised fifth edition 2007

Cover credits: AA WORLD TRAVEL LIBRARY/C Coe f/cover, b/cover (top), b/cover
(centre top), b/cover (centre bottom), b/cover (bottom)

A02697
Atlas mapping in this title produced from map data supplied by
Global Mapping, Brackley, UK. © Global Mapping

CONTENTS

ABOUT THIS BOOK

This book is not only a practical touring guide for the independent traveler, but is also invaluable for those who would like to know more about New England.

It is divided into the 6 states, each with its own city and driving tours. The driving tours start and finish in those cities considered to be the most interesting centers for exploration.

There are special features on Boston and the American Revolution, the beauty of the fall, and the rich heritage of the arts and the surrounding seas.

Each tour has details of the most interesting places to visit en route. Boxes catering to special interests follow some of the main entries – for those whose interest is in history, or walking, or those who have children. There are also boxes which highlight scenic stretches of road and which give details of special events, crafts and customs.

The simple route directions are accompanied by an easy-to-use map at the beginning of each tour, along with a chart showing how far it is from one town to the next in miles and kilometers. This can help you to decide where to take a break and stop overnight. (All distances quoted are approximate.)

Before setting off, it is advisable to check with the information center listed at the start of the tour for recommendations on where to break your journey, and for additional information on what to see and do, and when best to visit.

Torrington, Connecticut

ATMs (cash machines) are plentiful.

Currency
The American unit of currency is the dollar, consisting of 100 cents. Bills are mainly green, are the same size and have similar appearance, so be careful, though the $10, $20 and $50 have been redesigned. They range from one to 2, 5, 10, 20, 50 and 100 dollars. Coins are in denominations of 1 cent, (penny), 5 cents (nickel), 10 cents (dime), 25 cents (quarter) and – rarely – a silver dollar.

Tour Information
See pages 167–76 for addresses, telephone numbers, websites and opening times of attractions plus telephone numbers and websites of tourist offices.

Accommodations and restaurants
See pages 161–6 for a list of recommended hotels and restaurants for each tour.

Motoring
For information on aspects of motoring in New England see pages 159–60.

INFORMATION FOR NON-U.S. RESIDENTS
Banks
Banks set their own hours, opening at 9 and closing between 3 and 5 on weekdays. Some open on Saturdays.

Although foreign currency can be changed at big hotels or airports, U.S. dollar travelers' checks are recommended as they are accepted as cash everywhere from restaurants to gas stations.

Credit Cards
Major credit cards are accepted in New England. However, many small bed-and-breakfasts will accept only cash or travelers' checks.

Customs Regulations
Non-U.S. residents may take in, duty-free, one carton of cigarettes, a liter of alcohol and $100 worth of gifts. Customs officials are very strict about banning any fresh meat, fruit, plants and, of course, drugs (unless on prescription). Check for updates to regulations before traveling.

Electricity
Standard voltage is 110–120V, 60 cycles AC, using flat two-pin plugs. Bring the right adaptor.

Emergency Telephone Numbers
If you have an emergency, telephone 911 to be put in touch with

the right service. Otherwise, dial "0" and consult the operator.

Entry Regulations

Citizens of most European countries, plus Japan and New Zealand, do not need visas if they are visiting the U.S. on holiday, the stay will not exceed 90 days and they have a return or onward ticket.

However, requirements for travel to the US can change, so check the current situation with your tour operator or travel agent, as well as such official websites as www.travel.state.gov and www. dhs.gov. Some of the newer requirements relate to machine readable passports and being able to provide information such as the full address of your destination, where you will spend the first night in the US.

Health Matters

It is essential to have adequate health insurance before traveling to the U.S. While hospitals are usually excellent, treatment can be expensive. It may be delayed or refused without proof of proper insurance. Your hotel will be able to recommend a doctor or hospital. Alternatively, call the local hospital. No special inoculations are required.

See also Health Services on page 159.

Holidays

See page 159.

Post Offices

Stamps for postcards and letters are on sale in many stores and hotels; for larger packages, go to a post office. It is cheaper to send postcards and aerograms than letters. See also page 160.

Telephones

Each state has several area codes, with new ones opening up all the time as telecommunications expand.

Pay phones require 5, 10 and 25 cent coins, so use a telephone card for convenience. To call abroad, dial 011, then the country code:

Australia 61
Canada 1
New Zealand 64
Republic of Ireland 353
U.K. 44

Time differences

New England is on Eastern Standard Time (EST), 5 hours behind the U.K., 6 hours behind mainland Europe, and 15 hours behind Sydney, Australia.

Daylight Saving Time alters the time by one hour from March or April to October or November.

Travelers Aid Society

The Travelers Aid Society, 17 East Street, Boston, Massachusetts 02111 (tel: 617/542-7286), is dedicated to helping travelers. Staff provide crisis intervention, counseling, referrals to community sources, and emergency financial assistance to travelers in crisis.

Useful Addresses

As well as the listings on pages 161–6, these agencies and associations have a selection of places to stay:
Select Registry, Distinguished Inns of North America (tel: 800/344-5244; www.SelectRegistry.com);
Bed and Breakfast Agency of Boston, 47 Commercial Wharf, Boston, MA 02110. Tel: (in U.K.) 0800 895128 (in U.S.A. and Canada) 800/248-9262; www. boston-bnbagency.com.

Lobster boat at rest in Maine

MASSACHUSETTS

After 385 years of permanent European settlement, Massachusetts has acquired a "little history." Here, the Pilgrims landed and built their communities. A century and a half later, patriotic passion exploded in a series of events culminating in the American Revolution. Not surprisingly, that heritage has been preserved. Conservation has encompassed old houses and bridges, churches and farms, even entire villages.

Massachusetts is known as the Bay State because of the gaping Atlantic gulf enclosed by the flexed arm of Cape Cod. The shape of the state ensures a variety of landscapes. It stretches from the storm-tossed Atlantic to the rolling, wooded hills of the Berkshires, with the rich meadows of the Connecticut River Valley in between.

The seasons are distinct: crisp, clear winter days melting into an explosion of spring greenery and flowers, followed by muggy, soporific summers and, finally, the fall with its dazzling multicolored leaves (see pages 102–3).

Massachusetts, especially around Boston, was also America's cultural cradle (see pages 56–7). Artists and writers, poets and musicians have long been drawn together by the web of academia. Harvard University, founded in 1636, is the oldest American institute of higher learning, but there are numerous other colleges to be found throughout the state, as well as boarding schools (called "prep schools" because they prepare students for college).

Concord is a beautiful town with a rich and varied history

Outdoor festivals of music and drama are a bonus for visitors during the summer months.

But the region's focus always returns to history. Many of America's most treasured icons are here, from Plymouth Rock to Boston's Old North Church and Concord's historic bridge. Thanksgiving is celebrated with justifiable pride; after all, the tradition of eating turkey and pumpkin pie was "invented" here. They even have the cranberry bogs nearby to provide the accompanying sauce.

Tour 1

"Listen, my children, and you shall hear,
Of the midnight ride of Paul Revere ..."

Paul Revere is one of the best-known messengers in history, thanks to Henry Wadsworth Longfellow's poem. His ride from Boston to warn the Americans that the British were on the march has become legendary. The patriots assembled and took on the trained soldiers, first in Lexington and then in Concord. All the British wanted to do was capture the rebels' arms cache; they had no idea that the skirmishes of April 19, 1775 would spark the American Revolution. In both towns, historic sites have been preserved, while the visitor information centers provide details of "who did what and when." The route for this tour also has a literary focus. In the 19th century, Concord was the home of some of the best-known writers of the day: Henry David Thoreau, Louisa May Alcott, Nathaniel Hawthorne and Ralph Waldo Emerson.

Tour 2

Although Cape Cod has long been recognized as a playground for Bostonians, the North Shore, with its rugged, rocky outcrops is also a popular place to relax by the sea. Add to that atmospheric fishing villages and the gruesome history of witches in Salem, and this drive is fun as well as scenic. The sparkling light has long attracted artists, especially in Rockport. Castles and underwater rocks, whales, frozen peas and even clam chowder are threads in the rich tapestry of America's history which unravels along this shoreline drive.

Tour 3

Cape Cod enjoys a mystique matched by few holiday destinations. The names of its 300-year-old villages are reminders of English fishing ports, its history peopled with Native Americans and fishermen, whalers and sea captains. On Cape Cod Bay, the

Chatham Light, Cape Cod. Lighthouses are an important part of New England's heritage

sands are sheltered and the water is warmer than on the Atlantic Ocean shore, where strong waves buffet the dunes of the Cape Cod National Seashore.

This 40-mile (60km) coastline stretches from the elbow of the peninsula up to Provincetown, known for its bohemian lifestyle. The popularity of the Cape has taken its toll: roadside development sprawls around Hyannis on the south shore and traffic can be bumper to bumper on summer weekends. Off season, it is easier to get away from it all, and find what aficionados call "the old Cape Cod."

Tour 4

Western Massachusetts has an intriguing mixture of the rural and sophisticated, the historic and eccentric. The rolling Berkshire Hills inspired authors such as Herman Melville and Edith Wharton, and attracted millionaires, who built vacation homes away from the seaside. Now the hills resound to summer festivals of music and theater. Attractive towns and villages range from Deerfield, with its perfectly preserved 18th-century houses, to Williamstown with its excellent college and astonishing art collection. Stockbridge thrives on its "traditional America" image, ably reinforced by *Saturday Evening Post* cover artist Norman Rockwell, whose paintings are on display here. Drive down lazy back roads to old covered bridges arching over rocky streams; there are surprises around every corner.

BIRTHPLACE OF A NATION

The American perspective of the War of Independence is simple: the Colonists were oppressed by King George III and Parliament and justifiably rebelled. The issues were a little more complex. In the early days, there were no "states" as such. The Colonies differed in population and style of government: some depended on fishing and trade, others on farming and tobacco. Although links with the Mother Country were strong for economic and cultural reasons, the Colonists had become increasingly independent-minded during the century-and-a-half since the first settlers arrived.

Native Americans, boarded the newly arrived HMS *Dartmouth*. Its cargo of 300 chests of tea was thrown overboard. In response, General Gage and four British regiments were sent to Boston, and the port was closed down in 1774.

Below: the Boston Massacre, in which five Colonists died

A turning point in American history was the defeat of the French and the Native Americans in the war from 1756 to 1763. This gave the New Englanders, and the colonies along the coast to the south, a vision of vast lands stretching westward and a sense of "new" country to be developed. Relations with Britain, however, became strained when Parliament decided that the colonies should help pay for the seven years of war; after all, the English reasoned, they were defending Colonial lands. Moreover, a 10,000-strong army was still needed to protect the Colonies. A monopoly on trade was proclaimed, restricting Colonists to dealing only with Britain and other British possessions (notably the West Indies). Further, a ban was issued on new settlements west of the Appalachians.

Although these restrictions rankled, what inflamed Colonial passions was direct taxation. Traditionally, Britain had raised money by customs duties on shipping; the Stamp Act in 1765 set a new precedent. This placed a charge on all contracts, deeds, newspapers and legal documents. Protests forced its repeal within a year, but other revenue-raisers followed, only to be repealed. Parliament decided to stand firm on one, however. That was the tax on tea.

After the French and Indian War, economic times were hard for the Colonists, and the new rules hurt financially. But the

Colonists also protested on principle. "No taxation without representation" was the cry at public meetings and in pamphlets. Articles questioned the legality of such taxes, claiming that they infringed the charters of some of the Colonies.

Boston was an important focus of militant feelings, which periodically exploded into riots. One relatively minor event, on March 5, 1770, became a legend. A lone British sentry on duty at the Custom House was harassed by a crowd. Reinforcements arrived, but the mob continued to bait the soldiers, heckling them and throwing stones. Shots were fired; five Colonists died. This incident became known as the "Boston Massacre" and was used by leaders such as Samuel Adams to whip up emotions.

Three years later, in December, came one of the most colorful incidents of the era, the Boston Tea Party. As a protest against the tax of 3 pence per pound on tea, about 100 men, disguised as

Bottom: the "Sons of Liberty," disguised as Mohawks, throw East India Company tea into the water

The scene was set for the smoldering coals of resentment to be ignited. In April, 1775, it was reported to General Gage that farmers in Concord, a small village west of Boston, were stockpiling firearms. He ordered 700 British troops to march out, confiscate and destroy the Patriots' illegal cache. On route, they skirmished with the Minute Men (locals who could be ready "in a minute" to fight) in Lexington before being outnumbered in Concord. Instead of withdrawing in an orderly manner, the British confronted the militiamen, lost three soldiers and had to beat a hasty, undignified retreat to Boston.

cost was hundreds of lives. The psychological victory belonged to the Americans. King George III replied savagely by declaring the Colonies to be in rebellion. Mercenaries were hired in Europe and transported across the Atlantic to augment the troops.

Not all the Colonists were ready for war. About one-third remained loyal to the crown and another third were neutral. The rest, however, were vociferous and demanded to sever links with the Mother Country. Further British attacks on Falmouth (now Portland, Maine) in October, 1775 and on Norfolk, Virginia in January, 1776, only

Boston, never to return. Fighting, however, continued elsewhere. In May, representatives of all 13 Colonies met in Philadelphia, Pennsylvania. Freedom was the agenda of this Continental Congress. A short document drafted by Thomas Jefferson of Virginia set out the grievances and proclaimed that "these united colonies are, and of right ought to be, free and independent states." This was the Declaration of Independence, accepted unanimously by the delegates and signed on July 4, 1776.

Liberty did not come immediately, however. War raged for five years and even after the

Some 20,000 Minute Men rushed to Boston, penning the British forces in. In May, 1775, artillery powder and ammunition captured at Fort Ticonderoga in New York State was hauled overland by the Colonists and used to capture Bunker Hill. Although the Redcoats soon stormed and recaptured it, the

served to fan the fury. *Common Sense*, a pamphlet written by Thomas Paine, became a best seller, with 120,000 copies sold in January, 1776 alone. Although he was an Englishman who had lived in the Colonies for only a year, he argued strenuously for independence. In March, 1776, the British withdrew from

The citizens of Lexington reenact the events of April 19, 1775

formal British surrender in 1781, London refused to recognize the Colonies' independence. Finally, in September, 1783, a peace treaty was signed in Paris, acknowledging that a new nation had been born.

Lexington
& Concord

Concord and Lexington are two of the most famous towns in the United States, due to the skirmishes between locals and British soldiers in 1775 that triggered the American Revolution. Concord has an additional claim to fame: it was home to some of the great writers of 19th-century America. Today, Lexington feels like a residential suburb of Boston, while Concord has retained more of its historical flavor. The main themes of this route are liberty and literature, but at the end, the focus is strictly contemporary.

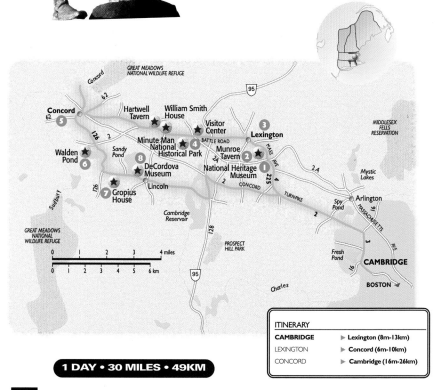

1 DAY • 30 MILES • 49KM

ITINERARY	
CAMBRIDGE	▶ **Lexington (8m-13km)**
LEXINGTON	▶ **Concord (6m-10km)**
CONCORD	▶ **Cambridge (16m-26km)**

i *Cambridge Visitor Information Booth, Harvard Square*

▶ *From Cambridge, take the Fresh Pond Parkway (Routes 16 and 3) to Route 2 west. Take this for 3 miles (5km) and then exit onto Routes 4 and 225. At the first stop sign, turn left onto Massachusetts Avenue (always known as "Mass Ave"). This was the route taken by Paul Revere on his way to Lexington. At the junction with the 2A, turn left onto 2A West to reach the National Heritage Museum.*

❶ National Heritage Museum

This bright and airy museum provides a useful background to the rest of the tour. As well as regular new exhibitions, a long-term display explores the background to the events that "sowed the seeds of liberty," including the notorious Stamp Act of 1765 – a major trigger of unrest in the Colonies. The museum's Heritage Shop has a wide range of American history books, plus cultural souvenirs.

▶ *Return to the Massachusetts Avenue junction and turn left to reach Munroe Tavern.*

❷ Munroe Tavern

On the afternoon of April 19, 1775, this fine old pub (1695) was the site of the temporary hospital and headquarters for British soldiers retreating from the battle at Concord. Fourteen years later, George Washington dined here in an upstairs room, while on tour in New England. Today it is the headquarters of the Lexington Historical Society.

▶ *Follow Massachusetts Avenue for about a mile (1.5km), straight into Lexington to the triangular green.*

❸ Lexington

This cradle of the American Revolution is dotted with significant sites, not least of which is Battle Green. Here, a bronze statue of Captain John Parker stands on a stone cairn, facing the line of the British approach. Behind him the Lexington militia would have stood. "Ye villains, ye rebels, disperse!" ordered the arrogant Major John Pitcairn. Faced by the superior numbers and strength of the

Headquarters of the Lexington Minute Men, 1775

British, Parker wisely told his men: "Don't fire unless fired upon, but if they mean to have a war, let it begin here!"

A shot rang out, no-one knows from where. Suddenly fire was exchanged; two British soldiers and eight Minute Men were killed or wounded. Seven of them are buried under the Revolutionary Monument farther along on the Green. The British, having beaten off this minor attack, marched on toward Concord.

In the nearby Visitor Center there is a diorama giving an overview of the events of that day. Next door to it is Buckman Tavern, a handsome three-story tavern (1710) where, in the early hours of April 19, 1775, several Lexington Minute Men had gathered to drink ale. Around 4am came the news that 700 British troops were just minutes from the Green. Bells rang out, drums rolled and the Minute Men, under the command of

Captain John Parker, filed out of the tavern. As the sun rose, they assembled on the Green, more as a protest than looking for a fight. The Tavern looks exactly as it did in 1775, with bar orders chalked on the tap room wall. The front door has a hole in it, allegedly from a bullet shot during the encounter.

From here go to the right of the Green and turn right on Hancock Street. Number 36 is the Hancock-Clarke House, where, at around 1am on April 19, 1775, John Hancock and Samuel Adams were awakened by a knock on the door. Paul Revere had arrived to warn these two important leaders that the British were on the march. This 1698 house is furnished as it would have been on that night. You can see Major Pitcairn's

The Old North Bridge, Concord

pistols (see previous page) and a drum belonging to Minute Man William Drummond.

[i] *1875 Massachusetts Avenue or Battle Green*

▶ *At the Minute Man statue, bear left (on Massachusetts Avenue) and follow the sign "West on 4/225." At the stoplight, turn right on 2A West, which takes you into the Minute Man National Historical Park.*

4 Minute Man National Historical Park
Although the actual road followed by the British troops has been largely covered over by Route 2A, a small section has been preserved in the Minute Man National Historical Park. About a half mile (800m) beyond the Visitor Center is the

site where Paul Revere was captured by a British patrol. His fellow messenger, Dr. Samuel Prescott, eluded them and rode on to Concord. In another half mile (800m), a narrow winding section of the original Battle Road bears off to the right. This is a typical "two rod road," named because of the 32-foot (10m) distance between the stone walls on either side of the road (a rod measures 16 feet/ 5m). Here, the William Smith House and the Ephraim Hartwell Tavern all reflect the style of architecture and the methods of construction used in the buildings of Colonial Massachusetts.

i   *Minute Man Visitor Center, Route 2A, Lexington*

▶   *Continue on **Route 2A**, and at the Battle Road and **Route 2A** split, bear right for Concord.*

5 Concord
Concord was founded in 1635, and is redolent with history, from its historic houses (many with date plaques) to its reminders of the Revolution, to its fine literary heritage.

The approach to the center of Concord is along Lexington Road, where two historic properties were once the homes of famous writers. The Wayside, with its distinctive red brick chimneys, was originally the home of the muster master, whose job was to summon the Minute Men if the British attacked. In the 19th century, it became first the residence of the Alcott family, then in 1852, Nathaniel Hawthorne bought it and changed the name from Hillside to The Wayside. He completed *Tanglewood Tales* in his study in the tower at the top of the house.

A little way farther up the street is Orchard House, to which the Alcott family moved after leaving The Wayside. It was here that Louisa May wrote much of *Little Women*. Researchers for the 1992 movie of the book took photographs

and made sketches here, then built a house in Canada especially for the filming. It was not an exact replica, however, and those taking the guided tour may notice a number of differences, particularly in the bedrooms. Carefully preserved furnishings and costumes reflect the family's 20 years here.

Closer to the town center, make a left onto the Cambridge Turnpike for the Concord Museum. This is a fine example of a small museum, and it

Orchard House, the home of novelist Louisa May Alcott

encompasses all aspects of Concord's history in a particularly engaging way. Relics of the Revolution include Paul Revere's signal lantern and the sword that belonged to Colonel Barrett, commander of the Concord militia. Literary mementos include Louisa May Alcott's tea kettle and doll, Henry David Thoreau's bed, writing desk and rocking chair from his cabin at Walden Pond (see below), and Ralph Waldo Emerson's study, brought from his former home across the street and reconstructed here.

When Emerson's original house was destroyed by fire in 1872, the philosopher-poet's reaction was unusual, to say the least: "But isn't it a lovely blaze!" was all he said. Sent away to recover from the shock, he returned after a year to find that his home had been rebuilt by his friends and neighbors. Emerson's life here was characterized by "plain living and high thinking" but he is less remembered for his essays than for quotes such as, "If a man can write a better book, preach a better sermon, or make a better mousetrap than his neighbor, though he builds his house in the woods, the world will beat a path to his door." The reconstructed house is exactly as he left it – except for the study, of course.

Off Concord's Green, along Route 62 East, is Sleepy Hollow Cemetery, every bit as peaceful as it sounds. Here, on top of "Author's Ridge," are the last resting places of Louisa May Alcott, Ralph Waldo Emerson and Nathaniel Hawthorne. The grave of Henry David Thoreau is marked by a simple headstone, inscribed with only one word: "Henry."

The most famous site in Concord is undoubtedly the Old North Bridge on Liberty Street, the "rude bridge" where, on April 19, 1775, "... the embattled farmers stood, And fired the shot heard round the world." These words are from the *Concord Hymn*, written by Emerson in 1837 to celebrate the completion of the Battle Monument. One of the most powerful American icons, it was sculpted by Daniel Chester French, who also created the figure of Abraham Lincoln for the Lincoln Memorial in Washington D.C.

On the day of the battle, some 400 Minute Men were waiting here to confront the 700 tired and worried British

Regulars. As they advanced across the bridge, the famous shot rang out. The sloping fields would have looked much as they do now, though the bridge is a modern replica. Across the river, at the edge of an open field, stands the Old Manse. It was from a window of this three-story wooden house that the parson, William Emerson, watched the bloody events. He was the grandfather of Ralph Waldo Emerson, who lived here as a little boy. In later years the house was rented to Nathaniel Hawthorne, and some of his possessions are still there, including his writing desk.

☐ *Concord Visitor Center, 58 Main Street; North Bridge Visitor Center, 174 Liberty Street*

▶ *Leave Concord following the sign for Route 2A, from the Green. After a short distance, turn right on Heywood Street, then left on Walden Street (Route 126). Continue for 1 mile (1.5km), crossing Route 2, to the Walden Pond parking lot.*

6 Walden Pond
Henry Thoreau came here and "lived alone, in the woods, a mile from any neighbor, in a house I had built myself, on the shore of Walden Pond." This two-year "back to nature" experience was the basis of his most famous work, *Walden*, published in 1854.

Seeking the solitude that he found may be difficult in summer, when families swim and picnic at "this pond ... so remarkable for its depth and purity ... a clear and deep well, half a mile long and a mile and three quarters in circumference ..." A replica of his cabin is conveniently close to the parking lot; to avoid the crowds, walk around to the far side of the water, where a cairn marks the site of the real cabin. The pond is surrounded by the 400-acre (160-hectare) Walden Pond State Reservation.

▶ *Follow Route 126 south for a short distance to Baker Bridge Road and turn left. At No. 68 is the Gropius House.*

7 Gropius House
This is the home of the German architect Walter Gropius, founder of the Bauhaus Movement, who moved to the U.S. in 1937 and lectured at Harvard for 14 years. The house was far ahead of its time, combining traditional architecture with the innovative use of modern materials, such as welded steel, glass blocks, and chrome. The house looks lived in: Coats hang in the hall, towels in the bathroom.

▶ *Continue to the end of the road and turn right onto Sandy Pond Road. On the left is the DeCordova Museum.*

8 DeCordova Museum
Dedicated to the work of contemporary American artists, this museum is located in 35

The Old North Bridge, actually a modern replica

Lexington & Concord

SPECIAL TO...

Around 1845, Concord was the literary epicenter of America, with four of the country's most revered writers living near one another. Ralph Waldo Emerson (1803–82) was a philosopher, poet and magnetic speaker. Today, he is best remembered for the *Concord Hymn*, encapsulating the events of the Old North Bridge (see page 14).

In 1837, he struck up a friendship with Henry Thoreau (1817–62). Thoreau came to live in Concord and spent two years in a small cabin that he constructed himself at the edge of Walden Pond. It was here that he wrote his most memorable book, *Walden*. The Salem-born novelist Nathaniel Hawthorne (1805–64), a Concord resident for a few years, was also part of the group. At that time, though Louisa May Alcott (1832–88) was just a child, she was already writing poems and romantic stories.

acres (14 hectares) of open fields and woods overlooking Sandy Pond. Around 80 sculptures are displayed outside in natural settings. The museum store sells original works of art.

▶ *Return to Sandy Pond Road, turn left and drive to the first*

RECOMMENDED TRIPS

Canoes can be rented at the South Bridge Boathouse (on Main Street, Concord) for trips through Concord and the Great Meadows National Wildlife Refuge.

Although there are 18 miles (29km) of navigable water, the paddle to the North Bridge and back is an easy two hours and is an excellent way to see parts of the town that haven't changed significantly since the Revolution.

If paddling is not your style, you can take the marked nature trail (3 miles/5km) in the wildlife refuge.

intersection. Cross Lincoln Road, and continue on Trapelo Road for 2½ miles (4km) to **Route 128**. *Go north on* **Route 128** *to* **Route 2** *east, the first exit, and return to Cambridge.*

FOR HISTORY BUFFS

"March with the Corps of Grenadiers and Light Infantry ... to Concord, where you will seize and destroy all Artillery, Ammunition, Provisions, Tents, Small Arms, and all Military Stores ... but you will take care that the Soldiers do not plunder the Inhabitants, or hurt private property."

Unfortunately the orders of General Gage were leaked to patriots in Boston and, as the British prepared to cross the Charles River on the night of April 18, two lanterns appeared in the belfry of the Old North Church. A waiting Paul Revere saw the signal and set off on horseback to tell the men of Lexington and Concord to be ready.

The North
Shore

One famous seaport after another follows the curve of the coast north of Boston, from the towns of Gloucester and Marblehead, to Salem and Newburyport. There are hundreds of handsome old houses, and dozens of high-quality museums and art galleries.

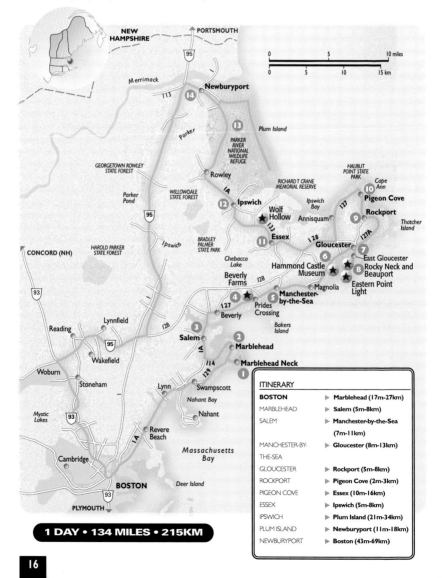

ITINERARY

BOSTON	▶ **Marblehead (17m-27km)**
MARBLEHEAD	▶ **Salem (5m-8km)**
SALEM	▶ **Manchester-by-the-Sea (7m-11km)**
MANCHESTER-BY-THE-SEA	▶ **Gloucester (8m-13km)**
GLOUCESTER	▶ **Rockport (5m-8km)**
ROCKPORT	▶ **Pigeon Cove (2m-3km)**
PIGEON COVE	▶ **Essex (10m-16km)**
ESSEX	▶ **Ipswich (5m-8km)**
IPSWICH	▶ **Plum Island (21m-34km)**
PLUM ISLAND	▶ **Newburyport (11m-18km)**
NEWBURYPORT	▶ **Boston (43m-69km)**

1 DAY • 134 MILES • 215KM

Salem Custom House where
Nathaniel Hawthorne worked

i *Boston Common Visitor
Information Center, 147 Tremont
Street*

▶ *Leave Boston via the Callahan
Tunnel, and follow* **Route 1A** *to
Lynn. After 8 miles (13km),
pass a rotary (roundabout),
and bear right onto Carroll
Parkway. Follow* **Route 129**
*along the sea wall to
Swampscott, and bear right
onto Puritan Road for 1 mile
(1.5km) until it rejoins* **Route
129**. *Go right on* **Route 129** *to
Ocean Avenue and turn right
to Marblehead Neck.*

① Marblehead Neck
On the road across the causeway,
look right for a view of the
Boston skyline. To the left, a
fleet of sailboats sits anchored in
Marblehead harbor. Bear right
and follow signs for the Bike
Route for about 2 miles (3km) to
Chandler Hovey Park and the
lighthouse.

From the park there are spectacular views all the way to
Manchester and Gloucester
harbors. Marblehead Neck itself
is all quiet residential streets.

▶ *Return to* **Route 129** *and turn
right to Marblehead.*

② Marblehead
The up-hill-and-down-dale style
of Marblehead's old town
reflects the West of England
origins of the fishermen who
settled here in 1629. On Front
Street, the oldest houses cluster
round the harbor of what was
soon known as the "greatest
Towne for fishing in New
England."

As overseas trade developed,
merchants built bigger and
better houses, such as the 1768
Jeremiah Lee Mansion. A few
steps away is the Marblehead

Museum and Historical Society.
Marblehead sailors played a vital
role in the Revolution, and a
local boat, the *Hannah*, takes
pride in being America's first
warship. Today luxury yachts fill
the moorings.

i *Information Booth, Pleasant and
Spring streets*

▶ *Leave Marblehead on* **Route
114**, *then join* **Route 1A North**
*and drive 5 miles (8km) to
Salem.*

③ Salem
One short period of hysteria in
the 17th century singled Salem
out from the rest of the North
Shore coastal ports. Now, more
than 300 years later, witchcraft
trials and executions have
become big business.

Those wanting to relive the
gruesome spectacles can visit
the Witch Museum, Witch
Village and Witch House, but
there is much more to see in this
historic town. The fine mansions
were so impressive that future-
president John Adams wrote in
1766: "the houses are the most
elegant and grand that I have
seen in any of the maritime
towns." Examples can be found
on Chestnut, Essex and Federal
streets.

Statue of Puritan Roger Conant, who founded Salem in 1626, outside the Salem Witch Museum

The Peabody Essex Museum, arguably America's oldest museum, is also one of New England's largest. It was started in 1799 by a group of sea captains wishing to display their souvenirs from far-flung voyages. The richest and most impressive section is the Asian Export Art Collection which contains beautiful oriental objects that were made specifically for sale to the West. Don't miss the Native American collection, with its contemporary and historic works, and the Oceanic collection, whose 20,000 pieces date back to the museum's founding.

The town's nautical traditions are portrayed in the admirable Salem Maritime National Historic Site that snakes along the harborfront.

i New Liberty and Essex streets

FOR HISTORY BUFFS

Salem comes from the Hebrew word *Shalom*, meaning peace. But the calm of Salem was shattered in 1692 when several young girls began to have fits and accused three women of casting spells on them. Panic followed, other accusations were made, and before common sense prevailed, 19 people had been hanged, and one man, Giles Corey, was crushed by rocks. The hysteria was stamped out the following year, when the governor ordered all the "witches" to be released from prison, probably because his wife had been one of the accused!

▶ Take **Route 1A North** across the bridge over Beverly Harbor, and follow **Route 127** through Beverly for 4 miles (6km) to the Prides Crossing railroad station.

4 Prides Crossing
When the railroad from Beverly was extended to Manchester in 1840, it crossed land once owned by the Pride family, who supposedly received the grant in the early 1700s from the King of England. The route was used by wealthy Bostonians who left the city and came out to spend the summers by the water in their large mansions. The railroad depot still has separate benches marked for use by Democrats and Republicans. Residents of this small village still commute to Boston's North Station. It's a 45-minute ride.

▶ Continue on **Route 127** for 3 miles (5km) into the center of Manchester-by-the-Sea.

5 Manchester-by-the-Sea
Originally settled by Englishmen from Manchester, the town's name was amended in 1990 to emphasize its position at the head of a pretty harbor, graced with its flotilla of sailboats. On one side of the town square is First Parish Church, built in 1807, with a clock face on each side of its distinctive steeple. Visitors come in summer, not just to walk along the waterfront, but also to spend the day on Singing Beach, where the wind "sings" as it whistles along the sand.

▶ Continue on **Route 127** for 3 miles (5km), then bear right for Magnolia. Continue through the town center and up the hill on Norman Avenue to Hammond Castle.

⑥ Hammond Castle Museum

Whenever you use a remote control button to switch television channels or open the garage from your car, the man to thank is Dr. John Hammond (1888–1965). This genius thought up over 800 inventions and was granted 400 patents, mainly to do with electronics. His quirky mind is reflected in the clifftop mansion he built in 1926, which incorporates bits of European buildings: there is an archway built with lava rock from Mount Vesuvius, and a Roman bath. There are even secret passages and a laboratory. Hammond is buried on the grounds with two of his cats and, as requested, poison ivy grows over his grave.

▶ Return to **Route 127** and continue for 2 miles (3km) to Gloucester.

⑦ Gloucester

The first landmark in town to meet your eye is *The Man at the Wheel*, the statue of a ship's pilot staring out toward the mouth of the harbor. The statue was set in place in 1923 to commemorate Gloucester's 300th birthday, and as a reminder that the town continues to be a working port, America's oldest. Learn more at the Gloucester Maritime Heritage Center.

The loss of the *Andrea Gail* in the early 1990s was the inspiration for the book *The Perfect Storm*. Now, visitors come to see where the movie (2000) was shot, as well as for whale-watching excursions and the annual

FOR CHILDREN

At the Gloucester Maritime Heritage Center, kids can handle sea stars, sea urchins, crabs and sand dollars in the touch tanks of the aquarium. They can also explore the reconstructed pilothouse of a 1936 Gloucester fishing vessel and listen to the voices of the family who fished her for more than 50 years. Using touch screen computer stations, children can learn about whales and shipwrecks.

The pier at Gloucester
Inset: *The Man at the Wheel*

Schooner Festival in early September. The Cape Ann Historical Museum is a tribute to artist Fitz Hugh Lane, who lived out his life here and specialized in seascapes.

ℹ *Stage Fort Park Information Center, Hough Avenue (seasonal) and 33 Commercial Street (year-round)*

SPECIAL TO...

There really was a Cap'n Birdseye. As early as 1912, Clarence Birdseye of Gloucester was intrigued to see how the Inuit people of Labrador preserved their food by freezing it. By 1924, he had perfected the bulk deep-freezing technique that is taken for granted today. The Freezing Company concentrated on fruit and vegetables in the early days, but as demand for his products grew, Birdseye needed to speed up the process, so he invented the multiple plate freezer, which is still used. In the 1950s, the company developed fish sticks, or fish fingers, a great favorite with children.

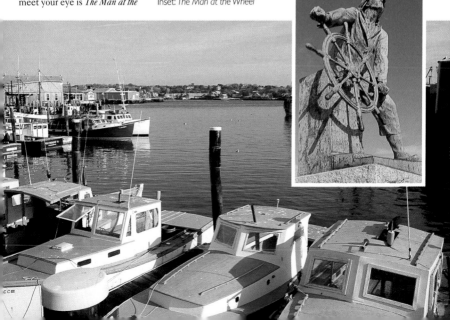

WHALE WATCHING...

Up and down the coast of New England, boats still set off to hunt for whales. Unlike the 19th century, however, the purpose is not to shoot the majestic mammals with harpoons, but with cameras. Tours depart regularly from Boston, but they also leave from Salem and Gloucester on the North Shore, from Portsmouth, New Hampshire and from Cape Cod towns such as Provincetown. The favorite places for spotting whales are the Stellwagen Bank and Jeffreys Ledge, both popular feeding grounds. Harbor porpoises and Atlantic white-sided dolphins, relatives of the whales, are also abundant, and have teeth rather than the baleen plates of the whales.

RIGHT WHALES
Named by Yankee whalers, because they were the "right" whales to catch, this is the most endangered species in the world. The whales are easily recognized by the callosities, crusty growths, on their backs. Reaching up to 50 feet and 60 tons (16m and 61,000kg), they can be spotted offshore from April through January.

HUMPBACK WHALES
The name comes from their habit of arching their backs before diving. They are also known to "breach," leaping clear out of the water, a particularly impressive sight, since humpbacks grow up to 50 feet (16m) long and 30 tons (30,500kg) in weight. They are resident off New England from spring through fall.

FIN WHALES
The largest whales in New England waters are also the most common. Reaching 70 feet (21m) in length and 50 tons (51,000kg), fin whales can be identified by their dorsal fin, as well as the white chevron on their backs. Like the humpbacks, they are resident from spring through fall.

SPECIAL TO...

The third weekend in May is Motif No. 1 Day in Rockport. It celebrates an old fishing shack, dating from the mid-1800s, that stands at the end of Bradley Wharf in Rockport Harbor. Local lore has it that, back in the 1920s, art teacher Lester Hornby was confronted by yet another student's sketch of this dark red hut, festooned with lobster traps and colorful lobster floats. "What? Motif number one again!" he exclaimed despairingly to the pupil. Would-be photographers and painters should walk to the end of the wharf to compose their own version of this picturesque icon.

▶ *Follow* **Route 127** *for 1 mile (1.5km), then bear right onto East Main Street for Rocky Neck.*

8 Rocky Neck and Beauport
Rocky Neck is a small settlement of working artists. The oldest such colony in the country, it has survived here since 1916. Some 30 people live on the tiny peninsula, with their studios in wood-shingled shacks. The roads are all one-way, narrow, and busy on weekends.

Farther toward Eastern Point lighthouse is Beauport. From the turn of the century, big spenders such as R. T. Vanderbilt and J. D. Rockefeller, as well as such stars as Joan Crawford, came out here to consult Henry Davis Sleeper (1878–1934), *the* interior decorator of his day. In Beauport, his own summer home, he gave

The town of Gloucester

each of the 40 rooms a design theme, from the Lord Byron and Paul Revere Rooms to the China Trade and India Rooms. The house is now a museum, full of his collection of antiques and art.

▶ *Return to Gloucester and follow signs for* **Alternate Route 127A** *to Rockport.*

9 Rockport
As its name implies, Rockport's early fame was founded on rock, in particular the granite quarried for many of America's 19th-century monuments, bridges, and civic buildings. For the past century, however, Rockport has been better known for its artists' colony and the town is full of galleries and craft shops exhibiting their work, principally the Rockport Art Association's galleries on Main Street.

The heart of the action in this popular resort is Bearskin Neck,

where old fishing lofts have been turned into studios and galleries, restaurants and stores.

Until 2005, Rockport was famously "dry," so liquor was not allowed to be sold. Years before Prohibition, Hannah Jumper led 200 women of Rockport in the Hatchet Gang raid of 1856. These militant teetotallers imposed their own ban on booze by smashing every cask, bottle, and flask they could find. And the men of Rockport didn't have the courage to ask for a drop after that. Now visitors can order drinks – as long as they are "in conjunction with the consumption of a meal."

i 3 Whistlestop Mall

▶ *Leave town, rejoining* **Route 127**, *and follow signs for Pigeon Cove (2 miles/3km).*

10 Pigeon Cove
Just off Route 127, this small community boasts an unusual building. At No. 52 Pigeon Hill Street stands the Paper House, built between 1922 and 1942 by Elis Stenman and his family. It took two decades and both the house and the furniture have been constructed out of 100,000 old newspapers. The walls are

215 sheets thick, the desk is made from the *Christian Science Monitor*, and a bookshelf uses only foreign papers!

▶ *Continue on Route 127 and after 1 mile (1.5km) is the turning for Halibut Point State Park. Route 127 continues past rocky points of land and art galleries to the rotary (round-about) at Route 128. Go west on Route 128, then turn right onto Route 133 west for Essex.*

🄻 Essex

The 30 or so antiques shops that line Main Street in this small, sleepy-looking town draw dealers and collectors from all over America for the quality and excellent value of their wares. The small Shipbuilding Museum, also on Main Street, recalls the town's heyday in the days of sail.

SPECIAL TO...

Woodmans of Essex is credited with inventing fried clams back in 1916, and is still one of the best-known clam shacks in New England. "Woodie's" is known for serving fresh, delicious fried clams, clam cakes, and New England clam chowder made with milk, butter, lots of potatoes, and clams.

▶ *Continue to Ipswich. Route 133 north joins Route 1A.*

🄼 Ipswich

Ipswich has several fine houses, particularly the 1677 John Whipple House, one of the oldest Puritan homes still standing, and the Heard House. This Federal-style mansion retains its period furnishings and has collections of art, toys, carriages and sleighs.

Out of town, some 6 miles (10km) along Argilla Road, is the home of Chicago industrialist Richard T. Crane, on the crest of Castle Hill. This 59-room Great House recalls the stately homes of England, with its 63-foot

(18.9m) long gallery and 16-foot (4.8m) high ceilings. It is open for tours, and there are also concerts and a popular Fourth of July event on the grounds in summer.

Down below, the 5-mile (8km) long beach is one of the most beautiful north of Cape Cod. Beware of the three weeks at the end of July and early August when the voracious, biting "greenhead" flies take over the strand.

▶ *Continue north on Route 133 and Route 1A for 11 miles (18km) to Rolfe's Lane. Turn right for Plum Island and the Parker Refuge.*

BACK TO NATURE

Located about 1 mile (1.5km) north of the turn-off to Crane's Beach on Route 133, Wolf Hollow is home to seven North American wolves. On weekends, visitors have an hour-long presentation and then watch the wolves as they respond to commands from their trainers. Fear not, for although they are at close range, a strong fence separates observers from the observed.

🄼🄴 Plum Island and the Parker River National Wildlife Refuge

With its vast expanse of salt marsh, this is a major stopping point for birds migrating north and south each year. Early spring and late fall are the ideal times to see some of the 300 species. The Joppa Flats Visitor Center has observation areas to view cranes, herons and Canada geese.

Plum Island, first visited by Samuel de Champlain in 1601, is a 6-mile (10km) long beach that acts as a breakwater to the coastal towns. Stop on the access road and follow the boardwalks across the dunes, but remember that swimming is dangerous here because of the cold water and the strong undertows.

▶ *Return to Route 1A and continue into Newburyport (11 miles/18km).*

🄼🄴 Newburyport

As in so many New England towns, the charming wooden houses of Colonial times were destroyed by fire and have been rebuilt in brick. A renovation program in the 1970s and 1980s tidied up the rundown sea front and restored the line-up of fine Federal and Greek Revival architecture. Now this ship-building town at the mouth of the Merrimack River is an attractive, if busy, place to spend time. The Custom House on Water Street is given over to a museum of all things maritime, including a re-creation of a ship's bridge.

Two centuries ago, the town commissioned Charles Bulfinch, the architect of the State House in Boston, to design the Courthouse on High Street. This street is often called "sea captain row," with mansions such as the three-story Cushing House, built in 1808 by John Cushing. His son, Caleb, was the first emissary sent by the United States to China, and his collection of fine porcelain, paintings, and cabinetware from China fills the 21 rooms.

▶ *Leave on High Street (Route 113) and follow signs to I–95 south and Route 128. (Do not take Route 1.) Take I–95 south, then west. After about 30 miles (48km), turn south onto I–93 for Boston.*

RECOMMENDED WALKS

Halibut Point State Park is a delightful place to stop and stretch your legs, with well-maintained nature and walking trails. The point is not named for fish; it was originally called "Haul About Point" because sailing ships had to "come about" here and tack to sail around Cape Ann.

Cape Cod

2 DAYS • 241 MILES • 387KM

This 62-mile (100km) long peninsula is one of the country's eminent vacation playgrounds. Route 6A, the Old King's Highway, passes through 300-year-old communities where every other house seems to be a craft shop, antiques store or bed-and-breakfast.

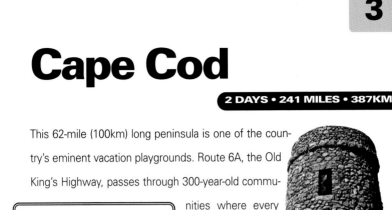

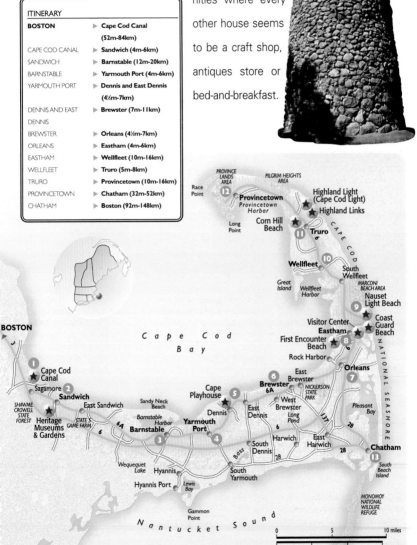

Fine example of Sandwich's famous glass, highly valued by collectors
Page 23: Scargo Tower

⒤ *Cape Cod Chamber of Commerce, Hyannis*

▶ *Leave Boston on **Route 93**; take **Route 3** south to the Sagamore Bridge, crossing the Cape Cod Canal.*

❶ Cape Cod Canal

Sailing from Boston around the outside of Cape Cod has always been dangerous. Indeed, even just a century ago, some 25 ships a year foundered on the 135-mile (216km) journey. Traders welcomed the opening of the canal in 1914, 300 years after Myles Standish of the Plymouth Colony first proposed the idea. Running 17 miles (28km) from Cape Cod Bay to Buzzard's Bay, the Canal is 160 yards (150m) wide. Nowadays, recreational yachtsmen take the short cut, watched by fishermen and cyclists on the Cape Cod Canal Bikepath.

⒤ *70 Main Street, Buzzards Bay*

▶ *Now on **Route 6A**, continue to Sandwich (4miles/6km).*

❷ Sandwich

Sandwich reeks of old-world charm, due to its fine collection of 18th- and 19th-century houses, the Wren-like spire on the First Church of Christ, and tree-lined streets. Overlooking Shawme Pond is shingled Dexter Grist Mill, still in working order, and one of the oldest houses on the Cape, the 1654 Hoxie House. In classic "salt box" style, with diamond window panes, it contains 17th-century furniture, tools, and tableware inside. The Eldred House, next door, is now a museum dedicated to the children's author Thornton W. Burgess, best remembered for his *Peter Cottontail* stories.

Despite its 300 years of history, however, Sandwich is no living museum: You can still

SPECIAL TO...

When Deming Jarves opened his Boston and Sandwich Glass Works in 1825, he banked on a plentiful supply of wood and sand to make his mass-produced household pressed glass. Unfortunately, the local sand was not satisfactory, so he had to import the raw material. The factory closed in 1888, but the highly collectible glass, along with glass-blowing demonstrations, may be seen in the Sandwich Glass Museum.

charter a boat to go fishing offshore for cod.

▶ *Continue on **Route 6A** to Barnstable (12½ miles/20km).*

❸ Barnstable

Off the road to the left, 4 miles (6km) before Barnstable, Sandy Neck is a rich nature reserve where the dunes were trampled by U.S. soldiers training for the North African Desert campaign during World War II. When a north wind blows, watch for windsurfers skimming across Barnstable Harbor.

In town, drop into the Sturgis Library to see the original home of the Reverend John Lothrop, one of the first residents of the 1639 settlement. The library's genealogical records are useful for those searching out family roots, especially if they are descended from the Lothrops, who occupy much of the cemetery. The main industries in the 19th century were growing cranberries, and making bricks, some of which are now collector's items.

▶ *Continue on **Route 6A** to Yarmouth Port.*

4 Yarmouth Port

The Captain Bangs Hallet House reflects the affluence and sophistication of a successful sea captain's life in the 19th century. Located near the Yarmouth Port Post Office, its handsome Greek Revival façade hides the original 1740 structure. It is now the headquarters of the local historical society, and the starting point for pleasant walks through a nature preserve along the Botanic Trails of Yarmouth.

The 1680 Thacher House and the 1780 Winslow-Crocker House next door, now run by Historic New England (formerly SPNEA), are filled with high-quality furniture and household objects made in Colonial and Federal times by New England craftsmen.

i Yarmouth Area Chamber of Commerce, 424 Route 28, West Yarmouth

▶ Continue on **Route 6A** to Dennis and East Dennis.

5 Dennis and East Dennis

Few men can match Josiah Dennis' claim of having five villages named for him. This 17th-century Congregational minister is immortalized in East, West and South Dennis, as well as Dennisport and Dennis. In his home, the Josiah Dennis Manse, visitors can see his portable pulpit, watch weavers at work and browse round the small maritime museum. There is a 200-year-old schoolhouse on the grounds.

Not quite as ancient, but still the oldest summer theater in the U.S., is the Cape Playhouse, where Bette Davis worked as an usherette. Gregory Peck and Henry Fonda also started their acting careers here. Don't miss the Cape Cod Museum of Art on the grounds, or the church-like building nearby which is actually an art deco cinema, complete with leather seats and a mural by 20th-century American artist Rockwell Kent.

Take time to see the lie of the land from the Scargo Tower where, on a good day, you can see Provincetown, 20 miles (32km) to the north.

i Dennis Chamber of Commerce, Junction Routes 134 and 28, West Dennis

▶ Continue on **Route 6A** to Brewster (7 miles/11km).

6 Brewster

On and behind Route 6A, which doubles as Main Street in Brewster, stand the elegant clapboard houses of 19th-century sea captains. At the height of New England's trading with China, as many as 100 lived here, and many are buried in the graveyard next to the "Captains' Church," the First Parish Church. Memories and records of that era are in the Brewster Historical Society Museum at Spruce Hill, East Brewster.

Other museums worth a visit include the New England Fire and History Museum, which has a unique 1929 Mercedes-Benz fire engine, and reconstructions

You can watch the process of corn being ground at Brewster

FOR CHILDREN

The Cape Cod Museum of Natural History at Brewster is popular for its aquarium and lively exhibitions, lectures and tours explaining the Cape's bird and animal life. As well as two short trails in the wildlife sanctuary, the longer John Wing Trail is a fine walk to the unspoiled beach. Remember, though, to check times of tides before setting out. The museum also organizes KidSummer, a range of nature-oriented programs for 3–12 year olds.

of a blacksmith's and an apothecary shop. More reminders of yesteryear include the Higgins Farm Windmill and Harris-Blake House in West Brewster.

i Brewster Chamber of Commerce, 2198 Main Street

BACK TO NATURE

The alewife, a type of herring,
spawns in fresh water every
three or four years. In spring,
these silvery fish swim up the
narrow Stony Brook creek,
using the fish ladder to bypass
the water-powered Grist Mill
on Stony Brook Road, just
north of Brewster, off Route
6A, and return to the ponds
where they were conceived.

▶ *Continue on **Route 6A** to
the Orleans roundabout.*

7 Orleans
The name rhymes with "beans,"
even though it commemorates
the French Duke of Orléans,
who fled here from the French
Revolution in 1797. This busy
town has been the "hub of the
Outer Cape" for two centuries.
Back then fish, and salt for
preserving the catch, were
shipped direct to Boston from
tiny Rock Harbor on Cape
Cod Bay.

▶ *Continue north for 4 miles
(6km) on what is now **Route 6**
to Eastham. Just before the
town, the road to Fort Hill, on
the right, provides panoramic
views above the cupola-
crowned Victorian house of
whaling captain Edward
Penniman.*

8 Eastham
The windmill opposite the
Town Hall in Eastham,
pronounced East-Ham, was
built in Plymouth in 1688,
rebuilt in Truro, then moved to
its present site in 1808. The
oldest windmill on the Cape, it
is celebrated on Windmill
Weekend in September.
Samoset Road leads to Cape
Cod Bay. Here, First Encounter
Beach is the legendary site of
the first meeting between the
Pilgrims and the Native
Americans. A metal plaque
explains how arrows and musket
fire were exchanged when the
newcomers encountered the
tribe, who remembered a slave
trader kidnapping some of

their people six years before.
Don't expect to find any arrow-
heads, though; the Pilgrims
gathered up the arrows and
sent them back to England as
curiosities.

From here to Provincetown,
the Cape is a landscape of steep
dunes tufted with grass. On the
Atlantic side, breakers pound
the flat beaches while lighthouses emphasize the sense
of solitude.

At the Salt Pond Visitor
Center, beyond Eastham,
displays and films explain the
ecology and wildlife of the
43,600-acre (17,650-hectare)
Cape Cod National Seashore, a
stretch of unspoiled coastline
some 40 miles long (64km). A
road leads to Coast Guard Beach
where, in 1929, Henry Beston
spent a year writing his classic
nature journal, *The Outermost
House*. The book is evocative,
and perhaps more readable than
Henry Thoreau's *Walden*. The
beach is superb.

Eye-catching façade on Cape Cod

The Nauset Light is a reminder of the region's seafaring heritage

[i] Eastham Tourist Information Booth, Route 6 at Governor Prence Road (seasonal)

▶ Detour east to Coast Guard Beach, on Doane Road, then turn left on Ocean View Drive to Nauset Light Beach.

SPECIAL TO...

The local Native Americans taught the Pilgrims how to cook shellfish and New Englanders still use the same method for a clambake on the beach. Dig a shallow pit into the sand, line it with stones and build a wood fire. When the wood has burned down, cover the hot stones with layers of damp seaweed, clean clams, more seaweed, corn on the cob and bluefish. Seal with a tarpaulin. Leave for an hour to steam, then uncover and eat.

9 Nauset Light Beach

As you drive through the typical scrub oak and pine that is the natural vegetation of Cape Cod, you will catch glimpses of the ocean to the right. You can venture down to a stretch of seemingly unending sandy beach, where the Atlantic waves thunder in, and you can get away from other people simply by taking a walk.

SCENIC ROUTES

The Cape Cod Central Railroad runs by cranberry bogs and marshes between Hyannis and the Cape Cod Canal. This should not be confused with the Cape Cod Rail Trail, where there is no longer a train. The Rail Trail follows the former Boston to Provincetown railroad route between South Dennis and Wellfleet. Here, the rail bed has been replaced by a smooth, 22-mile (35km) path. Its flatness makes it ideal for joggers, hikers, and cyclists.

▶ Loop back to **Route 6** via Cable Road and Nauset Road to Wellfleet (7 miles/11km).

10 Wellfleet

Famous for its oysters since Samuel de Champlain's Gallic taste-buds were tickled in 1606, this charming town, complete with picturesque harbor and photogenic old houses, now attracts artists, whose number is so great that their works fill its 22 art galleries. Fishing still goes on, and the clock on the First

Fishermen on the pier in Truro as the sun sets

Congregational Church reflects Wellfleet's nautical tradition by following ships' time, confusing landlubbers considerably by chiming, for example, two bells at one, five and nine o'clock. It is reportedly the only clock in the world to do so.

[i] *Wellfleet Chamber of Commerce, off Route 6, South Wellfleet*

FOR HISTORY BUFFS

"... I extend on behalf of the American people most cordial greetings and good wishes to you and all the people of the British Empire." President Theodore Roosevelt's transatlantic message to King Edward VII of England in 1903 was the first sent from Guglielmo Marconi's Wireless Telegraph Station in South Wellfleet.

At Orleans, the French Cable Station had already linked up with Brest in France in 1891. The stations were situated here because the Cape is one of the closest parts of the U.S. to Europe.

RECOMMENDED WALKS

The Great Island Trail is an 8-mile (13km) round-trip walk along a narrow spit of sand. The trail is covered at high tide, and has views up to Provincetown and down to Brewster. To get there, follow Holbrook Avenue from Wellfleet Center. Turn right on Commercial Street, keep the water on the left, continue to Chequesset Neck Road and drive to the parking lot.

▶ *Continue north on **Route 6** for 5 miles (8km) to Truro.*

⓫ Truro

Originally named Dangerfield, this is a small, quiet neighborhood. On the way to North Truro, the Highland or Cape Cod Light is on South Highland Road. Standing on the site of the Cape's first lighthouse (1791), it has been damaged and restored, moved and rebuilt. The oldest golf course on the Cape, Highland Links, is nearby.

Back on Route 6, turn down Corn Hill Road for Corn Hill Beach where, in the parking lot, is a little taste of Pilgrim lore. Soon after the Pilgrim Father's arrival, Captain Myles Standish

came across a cache of corn buried by a Native American in the sand. Desperate for food, he took it, but on meeting with the owner about a year later, Standish repaid him what was owed. Farther north, park the car and hike the short Pilgrim Spring Trail to the spot where legend has it that the Pilgrim Fathers first found "springs of fresh water" after their grueling transatlantic crossing.

▶ *Continue north on **Route 6** to Provincetown (10 miles/16km).*

⓬ Provincetown

Although the Vikings are reckoned to have landed here long before, in AD 1004, this is where it all started for the Americans on November 11 or 21, 1620, depending on which calendar you use. The *Mayflower* dropped anchor in what is now Provincetown Harbor, after a 65-day voyage. Of the 102 passengers, one had died, but a baby had been born. Myles Standish, a soldier of fortune hired by the Pilgrims for protection, rowed ashore. These days, a rather unimpressive plaque on Commercial Street marks the event. After five weeks, the Pilgrims continued on their way, hoping to find a more hospitable site for settlement. They are remembered with the Pilgrim Monument, found in the center of town. Built in 1910, the granite tower soars 252 feet (76m) high. The stairs are a real test of stamina, but climbers can read the plaques noting the founding dates of Massachusetts towns and *Mayflower* descendants. The reward is the observation platform at the top. The museum at the base tells the story of Provincetown.

The town's main industry of deep-water fishing for cod, mackerel and whales was established in the early 18th century. Although the fishing heyday passed over a century ago, boats still go out each morning to supply New York and Boston with fresh fish, and whale watching is popular in summer.

Today, in Provincetown, known almost universally as P-town, the fun really begins after the day-trippers have gone home. Artists have been coming here since Charles Hawthorne arrived in 1899. He taught for 30 years and his painting, *Fish Cleaners*, can be seen in the Town Hall.

Edward Hopper and Jackson Pollock are among the famous who joined the amateurs, working in the dazzling light on the shore. Playwright Eugene O'Neill wrote and produced his earliest plays in what was, and still is, a surprisingly bohemian town where everyone comes to have a good time.

i 307 Commercial Street

▶ Return on **Route 6**, but before the Orleans rotary (roundabout), turn off on **Route 28** for Chatham (32 miles/52km).

⓭ Chatham
Sitting right on Cape Cod's "elbow," Chatham relies on more than just tourism, thanks to its busy fishing fleet. The bounty of the sea is represented by the striking 1992 sculpture *Provider* on Fish Pier. Here, each afternoon, crates of flounder and

haddock, cod and halibut are transferred straight from the boats to waiting trucks. Take a walk along Main Street, with its clapboard houses, restaurants, stores, and 175-year-old Mayo House, restored and open to the public. Chatham Lighthouse, known as "The Light," is a favorite spot to park and admire the ocean views. In season, you can tour the lighthouse.

i 533 Main Street and 2377 Main Street

▶ Take **Route 28** out of Chatham. Turn north on **Route 137** and rejoin **Route 6** at Exit 11. Follow **Route 6** back to the Sagamore Bridge, then **Route 3** to **Route 93** and back to Boston.

Provincetown, overlooked by the Center Methodist Church
Inset: cranberries at Plymouth

SPECIAL TO...

The first export from Massachusetts back to the Mother Country was, reputedly, cranberries. They were not sent to be made into sauce or juice, instead they served as ballast in ships. The hard, bitter red berries grow wild in bogs and ponds along the Cape but in the 18th century, Henry Hall cultivated the wild berry. Later, Alvin Cahoon planted the first commercial bog, using a layer of sand to promote the growth of the bushes. Today, vitamin C-rich cranberries are a multi-million dollar business. Harwich has a popular Cranberry Harvest Festival in mid-September. Plymouth County growers have their festival over Columbus Day weekend.

2 DAYS • 181½ MILES • 292KM

The Berkshire
Hills

The Berkshires were once the exclusive playground of the rich. Now these forested slopes are a vacation destination for everyone, particularly music lovers who are drawn to the numerous summer festivals.

ITINERARY		
SPRINGFIELD	▶	**Monterey (32m-51km)**
MONTEREY	▶	**Gt Barrington (9m-15km)**
GREAT BARRINGTON	▶	**Sheffield (7½m-12km)**
SHEFFIELD	▶	**Stockbridge (20m-32km)**
STOCKBRIDGE	▶	**Lenox (7m-11km)**
LENOX	▶	**Pittsfield (6m-10km)**
PITTSFIELD	▶	**Williamstown (22m-35km)**
WILLIAMSTOWN	▶	**North Adams (3m-5km)**
NORTH ADAMS	▶	**Shelburne Falls (29m-46km)**
SHELBURNE FALLS	▶	**Deerfield (11m-18km)**
DEERFIELD	▶	**Northampton (16m-26km)**
NORTHAMPTON	▶	**Springfield (19m-31km)**

i *1441 Main Street, Springfield;*
Riverfront Park Information
Center, West Columbus Avenue

SPECIAL TO...

Basketball was invented in
Springfield, and the town
boasts the Basketball Hall of
Fame. Desperate to exercise
bored young men during the
winter of 1891, Dr. James
Naismith nailed up a couple
of peach baskets in the gymnasium of the Springfield YMCA
and tossed them a soccer ball.
Basketball was born. At first,
the players had to put up a ladder to retrieve the ball every
time there was a score. Then
someone had a brilliant idea:
remove the bottom of the baskets. First accepted at the 1936
Olympics, basketball has
become the world's most
popular indoor sport.

FOR CHILDREN

South of Springfield on Route
159 is the Six Flags New
England theme and water park.
Its eight thrilling rollercoasters
include Superman Ride of
Steel, a combination of height,
speed and weightlessness, and
Batman – The Dark Knight,
with its sensation of flying.
Gentler rides for younger
children include Poison Ivy's
Tangled Train and *Looney Tunes*
Animation Department.

▶ *From Springfield, take* **Route**
20 *west across the*
Connecticut River, through
West Springfield, passing the
Exposition grounds, site of the
huge "Big E," New England's
largest fair, held every
September. Bear left on **Route**
23 *west at Woronoco. Drive*
through Blandford and Otis to
Monterey.

❶ Monterey
The Mexican name of this town
honors General Zachary Taylor, a
hero in the Mexican-American

War (1846–8). So popular was
"Old Rough and Ready" Taylor
after his victories at Monterey
and Buena Vista, that one
Kentuckian predicted (correctly)
that the general would win the
1848 presidential election "by
spontaneous combustion." Born
in Virginia, Taylor had no known
connections with the village.

▶ *Continue on* **Route 23**, *past*
the Butternut Ski Area.

❷ Great Barrington
Local inventor William Stanley
assured that this small town
would have its place in the
history books. He first demon-
strated the potential of using
alternating current here in 1886
by lighting up 24 stores on the
main street. Stanley's system,
more efficient than Edison's
cumbersome direct current

lighting, led to more widespread
use of electricity. A lamp and
plaque in the small park at the
corner of Main and Cottage
streets tell the story.
   On five Saturdays in summer,
Simon's Rock College hosts the
Aston Magna Festival. It is the
oldest festival in America
devoted to baroque, classical and
early romantic music, all played
on period instruments.

▶ *Leave town on* **Route 7** *and*
head south for 7½ miles
(12km) to Sheffield.

❸ Sheffield
Back in the 18th century, two
minor events helped shape
American democracy. In 1773,

A cover image from the Saturday
Evening Post, painted by Norman
Rockwell

BACK TO NATURE

About 1½ miles (2km) south of Sheffield is one of several small, flat-topped hills known locally as "cobbles." Barthlomew's Cobble is a 500-million-year-old lump of limestone and quartzite, doubling as a nature reserve.
Ledges Interpretive Trail (20 minutes) winds through rugged, glacially formed rocks. Here, some 45 species of fern, many of them rare, grow in the summer. A small museum records some of the 900 types of plants and wildlife in the area.

the Sheffield Declaration demanded freedom for the individual, while in 1787, Shays' Rebellion ended here. Poor farmers, many of them Revolutionary War veterans, thought they were being overtaxed and rebelled under Captain Daniel Shays. The seven-month protest brought the end of imprisonment for debt, and also strengthened the case for federal and state laws. A century or so ago, local people carved a large slab of marble into a monument honoring the rebellion. It stands in a field north of the town. Today, antiques shops line the main street.

▶ *Leave Sheffield west on Berkshire School Road to* **Route**

41 and turn north. Join **Route** *23 and take it through South Egremont to Great Barrington. Rejoin* **Route 7** *and head north to Monument Mountain.*

4 Monument Mountain

This jumble of huge boulders has long been a favorite for picnickers and hikers. Back in 1850, two of New England's best-known authors, Herman Melville and Nathaniel Hawthorne, first met here. Caught in a thunderstorm, they took shelter, drank champagne with their companions, and listened to a recitation of *The Story of the Indian Girl*. The poem relates the local legend of a love-lorn girl who leapt to her death from this mountain.

FOR HISTORY BUFFS

The charming wooden Ashley House in Sheffield is named after Colonel John Ashley who campaigned for The Sheffield Declaration of equal rights in the late 18th century. His slave, Mum Bet, is better remembered, since she used her master's arguments to gain her own freedom in 1783. The woodwork and paneling in Ashley's upstairs study show the skill of the craftsmen who built the house in 1735.

RECOMMENDED WALKS

Two trails lead to Squaw Peak, the 1,735-foot (520m) summit of Monument Mountain. The easier trail takes about an hour; follow the sign for Indian Monument.
The longer hike (3 miles/5km) climbs through oaks, white pines, laurels and chestnuts, revealing mysterious caves under overhanging rocks and rushing streams. A fine view can be had from the top.

▶ *Continue north on* **Route 7** *to Stockbridge.*

5 Stockbridge

Stockbridge was created in 1722 as a well-meaning experiment by the London Society for the Propagation of the Gospel in Foreign Lands. The local Native Americans were invited to settle alongside the English Colonists in the hope that they would become "civilized," and follow Christian and English customs. Despite the support given by the Native Americans during the Revolutionary War, the Colonial ambitions of the settlers put an end to the experiment. Even today, the Berkshires remains picture-postcard pretty, with tall maples and elms. There is hardly a telephone or electricity pole in sight, the cables have been buried underground. The Red Lion Inn is the heart of the town, as it has always been since pre-Revolutionary days. Although this old coaching inn burned down in the 19th century, the Victorian replacement retains the wide porches, with rocking chairs for watching life pass by.

Installed on the old Linwood estate, the Norman Rockwell Museum has 600 of the illustrator's works, and contains his studio, which was moved here lock, stock, palette, and paintbrush. Rockwell's *Saturday*

The Norman Rockwell Museum
in Stockbridge

Evening Post magazine covers made him a household name, and many favorites are here. Freckle-faced boys, cuddly grannies all Thanksgiving turkeys all appear bathed in the glow of nostalgia.

Near by is Chesterwood, the summer home and studio of sculptor Daniel Chester French. The best known of his 1,000 works are national symbols: the solemn, seated figure of Abraham Lincoln in the Lincoln Memorial in Washington D.C. and *The Minute Man* statue in Concord, Massachusetts.

Besides attracting artists, the Berkshires became a resort for turn-of-the-20th-century millionaires. Up Prospect Hill is Naumkeag, the Choate family's magnificent estate. The 44-room mansion vies for attention with the landscaping, especially the famous "Blue Steps."

As you leave Stockbridge to continue the itinerary, look for the Berkshire Botanical Garden, 2 miles (3km) out of town at the junction of Routes 183 and 102. One of the oldest botanical gardens in the U.S., it is a beautiful and relaxing place to visit, with 15 acres (6 hectares) of colorful landscaped gardens that include water features, annual and perennial beds, vegetable plots, a children's garden and a woodland trail.

i Main Street

▶ *Leave town on Route 102 west. Turn right on Route 183 north at the Berkshire Botanical Garden and continue north for 6 miles (10km) to Tanglewood.*

6 Tanglewood

The former country estate of the Tappan family is now synonymous with music. Although the New York Symphony first performed here in 1934, it is the Boston Symphony Orchestra that has made Tanglewood its summer home since 1936. Over the years, millions have come to picnic on the grounds before

listening to concerts in the 6,000-seat Koussevitzky Music Shed. Great conductors such as Leonard Bernstein and Seiji Ozawa have directed here. In 1994, the 1,200-seat Seiji Ozawa Hall was added: the rear wall opens on to a grassy hillside. Jazz, folk and pop are also on the program, along with recitals by students from the prestigious Tanglewood summer music school. Also on the grounds is a reproduction of author Nathaniel Hawthorne's Little Red House, the summer cottage where he wrote *The Tanglewood Tales* and *The House of the Seven Gables*.

▶ *Follow Route 183 to Lenox.*

7 Lenox

Because of the movie *The Age of Innocence*, there has been renewed interest in the Pulitzer Prize-winning writer Edith Wharton (1862–1937). Visitors come to this attractive town because it was the haunt of some of America's richest families more than a century ago. The Vanderbilts, Carnegies, and other stars of New York's upper crust summered in what they referred to as "Berkshire cottages." Some of these grand estates still exist, others are charming small hotels such as the Wheatleigh and the Blantyre. The Mount, Wharton's 35-room mansion, was built to her own rigid specifications. She

Enjoying one of the summer concerts at Tanglewood

Williamstown's Gothic cathedral
Inset: Hancock Shaker Village

spent her happiest years here (1902–11), writing such novels as *Ethan Frome* in bed each morning. She delighted in looking east over the "outdoor rooms," the splendid gardens, and the pond that she designed.

Shakespeare & Co., the popular theater group, have moved to their own premises on Kemble Street.

> *i* Chamber of Commerce, 5 Walker Street

▶ *Continue north on **Route 7A/7** toward Pittsfield. On the right, just before the town, are signs for Arrowhead.*

8 Arrowhead
Author Herman Melville (1819–91) was inspired by the Berkshires. Between 1850 and 1863, he lived on this farm where the views reminded him of his seafaring days: "I look out of my window in the morning when I rise as I would out of the porthole of a ship in the Atlantic." He could see the humpbacked, whale-like shape of Mount Greylock, a constant influence as he wrote *Moby-Dick*. The novel did not sell, so Melville was forced to leave

Arrowhead and take a job as a customs officer in New York. He died a poor man.

> *i* Pittsfield Visitor Information Center, 111 South Street

▶ *Continue north for 2 miles (3km) to Pittsfield, turn left on **Route 20** and drive 6 miles (10km) to Hancock Shaker Village.*

9 Hancock Shaker Village
The Shakers, a socialist Christian sect, are remembered for their use of dance in religious services, and their exquisitely simple but practical furniture and architecture. The last of the Shakers left Hancock in 1960, after 170 years, but their homes, workshops, herb gardens, and farm have been restored and revived.

Typical is the three-story round barn, built in 1826, where one man standing in the center can feed 54 cows with ease. You can also enjoy Shaker picnics and suppers. The tranquility of the 1,200 acres (480 hectares) of meadows and woodlands clearly reinforces Hancock's original Shaker name: the City of Peace.

▶ *Return to Pittsfield and **Route 7**. Continue north to Williamstown on **Route 7**.*

10 Williamstown
Revolutionary soldier Colonel Ephraim Williams' gift of money ensured that both the town and college would bear his name. With that, he outdid earlier educational benefactors such as John Harvard and Nicholas Brown, who only have schools named for them. Today, Williams College is one of the country's most distinguished small colleges, and the town is one of the most attractive in New England.

There is plenty here for culture addicts. First on anyone's list should be the Sterling and Francine Clark Art Institute, housed in a stunning white, marble, temple-like

building. The art collection was created by the Singer sewing machine heir and his French wife and features works by European and American painters. Included are *At the Concert*, one of 30 paintings by Pierre Auguste Renoir; a study of Rouen Cathedral by Claude Monet; and *Rockets and Blue Lights* by J. M. W. Turner.

Next is the college's own Museum of Art, which concentrates on non-Western and ancient art. Contemporary works, such as Andy Warhol's yellow and black self-portrait are on display. For 50 years, the Williamstown Theater Festival has attracted such star names as Ben Affleck and Gwyneth Paltrow to participate in the summer season.

> *i* Routes 2 and 7; also 70 Denison Park Drive

▶ *Drive east on **Route 2** for 4 miles (6.5km) to North Adams.*

11 North Adams
The term Museum of Contemporary Art will never be the same after you have been to the innovative new Massachusetts Museum of Contemporary Art (MASS MoCA). Contemporary in every sense of the word, the museum embraces a new approach to putting visual, performing and media arts on show. The whole process of creativity is explored here, and the center not only stages exhibitions and performances by renowned artists, but also shows work in progress in its

---

BACK TO NATURE

Halfway between Lenox and Pittsfield is the Pleasant Valley Wildlife Sanctuary. With its hummingbirds and beavers, this is a delightful place for a stroll. Some 7 miles (11km) of marked trails meander through the 1,400 acres (560 hectares) of meadow and forest.

art fabrication shops, production studios, performance rehearsals and the use of multimedia technologies. The museum is housed in a converted mill complex consisting of some 27 buildings, linked by covered bridges and elevated walkways.

▶ Continue east on **Route 2**.

⓬ Shelburne Falls
Hamlets dot this rugged road as it passes through forests and along the edges of gorges where the gushing water once drove the mills. Shelburne Falls is enjoying a renaissance, and members of the local

---

SCENIC ROUTE

Three hundred years ago, Native Americans crossed the Berkshire Hills by walking a trail cut through the forest. Later, pioneer settlers broadened the route on their way through to what is now New York State. Opened in 1914 as one of America's first "scenic highways," the Mohawk Trail is a popular drive these days, especially in the fall (see pages 102–3). The Mohawk tribe is remembered with *Hail to the Sunrise*, the statue of a serene Native American brave, his arms raised to the east.

---

horticultural society have had the ingenuity to disguise a 400-foot (120m) long trolley bridge with a hanging flower garden, the Bridge of Flowers.

[i] *75 Bridge Street*

▶ Continue to Greenfield and turn south on **Route 5** to historic Deerfield.

⓭ Deerfield
Called simply "The Street," Deerfield's main thoroughfare is

The *Hail to the Sunrise* memorial at the entrance to the Mohawk Trail State Forest

lined with the most impressive collection of original Colonial houses in New England. The surrounding fields and absence of advertising completes the film-set effect. A dozen of the 65 18th- and 19th-century houses are open to the public for guided and self-guided tours, revealing a potted history of early American interior decorating, from furniture to textiles and silverware.

The modern Flynt Center of Early New England Life offers an excellent introduction. In 1675, Native Americans massacred farmers as they paused to eat grapes, giving a nearby stream its present name of Bloody Brook. In 1704, the French and Native Americans ravaged the town in the depths of winter, carrying off 112 prisoners to Canada.

The Indian House Door, with its gaping hole hacked by a tomahawk, is preserved in the Memorial Hall. The hall was once used by students at the 200-year-old Deerfield Academy, a well-known boarding school.

By contrast, the colors and restoration work in the Wells-Thorn House recall happier days. In 1774, residents raised a liberty pole, and declared their independence nine days before the historic Fourth of July, 1776.

FOR CHILDREN

Butterflies never fail to delight children, and they are sure to be captivated by Magic Wings, a butterfly conservatory and garden. Lush gardens house 4,000 colorful, free-flying tropical butterflies and moths, and outdoor gardens have been planted specially to attract indigenous species.

▶ You can either continue south for 16 miles (26km) on **Route 5** to Northampton or use the faster route, **I–91**.

14 Northampton

With its mixture of industrial and educational heritage, Northampton is a pleasant, balanced sort of town. Little evidence remains that it was first settled in 1654. In the 1980s, a vigorous program of downtown renewal sprouted restaurants and boutiques. It is the home of one of America's first women's colleges, founded in 1875 by Sophia Smith, and Smith College is still one of the nation's most prestigious schools.

i 99 Pleasant Street

▶ Return to **I–91** south and drive to Springfield.

Dwight House is a delightful example of early 18th-century architecture in Deerfield

FOR HISTORY BUFFS

"This is my letter to the world, that never wrote to me ..." penned the poet and recluse Emily Dickinson (1830–86) who lived in Amherst, northeast of Northampton, on Route 9. Of her 1,700 poems, only 11 had been published by the time she died. Hundreds were later found in her bedroom. Dickinson rarely left the house, but was a favorite with local children, lowering baskets of her home-baked gingerbread to them from her window. Most of her papers and belongings are kept at Harvard University and Amherst College, but her white dress hangs in her house. The garden at Amherst is a delight.

SPECIAL TO...

Sylvester Graham of Northampton was a health food fanatic who gave his name to Graham flour, a type of wholewheat flour which is more familiar when made into Graham Crackers.

BOSTON

With its unique blend of history and modern development, its "walkable" downtown and efficient public transport system, Boston is a delight for the visitor. Words like "sophisticated" and "civilized" are often used to describe this city that feels European but is the birthplace of American liberty. Balancing all this is a lively student population of more then 250,000, from around 60 colleges and universities.

The city owes its foundation to the sea. When the Puritans settled here in 1630, they found poor soil, but a fine harbor. By 1700, only the ports of London and Bristol outranked Boston. Until 1755, Boston was the largest city in North America. Its place on the American stage was guaranteed less by wealth and more by its independent thinkers, who had been in the forefront of the Independence movement (see pages 8–9).

Boston's great strength is that it has moved with the times. After the Revolution, Beacon Hill was developed for elegant housing, followed by Back Bay, a landfill project that is now an area of chic stores, galleries and cafés. In the 1960s, a bold plan of urban renewal revitalized Quincy Market. Even bigger is the Central Artery/Tunnel Project, nicknamed the Big Dig. Begun in 1991, this feat of civil engineering has diverted heavy commuter traffic into tunnels. The redundant elevated expressway has been taken down, removing the ugly barrier between Boston's downtown and the North End and waterfront.

As well as theater, music and art galleries, sport plays a major part in the life of the city. The professional teams boast proud histories in the nation's four favorite sports: baseball (the Red Sox), hockey (the Bruins), basketball (the Celtics) and football (the New England Patriots).

As for getting around, that is easy. "The T," as locals call the MBTA (Massachusetts Bay Transport Authority), was the country's first such subway system, opened in 1897.

The USS Constitution

Tour 5

The Boston Freedom Trail is a "must" for anyone interested in American history. A red line on the pavement leads visitors along the world's first self-guided walking tour of its kind. Along the route are buildings that played an important role in the uprising against British Colonial rule over 200 years ago. This is no dry re-run of history, however.

There is also tantalizing trivia, from America's oldest restaurant to the nation's oldest commissioned vessel. Plaques and cemeteries, sculpture and bullet marks are also pointed out to give a fascinating insight into the history of the city, known as the "Cradle of the American Revolution."

Tour 6

There is more to Boston than Revolutionary history. This walk shows off the contrasts in Boston, starting down by the water and the modern aquarium and ending at Copley Square, where the Boston Marathon ends. In between are the cobbled streets and Georgian front doors on Beacon Hill, the chic stores of Newbury Street, and the open-air elegance of the Public Garden. Always a city that has welcomed strangers, there are also moving tributes to Afro-Americans and victims of the Holocaust.

Tour 7

Harvard University is one of the world's great educational institutions. Its libraries and museums boast some of the finest collections in the world, housed in magnificent examples of architecture from the 17th century to the present day. At the same time, the student body, which now includes the women of Radcliffe College, adds zest to Cambridge, where coffee shops and boutiques, bookstores and art galleries are a pleasure for students and visitors alike. With huge mature trees along the Charles River, and New England clapboard houses, Cambridge retains its own character, totally distinct from Boston, just a bridge or two away.

Harvard University is one of the pre-eminent Ivy League establishments in the country

Boston's impressive skyline at night

The Boston
Freedom Trail

A local journalist, William Schofield, came up with the simple idea of linking Boston's historically important sites with a walking trailin 1951.

Since then, millions have taken the route, marked sometimes by a painted red line, at other times by red bricks.

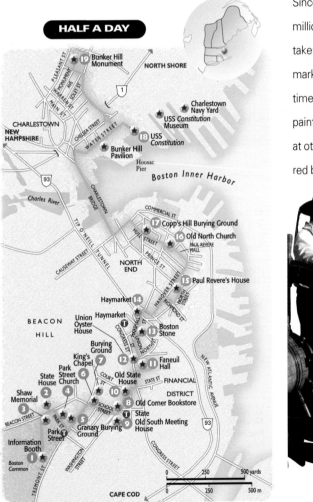

HALF A DAY

- 19 Bunker Hill Monument
- NORTH SHORE
- 1
- CHARLESTOWN
- NEW HAMPSHIRE
- Charlestown Navy Yard
- USS *Constitution* Museum
- 18 USS *Constitution*
- Bunker Hill Pavilion
- Hoosac Pier
- *Boston Inner Harbor*
- *Charles River*
- 93
- 17 Copp's Hill Burying Ground
- 16 Old North Church
- PAUL REVERE MALL
- NORTH END
- 15 Paul Revere's House
- 14 Haymarket
- Union Oyster House
- Haymarket
- BEACON HILL
- Burying Ground
- 13 Boston Stone
- King's Chapel 7
- Park Street Church 6
- 12
- 11 Faneuil Hall
- State House 2
- 4
- Old State House
- FINANCIAL DISTRICT
- Shaw Memorial 3
- 10
- 8 Old Corner Bookstore
- State
- BEACON STREET
- 5
- 9 Old South Meeting House
- 93
- Park Street
- Granary Burying Ground
- Information Booth
- Boston Common 1
- CONGRESS STREET
- 0 250 500 yards
- 0 250 500 m
- CAPE COD

Allow half a day, longer if you want to explore the Charlestown Navy Yard, located near the end of the trail, home of the USS *Constitution*. Remember that in summer long lines build up to see this historic ship.

▶ *Start at the information booth on the Tremont Street side of Boston Common, near the Park Street MBTA stop.*

❶ Boston Common
Often called America's first public park, this common land in the very heart of Boston was set aside in 1634 for "the feeding of Cattell" and as a "trayning field" for militia. Once the cattle left around 1830, the Common was used for recreation and oration. In 1851, Amelia Bloomer, wearing her manly "bloomers," campaigned for women's rights.

In the coming century, charismatic speakers such as Martin Luther King, Jr. and Pope John Paul II have also addressed large crowds here. Today it is an area of lawns, trees, and even baseball diamonds.

▶ *Follow the red line to the State House.*

❷ State House
Built in 1795, this "new" seat of state government replaced the Old State House of 1713. The original red-brick structure was designed by Charles Bulfinch, the most able and sought-after architect of his day. His original dome of wood was replaced first with a copper one, then gilded with 23-carat gold leaf in 1861.

▶ *Just across Beacon Street is a large monument.*

❸ Shaw/54th Regiment Memorial
The lively bronze bas-relief by Augustus Saint-Gaudens pays tribute to the local black soldiers who volunteered to fight for the North in the American Civil War. Prejudice confined blacks to the ranks, but wealthy white Bostonian Robert Gould Shaw led what became the 54th Massachusetts Regiment. He was killed, along with 32 of his soldiers, in the assault on Fort Wagner, South Carolina. Their heroism inspired the 1989 movie *Glory*, which won three Academy Awards.

The Robert Gould Shaw/54th Regiment Memorial

▶ *Walk through the Common to Park Street Church.*

❹ Park Street Church
Founded in 1809, this is where anti-slavery campaigner William Lloyd Garrison made his first speech in 1829. Two years later, the hymn *America* was first sung on the steps, and it remains part of the church's Fourth of July tradition. It is ironic that the melody is the same as the British national anthem.

▶ *Adjacent to Park Street Church, facing Tremont Street, is the Granary Burying Ground.*

❺ Granary Burying Ground
Buried here are some of the best-known leaders of the patriot cause: John Hancock, Samuel Adams, John Otis, and Paul Revere (see page 12). One of the most popular graves, however, is that of Mary Goose, also called Elizabeth Vergoose, and supposedly the original Mother Goose. The mother and step-mother of a total of 20 children, she was buried here in 1757. Her son-in-law is

SPECIAL TO...

The Omni Parker House, a hotel since 1855, overlooks King's Chapel and the Burying Ground. Parker House rolls became widely known and served, perhaps because they were considered the "patrician accompaniment to formal dining." Ironically, these popular rolls were served to customers by two of the 20th century's most radical figures who both worked here as waiters: Ho Chi Minh, later leader of North Vietnam, and Malcolm X, the 1960s militant black leader.

supposed to have published *Mother Goose's Melodies* (*Songs for the Nursery*).

▶ *Turn left on Tremont Street. Cross to King's Chapel, on the corner of School Street.*

❻ King's Chapel
Dating from 1749, King's Chapel was seen as a symbol of British rule in North America. The colony's governors worshipped in a special canopied pew. George Washington also used it in 1789; perhaps one reason

that it has survived. Today's congregation follows a mixture of Church of England and Unitarian liturgy.

▶ *Walk down School Street. Behind the chapel is the graveyard.*

7 Burying Ground

This cemetery contains the graves of several historic figures, including Mary Chilton, the first of the *Mayflower* pilgrims to reach Plymouth Rock, and John Winthrop, first governor of the colony. Others buried here include William Dawes, who joined Paul Revere in his "midnight ride," as well as Elizabeth Pain, who provided the inspiration for Hester Prynne in Nathaniel Hawthorne's *The Scarlet Letter.* The oldest gravestone in Boston remembers William Paddy, who died in 1658.

▶ *Continue on School Street, passing Old City Hall.*

8 Old Corner Bookstore

Once a famous bookstore (now a jeweler), this is one of Boston's oldest buildings. Starting out as an apothecary shop in 1712, it became famous in the mid-19th century as the publishers Ticknor and Fields. Their best-selling authors included Nathaniel Hawthorne, Henry Wadsworth Longfellow, Henry David Thoreau, and Julia Ward Howe, who penned *The Battle Hymn of the Republic*, the anthem of the North during the Civil War.

▶ *Turn right on Washington Street.*

9 Old South Meeting House

Standing in the quiet simplicity of this 1729 Congregational church, it is hard to imagine the fiery debates that inflamed political passions and led to the Revolution. Back then, "Old South" was the largest space

Union Oyster House where Daniel Webster used to dine

available for public assemblies. After the Boston Massacre in 1770, protesters marched from here to confront the lieutenant-governor.

More than three years later came the meeting that triggered the Boston Tea Party (see page 8). Today, the second-oldest church in Boston is a museum recording those tumultuous days.

i Boston National Historical Park Visitor Center, 15 State Street

▶ *Turn back and follow Washington Street past the Corner Bookstore. Just before the Old State House, a walk-way to the right leads to the Old State House.*

10 Old State House

The lion and unicorn symbolize the connection with the Mother Country, a link which James Otis demanded be cut as early as 1761. Five years later, the hated Stamp Act was debated here and, on July 18, 1776, Colonel Thomas Crafts stepped on to the balcony to read the Declaration of Independence. Two hundred years later, Queen Elizabeth II stood on the same spot and spoke in celebration of the American bicentennial. Note the ring of cobblestones outside

the seat of the Massachusetts Assembly, recording the Boston Massacre of 1770, when five Bostonians were shot by British soldiers (see page 8). The museum inside tells the story.

▶ *Cross Congress Street diagonally.*

11 Faneuil Hall

In Boston, Faneuil rhymes with Daniel, and the name recalls the French merchant who funded the construction of Boston's marketplace in 1742. In the meeting hall above, freedom of speech was a prerogative. Locals congregated in 1764 to object to the Sugar Act. In the following years, their topics of protest were taxation and English troop movements. Samuel Adams' rebellious speech in 1772, stirring up anti-British feelings, was particularly provocative. But debate did not stop with Independence.

Over the centuries, Bostonians have spoken their minds here on issues such as slavery, alcohol, the Vietnam War and women's rights. Like the Old State House, there is a reminder of England: the grasshopper that tops the building is thought to be a copy of the weathervane on the Royal Exchange in London.

Boston's oldest public building, the 1713 Old State House

▶ *Turn right into Haymarket.*

🄼 Haymarket

Vendors still set out their produce here on Fridays and Saturdays as their predecessors have done for 300 years. In contrast to modern air-conditioned supermarkets, this is a noisy, bustling market, with a huge variety of fruit and vegetables, locally grown and from around the world. Although the Big Dig is finished and the overhead expressway taken down, much landscaping work remains to be done in the area.

▶ *Follow the Freedom Trail red line to Hanover Street. Turn right on Richmond Street, then left on North Street to North Square.*

🄵 Paul Revere House

Revere's talent as a silversmith, bell-maker, engraver, and even false teeth-maker fade away in the light of his fame as messenger. He rode to Lexington on the night of April 18, 1775 to warn that "the British are coming!" (see page 12). His tiny wooden home, at No. 19, is the oldest in Boston (1680) and is as plain and simple inside as Revere left it.

▶ *Leave North Square on Prince Street, turn right on Hanover*

FOR HISTORY BUFFS

Among the pages of history devoted to the men of the Massachusetts Bay Colony, Ann Hutchinson is only a footnote. Yet this woman dared to discuss her own views of what was, then, the "official" religion. The punishment for such a challenge to the Puritan hierarchy was exile. In 1638, she left home and, with her followers, moved south. They founded the second settlement in New England in what is now the state of Rhode Island.

▶ *Follow the red line across North Street to Union Street. (For the Holocaust Memorial, see page 46.)*

🄬 Union Oyster House

Dating back to 1826, this place enjoys the title of the "oldest continuously operated restaurant in America." It started life as a store, but became a place to eat in 1826. Lawyer Daniel Webster used to sit at the bar, consuming up to six glasses of brandy and three dozen oysters at a sitting.

▶ *Turn onto Marshall Street for the Boston Stone.*

🄭 Boston Stone

Myth insists that this millstone marked the true center of Boston, and that all distances were measured from here. This is a tribute to the public relations skills of a tavern owner who set the stone up as a publicity stunt back in 1737. The stone itself was used originally for grinding pigment by Thomas Child, a painter from London.

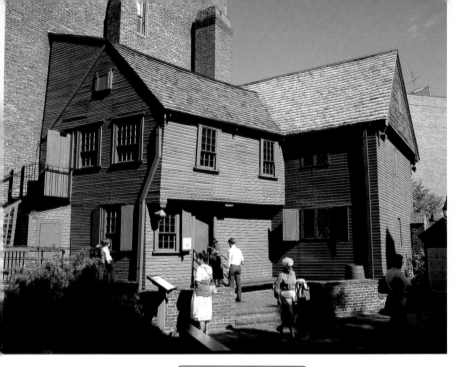

Paul Revere's House, restored to its original appearance, now operates as a small museum

Street, then left on Paul Revere Mall to the Old North Church.

16 Old North Church

Sexton Robert Newman had to flash lanterns ("One if by land, and two if by sea") to fellow patriots across the Charles River to warn them of British troop movements. He hung up two from the 191-foot (58m) steeple that is still visible in many parts of the city. Supposedly, one John Childs *flew* from the steeple in 1757, though contemporary reports do not explain how. Officially named Christ Church, it is the oldest in Boston (1723), and remains a place of worship. On the "Behind the Scenes" tour, you can go up into the bell-ringing chamber and down into the crypt. Here is the tomb of British Major John Pitcairn (see page 11).

▶ *Go uphill on Hull Street.*

17 Copp's Hill Burying Ground

This is not a resting place of famous historic figures, though Sexton Newman is buried here,

SPECIAL TO...

One of the most bizarre accidents in Boston's history took place on Copp's Hill Terrace. In 1919, 21 people were killed by a tidal wave of molasses when a giant tank burst open releasing 2.5 million gallons (11 million liters) of the sticky liquid.

as is early African American community leader Prince Hall. The old headstones are worth a look, particularly that of Daniel Malcolm. Used for target practice by the British soldiers who camped here, the scars are still clear to see.

▶ *Continue downhill on Hull Street; turn left on Commercial Street, then right across Charlestown Bridge on the right-hand sidewalk. At the north end of the bridge, follow the red line down the steps and along Water Street.*

18 USS *Constitution*

Like HMS *Victory* in England, this is still a commissioned ship and an icon for the navy. A magnificent example of a

wooden warship, her greatest glory came in the war of 1812 against the British, who were then masters of the sea. She destroyed four enemy frigates and sloops and earned the nickname, "Old Ironsides," when, as cannonballs bounced off her hull, a seaman shouted "Huzzah! Her sides are made of iron!" In fact, the ship is made of live oak, a particularly tough wood from southeastern U.S.A.

▶ *From the Navy Yard follow the trail to the Bunker Hill Monument.*

19 Bunker Hill Monument

A 221-foot (67m) obelisk commemorates the first major battle of the Revolutionary War, which was fought on this hill on June 17, 1775. Facing a mighty British force, the ill-equipped Colonists stood their ground, mindful of the now legendary order, "Don't fire until you see the whites of their eyes!" Though the Colonists were eventually routed, they reduced the British army's numbers considerably and the battle was significant in their ultimate victory. There is an exhibition on the site, and musket firing takes place in summer.

TOUR
6

Boston
Old & New

Boston's development started by the water, then moved inland to Beacon Hill where the wealthy lived. Later, it included Back Bay, which was reclaimed land. Allow a full day for this tour, which traces highlights of that growth, from narrow streets to grand boulevards, with Georgian houses and modern skyscrapers.

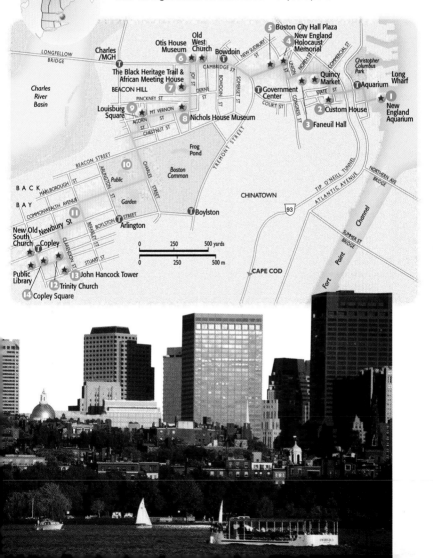

⌐i⌐ *147 Tremont Street; 15 State Street*

▷ *Start at the Aquarium MBTA stop. Walk to the New England Aquarium on Central Wharf.*

❶ New England Aquarium

By 1960, Boston's waterfront was an area of vacant warehouses and unused wharves. The decay was reversed in the 1970s by a renewal program that reestablished and emphasized the city's age-old role as a port. One of the first projects was the New England Aquarium, at the end of Central Wharf (1817). At low tide, the smell of the sea and the tidal flats permeates the outdoor plaza in front of the aquarium, where seals swim in the open-air pool and the *Discovery*, an auxiliary boat, hosts shows by trained sea lions.

Indoors, the centerpiece of the aquarium is a huge three-story-high glass salt-water tank (187,000 gallons/41,555 liters), one of the largest in the world, where sharks and eels prowl up and down past Myrtle, a 500-pound (227kg) green sea turtle who likes to have her back scratched by the aquarium's divers.

Whale-watching cruises leave daily from Long Wharf (April to October).

▷ *Return to the Aquarium MBTA Stop. Cross to State Street. At McKinley Square is the Custom House.*

❷ Custom House

This massive 1847 granite building was described as "one of the noblest pieces of commercial architecture in the world" by 19th-century poet Walt Whitman. Certainly it is one of the biggest Greek Revival structures in the country and took ten years to build, with 3,000 pilings each weighing more than 40 tons (36,363kg) being driven into the soggy soil.

In 1915, the 495-foot (148.5m) high tower was added. This shattered the city's height limit and won it the title of the "tallest building in New England." The four clock faces are notorious for showing different times.

▷ *Turn right on Commercial Street and continue into Quincy Market. Turn left.*

❸ Faneuil Hall/Quincy Market

The well-traveled visitor may see nothing remarkable about this array of stores and restaurants in restored 19th-century buildings. Yet this 1976 urban redevelopment was the first of its kind, and its success has been copied all over the world ever since.

In Colonial days, when sailing ships tied up at Long Wharf, the Marketplace was used by vendors of fruits, vegetables, and other commodities. By 1825, Faneuil (rhymes with "Daniel") Hall was too small, so Mayor Josiah Quincy authorized the construction of the Quincy Market and its two offspring, the North and South markets. Today, restaurants, pubs, and fast-food counters satisfy the hunger of over 14 million visitors a year. (See also page 42.)

▷ *At Faneuil Hall, cross North Street to Congress Street. Turn right and continue to the Holocaust Memorial.*

Quincy Market, a lively collection of eating places and stores

❹ New England Holocaust Memorial

This memorial, both dramatic and intimate, is located on a busy traffic island between City Hall Plaza and the 18th-century Blackstone Block. The six glass towers are lit from within at night. Each is six stories high and etched with six million random numbers, symbolizing the victims of the concentration camps. On the base of each tower are quotes from survivors, which tell of love, hope, and despair. One, from Gerda Weissman Klein, recalls a 13-year-old's gift to her best friend in the camp: "Imagine a world in which your entire possession is one raspberry, and you gave it to your friend."

▷ *Cross Congress Street and continue up the steps to the City Hall Plaza.*

❺ Boston City Hall Plaza

The area around City Hall was once the red-light district, with its attendant slums, burlesque theaters, and boarded-up stores. Known officially as Scollay Square, it once deserved its "Combat Zone" nickname. In the 1960s, the run-down buildings were demolished and replaced by the John F. Kennedy federal office buildings and a new City Hall, a pyramid standing on its head, designed by I. M. Pei. In winter the plaza

looks barren, but in summer it becomes a lively meeting-place, with pushcart vendors, office workers, and free evening concerts on the stage behind City Hall.

▶ *Continue through the Plaza to Cambridge Street; turn right.*

SPECIAL TO...

Beacon Hill looks like a movie-set for a costume drama, with brick sidewalks, gaslights, and handsome houses with shutters and window boxes. Acorn Street, one of the last remaining cobbled thoroughfares in the city, is the narrowest on the hill, yet wide enough to comply with building regulations of the period, which insisted that two cows must be able to pass by one another. Note the odd purple panes of glass. Back in 1818, a batch of window glass shipped over from Hamburg was tainted with manganese oxide that gradually turned purple after exposure to light.

---

6 Otis House Museum

Beacon Hill, with some of the most elegant homes in Boston, dates back to just after the Revolution, when Harrison Gray Otis started to build houses here. This lawyer, mayor of Boston, and U.S. senator was also a property developer, so he could afford to have Charles Bulfinch, the noted architect of the day, design a home for him here at 141 Cambridge Street. Often called the First Otis House, its perfectly proportioned, if rather dull, brick exterior hides a sophisticated and surprisingly colorful interior. At the top of a handsome staircase, the grand drawing-room looks much as it did 200 years ago. Today this is the headquarters of Historic New England (formerly SPNEA), an organization that looks after some 70 historic properties throughout New England.

▶ *Cross Cambridge Street and go up Joy Street.*

7 The Black Heritage Trail

At this point the itinerary and Boston's Black Heritage Trail meet. Celebrating the history of the city's African-American community, the Trail encompasses 14 significant sites. Two are on this route and are part of the Museum of Afro-American History, which traces the civil rights movement. The Abiel Smith School in Joy Street contains displays relating to the long struggle for equal education for African-American children in the city, which started in 1787 and ended when segregation was finally abolished in 1855. Established with an endowment from white businessman Abiel Smith, the school educated African American children for 20 years of that interim period.

Just off Joy Street, in Smith Court, is the African Meeting House (closed for renovation; due to re-open 2007), which is the ending point of the Trail. It was built by black Americans in 1806 as a place where they could worship without being relegated to the gallery, as was the case in "white" churches. The meeting house became the home of the New England Anti-Slavery Society – such a force in the Abolitionist Movement that the building became known as the Black Faneuil Hall.

▶ *Continue up Joy Street; turn right on Mount Vernon Street. At No. 55 is Nichols House.*

8 Nichols House Museum

Red-brick houses line Mount Vernon Street, one of the loveliest streets in Boston. The museum is a time-warp, where nothing has been changed since the owner, Rose Standish Nichols, died in 1960. Her will ensured that "people from around the world without a letter of introduction could see the inside of a fine house." From a wealthy Boston family, she is remembered as a landscape gardener and a fervent

worker for international peace. Her needlework and paintings lend a personal touch to the 1804 mansion, which also has bronzes by her uncle, the sculptor Augustus Saint-Gaudens.

▶ *Continue west along Mount Vernon Street to Louisburg Square.*

9 Louisburg Square

The name of this square recalls the struggle between France and Britain for supremacy in North America. Even though local troops had fought successfully for the Crown against the French at the Fortress of Louisburg, Nova Scotia, back in 1745, this elegant square, named after their victory, was built a century later. Much like a London square, the grassy quadrangle is a private park for owners of the surrounding smart homes. Residents included celebrities such as writer Louisa May Alcott (No. 10). Opera singer Jenny Lind, the "Swedish Nightingale," was married at No. 20.

▶ *Across from Louisburg Square is Willow Street. Take the first right, Acorn Street, then go left*

SPECIAL TO...

The early 19th-century equivalent of smoking a joint after dinner was sniffing ether. Dr. William Morton, a dentist, noticed that participants in these "ether frolics" felt no pain if they bumped into the furniture. He experimented with ether, using it on patients before extracting a tooth. On October 16, 1846, in Boston's Massachusetts General Hospital, he supervised an operation that successfully removed a tumor from a patient, using ether as an anaesthetic. This major breakthrough for surgery is commemorated with the statue *The Good Samaritan* in the Public Garden.

---

on West Cedar Street, then right on Chestnut Street and, finally, left on Charles Street. Across Beacon Street is the Public Garden.

⑩ Public Garden

Boston can thank a group of public-spirited green thumbs for America's first botanical garden. From 1837 until their success over 20 years later, they battled to protect the city's green heart from developers. Today, their triumph provides a retreat for locals and visitors alike. In spring and summer, flowers bloom by the paths, while the swish of fountains masks the noise of the traffic.

Children plead for rides on the slow, stately, foot-pedaled swan boats, introduced in 1877, and peer at the fountain sculpture of Bagheera, the panther immortalized in Kipling's *Jungle Books*. A home-grown favorite is the sculpture of Mrs. Mallard and her eight ducklings, at the corner of Charles and Beacon streets. Robert McCloskey's *Make Way for Ducklings* is a much-loved children's tale of a mother duck stopping Boston traffic as she shepherds her brood from the Charles River to the pond in the Boston Public Garden. A children's parade each spring retraces the ducklings' route.

▶ *Cross the Garden using the suspension bridge and exit through the Arlington Street gate onto Commonwealth Avenue. Walk one block, then turn left on Berkeley Street, then right on Newbury Street.*

⑪ Newbury Street

Water covered this area of Boston until the second half of the 19th century when Back Bay was filled in and transformed into a residential district. The backbone is Commonwealth Avenue, a Parisian-style boulevard, lined with fine trees and grand statues of long-forgotten worthies. Running parallel to "Comm Ave" is Newbury Street, known for its upscale and trendy art galleries, boutiques and cafés. Yet, the apartments on and around the street create a neighborhood atmosphere. Old buildings have new uses: What was built as a Temple for the Working Union of Progressive Spiritualists is now a major bookstore. Boston's former Museum of Natural History is full of expensive menswear; and the severe face of the New England Insurance Company fronts trendy fashion stores. You will also find fashion in the former

The pedal-powered swan boats on the pond in Boston's Public Garden are popular in summer

Trinity Church reflected in the John Hancock Tower

many of the original glass panels off the 62-story skyscraper. The difficulty was rectified and now the glass acts as a mirror, reflecting Trinity Church.

▶ *Copley Square is a huge plaza, bounded by the Boston Public Library, Trinity Church, New Old South Church, the Fairmont Copley Plaza Hotel and the John Hancock Tower.*

14 Copley Square

Copley Square was described by one observer as a "desert of dirt, dust, mud, and wind." Now it is a pleasant place of fountains, benches...and skateboarders. The bronze sculpture, *Tortoise and Hare*, commemorates all those who have run in the Boston Marathon, the world's oldest, which finishes here on the square. The Boston Public Library, the first in America to lend books for free, is Charles McKim's adaptation of an Italian Renaissance palazzo. Constructed with a quarryful of yellow Siena marble, the 1895 building was decorated with works by then-contemporary artists and sculptors such as John Singer Sargent and Daniel Chester French.

▶ *There is an MBTA stop at Copley Square to return to the Aquarium, or travel elsewhere in the city.*

Museum of Natural History and the former American Academy of Arts and Sciences.

▶ *After one block, turn left on Clarendon Street and continue to Boylston Street. Turn right, left and onto Copley Square.*

12 Trinity Church

Two of America's finest architects, Charles McKim and Henry Richardson, worked on Trinity Church in the late 19th century. Richardson's design was inspired by medieval Europe, while the interior coloring was a tribute to William Morris's pre-Raphaelite movement. On the Boylston Street side of the church, the statue of the Rev. Phillips Brooks commemorates the passionate preacher who used to ride his horse at breakneck speed. He also wrote *O Little Town of Bethlehem*.

▶ *Across Stuart Street is the John Hancock Tower.*

13 John Hancock Tower

Once the tallest building in New England, the headquarters of the John Hancock Life Insurance Company has had its problems. Architect I. M. Pei's unusual rhomboid shape was beset by air currents that sucked

SATURDAY, NOV. 13
5·00-7·00 PM
BAKED BEAN SUPPER
ADULTS $5 CHILDREN $2
CHRIST CHURCH, UNITED METHODIST

HALF A DAY

Cambridge &
Harvard University

Established as Newtowne back in 1630, this was the first capital of the colony. Two years after Harvard College was founded in 1636, the town changed its name to Cambridge, to give it the same kudos, no doubt, as the English university city. Today, the mixture of grand museums, historic houses, wealthy residents, and student *joie de vivre* makes it one of the most vibrant and attractive places in New England.

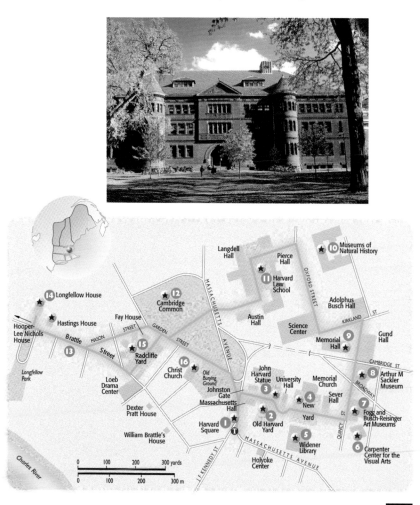

i Cambridge Visitor Information
   Booth, Harvard Square

▶ Start at the Harvard Square
   MBTA stop.

❶ Harvard Square

All around the traffic island is
the bustle and noise of "the
square." Here you can buy international newspapers at the
kiosk, eat international cuisine at
the numerous restaurants, then
buy all-American sportswear at
the Harvard Cooperative, the
large department store, known
locally as "the Coop" (rhymes
with hoop).

▶ Walk up Massachusetts
   Avenue and turn right through
   Johnston Gate, the entrance to
   Old Harvard Yard.

❷ Old Harvard Yard

Harvard is not only the oldest
university in America, but also
one of the most influential.
From its earliest days, it has
symbolized the independent
attitude of the Colonists and,
significantly, America's first
printing press was set up here in
1640. Harvard Yard, the center of
the campus for more than 350
years, is really two vast, open
quadrangles, totalling 22 acres
(8.8 hectares). The first yard is

FOR HISTORY BUFFS

America's oldest university is
also one of its most
prestigious. One of the seven
so-called Ivy League schools
(so old that ivy grows on their
hallowed walls), Harvard
emphasizes academic
excellence, shunning the sports
scholarships and razzmatazz of
the country's younger universities. The 7,000 undergraduates
now include the women of
Radcliffe (see page 55), but
there is also an impressive
graduate program ranging from
the prestigious Harvard Law
and Medical Schools, to newer
disciplines, such as Business
Administration and
Government.

the home of the Freshmen (first-
year students) who live in the
red-brick dormitories. On the
right is Massachusetts Hall, the
university's oldest surviving
building. Established as a laboratory and dormitory in 1720, it
housed American troops at the
start of the Revolution.

i Harvard Information Center,
   Holyoke Center

❸ John Harvard Statue

Directly across the yard, in front
of the granite University Hall
(1815), this seated statue is
labeled "John Harvard, founder
1638." The sculpture is wittily
referred to as the "Statue of the
Three Lies." Harvard was a
benefactor rather than a founder,
the foundation year was 1636,
and the statue is actually of
Sherman Hoar, a Harvard
student who modeled for
19th-century sculptor Daniel
Chester French.

▶ Continue past University Hall
   and enter New Yard.

Johnston Gate, the main entrance
to Old Harvard Yard

❹ New Yard

The second, larger portion of the
Yard is also called Tercentenary
Theater because it was here that
the 300th graduation ceremonies
were held in 1936. Criss-crossed
by walking paths, a figurative
bridge links the spiritual and
intellectual centers of the
university. To the left is
Memorial Church, "Mem
Church." It was completed in
1932 as a tribute by Harvard
alumni to classmates killed in
World War I, and has been
updated for victims of World
War II and, later, the Korean
and Vietnam conflicts.

▶ To the right is the Widener
   Library, the world's largest
   university library.

❺ Widener Library

In this temple to the written
word, information spans the
centuries, from a first folio of
Shakespeare and a Gutenberg

Bible, to microfilm files and computer screens. Built between 1913 and 1915, the library was given in memory of Harry Elkins Widener, a wealthy graduate who drowned on the *Titanic*. Unfortunately the library is not open to the public.

▶ *Straight ahead is Quincy Street.*

6 Carpenter Center for the Visual Arts
This glass and concrete block at No. 24 Quincy Street is the only example in America of a building by the 20th-century Swiss architect Le Corbusier. As well as art exhibitions, it houses the extensive Harvard Film Archive. Screenings of unusual or historic movies are often held here.

7 Fogg and Busch-Reisinger Art Museums
Many institutions of higher learning have their own museums. Harvard has eight on campus, of which the Fogg, Busch-Reisinger and the Arthur M. Sackler have world-class reputations.

The Fogg, which opened in 1895, is the oldest of the three. Behind the neo-Georgian façade on Quincy Street is a courtyard modeled after a 15th-century Italian palazzo. The collection concentrates on European art from the Middle Ages to the present, with a strong line-up of Italian Renaissance paintings, as well as a self-portrait by Van Gogh, and *Red Boats* by Claude Monet.

Directly behind the Fogg is the Busch-Reisinger Museum, in the Otto Werner Hall. Here, the main focus is works by the Expressionists, Europeans such as Franz Marc, Paul Klee, Wassily Kandinsky, and Emile Nolde.

▶ *Go north on Quincy Street, cross Broadway, and the Arthur M. Sackler Museum is on the right.*

8 Arthur M. Sackler Museum
This is the university's third art museum, in British architect James Sterling's strikingly

contemporary building, opened in 1985. Famous for its exquisite collection of Chinese ceramics, bronzes and jades, it specializes in Ancient Greek, Islamic and Asian art, from Indian miniatures to Japanese prints. On the fourth floor, among the Greek art, are several large ceramic vases dating from about 340 BC. There are also jade dragons, bronze ritual bells and a large bronze wine container, more than 3,000 years old, from China.

▶ *Continue along Quincy Street, crossing Cambridge Street. Memorial Hall is on the left.*

9 Memorial Hall
Memorial Hall reopened after a major restoration in 1996. Built in 1878 to honor the Harvard men who died in the Civil War, it epitomizes the Gothic Revival style, with a Great Hall soaring up to a jig-saw puzzle roof of

Well-displayed period furnishings complement the Fogg's paintings and sculptures

carved beams and timbers. Here, Winston Churchill was given an honorary degree in 1943. The stained-glass windows portray stories and heroes from the Bible, American history and Greek mythology. In a controversial move, "Mem Hall" has been made into a dining room. Where nervous undergraduates once took exams, first-year students gossip at mealtimes under the chandeliers. To one side is Sanders Theater, an intimate auditorium finished in dark wood. It was the setting for Harvard graduations up until 1911, but is now used for the performing arts.

▶ *At the end of Quincy Street bear left across Kirkland Street, then turn right onto Oxford Street.*

10 Museums of Natural History
Don't be put off by the fusty-sounding names of the four museums: there is plenty to fascinate adults and children alike in this brick building. Highlights include the 22-pound (10kg) meteor which fell from the sky in 1992, and landed on a car in Peekskill, New York, and the life-size skeleton of a 42-foot long (12.5m) *Kronosaurus*. This gigantic crocodile lived 135 million years ago.

Best known of all is the unique Ware Collection of Glass Flowers, 3,000 scientifically accurate, life-size models of flowers and plants made out of blown glass.

▶ *From Oxford Street, go into Harvard Law School. Pass under the arch to the right of Pierce Hall, and bear left on the path along Langdell Hall.*

11 Harvard Law School
The Law School was started in 1817, with six students. Today, each new class of 540 students has been selected from over 7,000 applicants. Langdell Hall, on the right, has the largest law library in the world, and a public reading room on the fourth floor that stretches the length of two football fields.

Next is Austin Hall, a small brownstone building completed in 1881 by Henry Hobson Richardson. Each spring in the Ames Courtroom, on the second floor, finalists in the third-year competition argue their cases before a Justice of the U.S. Supreme Court. In the sessions, seating is by ticket only; students have priority.

▶ *Bear right upon leaving Austin Hall and follow the path between Hemenway Gymnasium and Gannett House. Cross Massachusetts Avenue at the traffic light and walk across Cambridge Common.*

Longfellow House: this clapboard building was abandoned by its Loyalist owner in 1774

12 Cambridge Common
This small green park is all that remains of the fields and pastures where the American army assembled after the 1775 battles of Lexington and Concord (April) and Bunker Hill (June). On July 3, George Washington took command of the American army here, and a plaque marks the location of the Washington Elm beneath which this event took place. At least, that is the story ...

▶ *On the far side of the Common, turn right on Garden Street, then left on Mason Street. Turn right on Brattle Street and continue to No. 101.*

13 Brattle Street
All along Brattle Street are fine houses, built before the American Revolution. Since most were then occupied by supporters of the Crown, it was called "Tory Row." The owners left hastily, and all that remains are their names, recorded in blue plaques. Hastings House, No. 101, is a fine example, as are Nos. 113 and 115, which belonged to the daughters of Henry Wadsworth Longfellow, who lived at No. 105.

Built in 1685, the Hooper-Lee Nichols House at No. 159 is

now the headquarters of the Cambridge Historical Society, who also organize guided walks.

14 Longfellow House

The Tory, or British sympathizer, John Vassall lived in this yellow clapboard mansion. He built it in 1759, in anticipation of his marriage to Elizabeth, the sister of the last Royal Lieutenant Governor. In 1775, he was thrown out by the patriots, who moved in with the wounded from the Battle of Bunker Hill. Next, the hospital became George Washington's headquarters for nine months. Washington enlarged it to make room for guests.

In the following century, the celebrated American poet Henry Wadsworth Longfellow rented a room here. Later, he received the house as a wedding present and lived here from 1837 to 1882. During that period he wrote *Hiawatha* (1855) and *The Village Blacksmith* (1839) here, and completed his translation of Dante, among other works. Here, also, he entertained fellow writers Dickens, Emerson, Hawthorne, Twain, and Wilde. Longfellow was particularly fond of the view across to the Charles River, and it remains unspoiled, thanks to his children, who gave the land to the City of Cambridge in 1913.

After extensive restoration, the Longfellow House is again open to the public. Visits are by guided tour only but the gardens are always open.

▶ *Retrace your steps on Brattle Street and turn left into Radcliffe College.*

15 Radcliffe Yard

Radcliffe College started out in 1879 with just 27 women students in a small two-story house. It was named in honor of Londoner Lady Anne Radcliffe, who gave £100 to Harvard back in the 17th century. Admissions to Radcliffe have always been highly competitive, and many "Cliffies" have become well known, including Helen Keller,

whose life was portrayed in the movie *The Miracle Worker*. Nearly a century after its founding, Radcliffe merged with Harvard. The name, however, lives on thanks to the Radcliffe Institute for Advanced Study, founded in 1999. In Radcliffe Yard, the Federal-style Fay House was built in 1807 and was the first building acquired by the college. Today it is used as an administration building.

▶ *After crossing the Yard, exit onto Garden Street, and bear right to Christ Church.*

16 Christ Church and the Old Burying Ground

In the lobby, just inside the outer door of Christ Church, a plaque in front of you marks a bullet hole made, so the story goes, when the British were

Christ Church, designed by Peter Hamson, the architect of King's Chapel in Boston

marching to Lexington in April, 1775. Later that year, George and Martha Washington attended services here, using the pew directly below the pulpit, on the left. Between the Christ Church and the First Church is Cambridge's oldest cemetery, God's Acre. The earliest grave is that of Anne Erinton, a settler who passed away on December 24, 1635. Eight presidents of Harvard are also buried here.

▶ *Continue down Garden Street to Massachusetts Avenue and bear right to Harvard Square and the MBTA stop.*

SPECIAL TO...

Close by the sidewalk is a stone milestone, carved in 1734. On the back are the words: "Boston 8 miles." Today that distance is covered in 8 minutes on the MBTA.

CULTURAL CRADLE

America's culture, as well as its sense of history, started in New England. The 19th century, in particular, saw the development not just of American themes but of a distinctive American "voice" and viewpoint. What binds the most talented artists and writers together is their sense of New England, in print and on canvas, set to music or presented on stage. Names such as Robert Frost (poet), Nathaniel Hawthorne (novelist), Winslow Homer (painter), Norman Rockwell (illustrator), and Eugene O'Neill (playwright) conjure up bleak landscapes and clapboard houses, glistening seas and "salt-of-the-earth" families, while Charles Ives' music interprets the moods of the countryside.

Literature

The first New England writer to make an international name for himself was Henry Wadsworth Longfellow (1807–82), a poet who was also a professor at Harvard. Hugely popular, his narrative poems told home-grown tales, from *The Song of Hiawatha*, a story of Native Americans, to *The Midnight Ride of Paul Revere*, which encapsulates the start of the American Revolution. Nathaniel Hawthorne (1804–64) also took inspiration from New England history, though he explored the psychological effects of Puritanism in novels such as *The Scarlet Letter* and *The House of the Seven Gables*. His friend Herman Melville (1819–91) received little critical acclaim in his lifetime. A New Yorker who wrote at Arrowhead in Western Massachusetts, Melville's most famous novel was *Moby Dick*, an allegory of good and evil which drew on his experiences aboard a New England whaler as a young man.

While Hawthorne and Melville relied on the realism of history, two authors, Emerson and Thoreau, took a more spiritual path. Transcendentalism was a movement led by Ralph Waldo Emerson (1803–82), a charismatic speaker and writer whose philosophy is best summed up by his often quoted saying: "who so would be a man must be a non-conformist." He appealed to Americans to throw off the yoke of European tradition and to look at their individual experiences. His friend, Henry David Thoreau (1817–62), did just that, going "back to nature." The result of his simple life by Walden Pond, on the edge of Concord, was the idealistic book *Walden: Or Life in the Woods* (1854).

Both men spent time in Concord, where Louisa May Alcott (1832–88) also lived and wrote *Little Women*, a huge best-seller, based on family life. Another woman writer, Harriet Beecher Stowe (1811–96), brought the issue of slavery to thousands of homes with *Uncle Tom's Cabin*. The book, which was originally published as a weekly serial, sold 300,000 copies. While Stowe wrote to further a cause, Emily Dickinson (1830–86) wrote for herself. A recluse whose poems were only discovered after her death, she lived her entire life not just in Amherst in Western Massachusetts, but also in the same brick Federal house where she had been born.

New England also attracted writers from elsewhere in the States. Samuel Longhorne Clemens, better known as Mark Twain (1835–1910), was born in

Left: Henry Wadsworth Longfellow
Below: Topsy, from Harriet Beecher Stowe's *Uncle Tom's Cabin*

(Mrs Keeley as Topsy, "'s dretful wicked")
"SLAVE LIFE," OR "UNCLE TOM'S CABIN"

Missouri, but many of his best-loved stories, such as the antics of Huckleberry Finn and Tom Sawyer, were written in his Hartford home. His tales of the American West, written with humor and an easy style, brought him a wide audience. By contrast, high society was the subject of novelist Edith Wharton (1862–1937). The author of *The Age of Innocence* did much of her writing at The Mount, her retreat in Lenox, Massachusetts.

The quintessential New England poet was Robert Frost (1874–1963), who spent most of his life in New Hampshire and Vermont. So great was his stature that he was the first poet to participate in a presidential inauguration. In 1961, he read his poem *The Gift Outright* at President John F. Kennedy's swearing-in. His descriptions of a Vermont snowstorm and swinging on birch trees are easily remembered; his forthright expression of universal truths have a darker side.

Theater

New York was always the cradle of American theater, but America's first major playwright, Eugene O'Neill (1888–1953), learned his craft in New England. The New Yorker studied at the 47 Workshop of George Pierce Baker in Harvard before making an impact with the Provincetown Players on Cape Cod. Ten of his plays were produced from 1916 to 1920. A Nobel and Pulitzer prize winner, O'Neill is remembered at the theater bearing his name near New London, Connecticut. The cottage where he spent his boyhood summers was the setting for *Long Day's Journey into Night*.

Music

While Puritan influences restricted early New Englanders to music in churches, the region was a powerhouse of classical music in the 20th century. The best known composer is the avant-garde Charles Ives (1874–1954), born in Danbury, Connecticut, the son of a bandmaster. Fiercely proud and inde-

The Boston Symphony Orchestra performs at Symphony Hall from the beginning of October to the end of April

pendent, Ives bucked European tradition to draw on traditional American folk songs, hymns, and marches. The result was his *New England Symphony, Three Places in New England*, and *Sonata No. 2* for piano and flute. The last was nicknamed *Concord, Mass 1840–1860*, perhaps because of its dedication to the town's literary circle of Emerson, Thoreau, Hawthorne, and the Alcotts.

New Englander Colonel Henry Higginson enjoyed the Austrian attitude to music so much that he set up the legendary Boston Pops in 1885, based on the romance and fun of Viennese orchestras. In 1929, the Pops went outdoors to perform, as they still do to this day. The Boston Symphony, now one of the world's great orchestras, has extended its popularity and fame thanks to the summer season in Tanglewood, in western Massachusetts.

CONNECTICUT

Fall foliage in the Litchfield Hills

Connecticut is rarely recognized as a vacation destination. Although popular with Manhattanites for weekends, many Americans and overseas visitors overlook it when planning a trip to New England. Yet it has a history dating back to 1635, a rich tapestry of villages and towns, countryside that looks softer than elsewhere in the northeast, and miles of unspoiled shoreline. Contrasts are to be found everywhere. Although well over half the state is heavily forested, Connecticut is also heavily populated. Most residents live in the suburbs, on the southwest coast and alongside the Connecticut River that cuts through the middle of this rectangular state.

From the early days, the state has been the home of a host of inventors whose ideas still provide employment. Eli Whitney's cotton gin brought mass production techniques to the world. Sam Colt, inventor of the Colt 45 revolver, set up an arms and ammunition industry that survives today. Clocks and door locks, tires and the pay telephone were all developed here. Now, chemicals, jet engines, and insurance are major employers. One of the wealthiest states in the country, in 2004 it also boasted the highest per capita income.

The affluent southwestern corner of Connecticut is virtually a suburb of New York City. Farther north, the Litchfield Hills, idyllic for artists and craftsmen, are also a retreat for show business celebrities. Two hundred years ago, the same wooded hills were stripped to fuel the furnaces and forges that processed iron for the guns used during the Revolution.

The coast, especially the eastern strip, is most popular with visitors. Mystic Seaport is an admirable re-creation of an early 19th-century seafaring village, complete with sailing ships.

There is a rich cultural heritage, because of the influence of Yale University and writers such as Mark Twain, Harriet Beecher Stowe, and dictionary-writer Noah Webster. Painters and actors have also made their homes here, and antiques shops and art galleries abound.

Tour 8

Hartford is known as the "Insurance Capital of America." The business began in 1794. It is also a city of "firsts" and "oldests." It claims the first municipal rose garden and development of the first American dictionary; the oldest newspaper, the *Hartford Courant*, and oldest state house. Two of America's most revered writers also lived here: Mark Twain and Harriet Beecher Stowe, who was Twain's neighbor. Twain's Victorian house is one of the most intriguing you'll see, deliberately designed to be unusual.

Tour 9

When it comes to universities, Yale and Harvard go together like Oxford and Cambridge, in England. Just as Harvard and Cambridge are in attractive towns, so Yale and Oxford are in industrial cities. Yale, with its ivy-covered buildings, is one of the finest academic institutions in the country, with impressive museums and art galleries. Countering all this culture, the Frisbee was supposedly invented here, along with two of America's most popular fast foods: the hamburger and the pizza.

Tour 10

Western Connecticut has bumpy, wooded hills dotted with villages that don't seem to have kept up with the 20th century, let alone the 21st. Although New York City is within commuting distance, urban frenzy is banned here. This is the countryside the way urban folk prefer it, with waterfalls and covered bridges, pleasant stores and small art galleries. Litchfield boasts the first American law school, which was set up in a tiny house over 200 years ago. The innocent-looking town of Lakeville turned out tons of arms to fuel the battle against Britain, winning itself the nickname of the "Arsenal of the Revolution."

Tour 11

Connecticut's coast was settled in the early 17th century by British emigrants who named the small towns after their homes: New London, Guilford, Essex and Old Lyme. The oldest stone house in New England, complete with fortifications, was built back in 1640. Later, locals turned their hand to building ships and submarines. The finest maritime museum in the States is at Mystic, where boats and docks re-create the romance, if not the reality, of life aboard the sailing ships of the 18th and 19th centuries.

Later, the seaside attracted artists and writers, while the Eugene O'Neill Theater Center outside New London gave actors such as Al Pacino and Meryl Streep their early opportunities. Despite the popularity of the bigger towns, there are still sleepy corners where visitors can sit and munch a sandwich in peace, overlooking tranquil Long Island Sound.

Mystic Seaport is a re-creation of a 19th-century seaport

Hartford

One of the oldest cities in the country, Hartford was founded in 1636 by a native of Hertford, England. There is an English flavor to the narrow streets and parks of Hartford, downtown is easily navigable, and skyscrapers rise high above the Connecticut River with its renovated riverfront. In this state capital are well-preserved historic places, the nation's oldest public art museum, a world-famous rose garden, and the homes of two of America's best-known and best-loved writers, Harriet Beecher Stowe and Mark Twain.

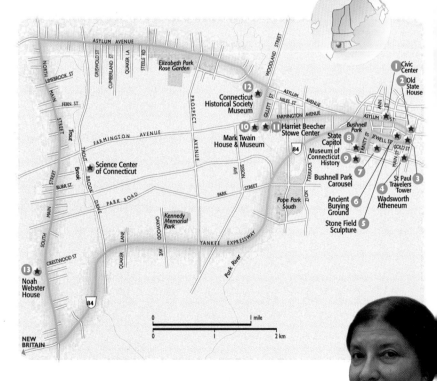

HALF A DAY

The Senate Chamber of the Old State House – the first state house in a newly independent United States

i / Civic Center Plaza

▶ *Park your car in the Civic Center garage, entrance on Asylum Street.*

❶ Civic Center

Downtown Hartford is undergoing a vigorous program of regeneration. Off Trumbull Street, at the side of the Civic Center is cobblestoned Pratt Street, with its variety of restaurants and shops. Inside the Civic Center, the outstanding University of Connecticut basketball squad consistently fills the arena, while the Hartford Wolf Pack, an affiliate of the New York Rangers hockey team, now faces off here.

▶ *Leave the Civic Center and walk east on Asylum Street to Main Street. Cross and enter the Old State House.*

❷ Old State House

Abandoned in 1878, the US's oldest state house has been carefully restored. Designed in 1792 and completed in 1796 by New England's star architect Charles Bulfinch, it stands on Meeting House Square, where the Colony was founded in 1636. This is where the first written constitution guaranteeing the right to representative government was enacted by the English colonists. That is why Connecticut is nicknamed "The Constitution State". Lafayette was made a citizen here, and the trials of Cinque and the *Amistad* opened here in 1839. One of the highlights of a visit is to see the original version of Gilbert Stuart's famous portrait of the first president of the US, George Washington. Also in the Old State House is Mr. Steward's Museum of Natural and Other Curiosities, established in 1797, featuring a two-headed calf and an 8.5-foot (2.5m) alligator. In summer, a farmers' market follows the Colonial tradition of setting up stands by the meeting house (Mon, Wed, Fri mornings).

▶ *Walk south one block to Travelers Tower, on the corner of Gold Street.*

SPECIAL TO...

The Connecticut Freedom Trail was established in 1995 to honor the history of the state's African American community, and covers a series of buildings and sites that represent the concept of freedom. Hartford's Old State House features in the trail for the part it played in the famous *Amistad* trials, a two-year legal battle that ultimately set free and repatriated to Sierra Leone a group of Africans who, in 1839, had taken control of the Spanish vessel carrying them to a life of slavery in Cuba. The story was told in Steven Spielberg's movie *Amistad* (1997).

⑧ St Paul Travelers Tower

Soaring 527 feet (160m) above street level, the "free Renaissance"-style, pink-granite Travelers Tower is capped by a prominent beacon light. From the observation deck atop the tower, visitors are rewarded with a breathtaking view of downtown Hartford, the Connecticut River and the entire Connecticut Valley from Mount Tom to Meriden Mountain in the south.

▶ *Across the street, on the corner of Main and Gold streets, is the Wadsworth Atheneum.*

④ Wadsworth Atheneum

One of New England's leading "must-see" museums, "the Wad" was founded in 1842, so it takes the title "the nation's oldest public art museum." Housed in an impressive neo-Gothic building, it boasts masterpieces from the 16th through the 20th centuries, including classics by Picasso (*Harlequin*) and Van Gogh (*Self Portrait*). The most intriguing painting is *House Fronting New Milford Green* by Ralph Earl, painted in 1796. The house still stands. Other home-grown talent includes members of the Hudson River School, the

FOR HISTORY BUFFS

Connecticut was proud of the royal charter it was granted by King Charles II, in 1662. When the next monarch, James II, wanted to revoke the colony's liberties in 1685, he sent Governor Andros to collect the document. Mysteriously, the candles blew out at the handover and the charter disappeared. Legend insists that Captain Joseph Wadsworth snatched it, ran off and hid it in a hollow oak tree, later called the Charter Oak. The privileges were restored four years later, after William and Mary came to the English throne. When the U.S. Constitution was drawn up, the Connecticut Charter served as a model.

The Hartford Fire Insurance Company building in Hartford, America's insurance industry capital

Downtown Hartford is dominated by high-rise office buildings

show dates of birth from the 1590s to the early 1600s, in Hertford, England.

▶ *Continue walking down Gold Street to Bushnell Park. Turn right along the border, Jewell Street. Opposite Ann Street, across from the YMCA, the Bushnell Park Carousel is in the park.*

🄇 Bushnell Park Carousel

The carousel is a Stein and Goldstein, hand-carved merry-go-round built in 1914, with 48 prancing horses and chariots rollicking to the tunes of a 1925 Wurlitzer band organ. At only 50 cents a ride, it is one of New England's bargains. Hot dogs and other snacks are available when the park is open.

▶ *Walk a few steps west to Trinity Street. Look right to the Sailors and Soldiers Memorial Arch, built in 1886 to honor the 4,000 Hartford citizens who served in the Civil War. Turn left and proceed up the hill half a block to the State Capitol. A statue of the French General Lafayette, ally of George Washington, sits on horseback in the middle of the street at the driveway entrance.*

🄈 State Capitol

Another refurbished landmark (built 1879), the Capitol is the home of the House of Representatives and Senate, Connecticut's legislature. Against a backdrop of white Connecticut marble are Gothic spires, a gleaming gold dome, statues, medallions, and bas-reliefs commemorating important people and events in state history. Gaudy to the point of being brash, architect Frank Lloyd Wright called it "The most ridiculous building I know of." Open to the public, the assemblies are in session from February through May in even years and January through June in odd years. More statues and historical relics decorate the interior.

🄄 Stone Field Sculpture

"$250,000 for a pile of rocks? That's ridiculous!" That was the reaction of many locals when the Hartford City Council voted to fund the sculpture created by Carl Andre in 1977. His work of art consists of 36 large stones laid out in rows to form an isosceles triangle. A similar furor erupted in England when London's Tate Gallery bought "a pile of bricks," a total of 120 bricks in two layers which the American sculptor entitled *Equivalent VIII*.

🄅 Ancient Burying Ground

Center Church, built in 1632, is Hartford's oldest church. Behind it, the Ancient Burying Ground is one of the city's few surviving historic sites from the 17th century. In the small, green, fenced-in graveyard, more than 400 brownstone markers stand at attention, marking the final resting places of Hartford's founding families. Epitaphs record lives that were only occasionally lengthy, more often short. Many

19th-century group of landscape painters who achieved a definite American style. There is also a fine collection of African-American art, decorative arts, costumes and textiles.

▶ *Cross the street diagonally to the north side of Gold Street and proceed down Gold Street, stopping at the Stone Field Sculpture and the adjacent Ancient Burying Ground.*

TOUR
8

▶ *Cross Capitol Avenue to No. 231.*

9 Museum of Connecticut History

The State Library and Supreme Court sandwich this museum, which contains the Fundamental Orders of Connecticut and the Colt Firearms Collection. The latter showcases Samuel Colt's genius for the invention, making and marketing of his patented revolvers and rifles. The museum also has a variety of political, industrial and military artifacts, with an emphasis on the Civil War era.

▶ *Return to the Capitol. Walk through it (round it, if closed) to the rear exit and continue north down the hill and through the park to Asylum Street. Turn right and walk one block back to the Civic Center to retrieve your car. Leave downtown, driving west on Asylum Street under the railroad bridge. Bear left at the fork onto Farmington Avenue. After 1 mile (1.6km), on the left is the home of Mark Twain.*

10 Mark Twain House and Museum

The internationally known writer and wit Samuel Clemens, alias Mark Twain, lived in this spectacular orange and black brick Victorian mansion for 17

The State Capitol; its exuberant design reflects Victorian pride

years. He commissioned this Gothic eccentricity in 1871, when he settled in Hartford with his family. In 1881, he had the 19-room home completely refurbished by Louis Comfort Tiffany. The library is the epitome of Victorian opulence, with carved wood, patterned carpets, and lavishly decorated walls and ceilings. Guides describe the life of the writer, his soirées with guests such as English writer Rudyard Kipling, and the way he retired to the billiard room to write books such as *The Adventures of Tom Sawyer* and *Huckleberry Finn*, because his children had commandeered his study. One of the first private

citizens in Hartford to have a telephone, Twain had so many problems with the new-fangled instrument that he kept a chart to record its inefficiencies.

In the museum, established in 2003, you can watch Ken Burns' revealing documentary on Twain.

▶ *Next door to the Twain house, at Forest Street, is the home of Harriet Beecher Stowe.*

11 Harriet Beecher Stowe Center

The "little lady who started the big war" (Civil War, 1865–70), was how President Abraham Lincoln referred to the author of *Uncle Tom's Cabin*. Published in 1852, the book was a blockbuster, selling over 300,000 copies in the first year alone. A stage version was even performed. The sentimental story of slaves in the south was unabashed, though successful, propaganda for the Anti-Slavery Movement. Nowadays, no-one remembers any of her other 30 books. Moreover, the term "Uncle Tom" has come to mean an African American who doesn't stand up for the rights of his race.

This house, in what was quiet farmland a century ago, was Stowe's home from 1873 until she died in 1896. Her home is now restored and paintings by

---

SPECIAL TO...

Samuel Colt (1814–62) was a self-taught and persistent inventor who revolutionized hand guns. Aged 21, he patented his Colt Paterson revolver and used the assembly-line techniques of fellow Connecticut inventor Eli Whitney to mass produce weapons. His 1848 Colt Dragoon was the first U.S. Army regulation revolver and, years later, the American West was won with what was, ironically, called the Colt Peacemaker.

FOR HISTORY BUFFS

On the Mississippi River, when a boatman called out "*Mark Twain*," the pilot knew that the depth was two fathoms. This was the pseudonym taken by Samuel Clemens, in 1862, when he became a newspaper reporter. Born in Missouri in 1835, Twain popularized life in the West with books such as *The Adventures of Tom Sawyer* (1876) and *The Adventures of Huckleberry Finn* (1884). Despite his folksy stories, he was no hayseed, but a well-traveled man, awarded an honorary degree by Oxford University in England in 1907.

---

her and her writing table, plus memorabilia of her career and her family lend a personal touch.

▶ *Continue west on Farmington Avenue for half a block. Turn right on Woodland Street, then take the first left onto Asylum Avenue. Just before the first traffic light, the Connecticut Historical Society is on the left.*

12 Connecticut Historical Society Museum

Inside, the museum offers rotating exhibits on state history, plus permanent displays of furniture and the decorative arts from Connecticut craftsmen of the 17th, 18th and 19th centuries. The exhibition "*Amistad* – A True Story of Freedom" tells the story (popularized by Stephen Spielberg's 1997 movie) of the African slaves who gained their freedom.

Mark Twain's House, in the Nook Farm district of Hartford

▶ *Back on Asylum Avenue, continue through the traffic light and take the right fork. After a mile (1.6km), having passed through two more traffic lights, the Elizabeth Park Rose Garden is on the left (see **Back to Nature** panel).*

▶ *Return to Asylum Avenue and drive for 1½ miles (2.2km), through two traffic lights. At the third light, turn left on North Main Street and go 2 miles (3km) through the West Hartford Center shopping district. North Main becomes South Main. Continue to No. 227, on the right.*

13 Noah Webster House

Born in 1758, Noah Webster graduated from Yale and became a teacher. He soon saw the need to standardize spelling, so published his *Bluebacked Spellers*, which sold some 70 million copies and became the basis for elementary education

---

BACK TO NATURE

The Elizabeth Park Rose Garden was the first municipal rose garden in the nation and now boasts some 15,000 rose bushes in about 800 varieties, which bloom and perfume the air from late May until late October. There are also swaths of tulips, plus rock gardens, ornamental grasses, and unusual collector specimen trees and nature walks.

---

throughout the country. The "Schoolmaster of the Republic" did not stop there. He recognized that the language of America was evolving from the original English words, spelling and pronunciation, and spent 20 years compiling *An American Dictionary of the English Language*. Published in 1828, the two volumes contained some 70,000 words.

Inside the house are a first edition of his dictionary, his spellers and some 200 editions of his works. Guides in 200-year-old Colonial dress lead the way through the authentically furnished rooms. On special days there are demonstrations of carding wool, weaving on the massive loom, cooking, bread baking and butter churning.

▶ *Continue south on South Main Street and turn left onto I–84 eastbound at exit 41 to return to downtown Hartford.*

FOR CHILDREN

The Science Center of Connecticut on Trout Brook Drive (roughly parallel, and to the east of South Main Street), is a great place for children, with lots of hands-on exhibits and other fun things to do. There's a Kids' Factory, Idea Zone, Turtle Town, a planetarium, a computer laboratory, and much more.

HALF A DAY

New Haven &
Yale University

Founded in 1638 by a group of settlers, the town first depended on seafaring. In the 19th century, thanks to inventors such as Eli Whitney, assembly lines turned out clocks, carriages, and guns by the thousand. More recently, New Haven has undergone a downtown regeneration, with Crown and Chapter streets particularly busy with bars, restaurants and nightlife. At the heart of the city is Yale, one of America's leading universities, adding an enviable cultural dimension to the city.

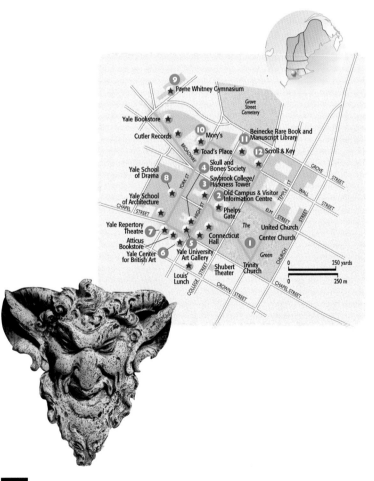

⌐i⌐ *Corner of College and Chapel streets; Yale University, 149 Elm Street*

▶ *Start on The Green, corner of Temple and Elm streets.*

❶ The Green

New Haven has been called "the first planned city in the U.S.A." because of its original (1638) grid-like street design, visible from the 16-acre (6.4-ha) Green. Here, residents came to gossip, to debate, and to pray at the trio of handsome churches, each with its different architectural style, but all built in the early 1800s.

The United Church, often compared with London's St. Martin-in-the-Fields, has long held public meetings and debates on topics ranging from slavery in the 1800s to Civil Rights in the 1970s. It is also sometimes referred to as the North Church.

In the middle of The Green is Center Church, and ever since the mid-1600s, a meeting house or church has stood on this site. Cool and elegant within, handsome Tiffany stained glass fills the arched window above the altar. Trinity Church, the third, was the first Gothic Revival church in the country, and was constructed with materials

Neo-Gothic Harkness Tower, a New Haven landmark

allowed to pass through the British blockade of New Haven harbor during the War of 1812. Compared with the white cupola and steeple of its neighbors, the tower seems heavy and ponderous. Two impressive buildings, City Hall and the Post Office, overlook the Green.

▶ *Walk diagonally north across The Green toward the imposing battlements and towers of Yale University and enter the Old Campus through the Phelps Gate.*

SPECIAL TO...

Ever wondered who invented the hamburger? One of the strongest claims comes from Louis Lassen of New Haven who served them here at Louis Lunch. That was back in 1900, and the simple brick house with a communal table and two booths probably looks much now as it did then. It stands in the middle of a parking lot at 263 Crown Street. The hamburgers, however, come as a surprise. Forget the griddle and the buns, these beef patties are cooked in front of diners on a vertical gas grill and served on toast.

❷ Old Campus

Phelps Gate, the front door to Yale, leads to the Old Campus, a typical university quadrangle. The oldest building here is also the oldest in town. Connecticut Hall, with its handsome windows and brick, was built between 1750 and 1753. Nathan Hale, Class of 1773, whose green patina statue sits outside, lived here during his student years. Three years later he was hanged in New York by the British who caught him spying. His last words: "I only regret that I have but one life to lose for my country" became a rallying cry. He was only 21. The right foot of Theodore Woolsey's statue is particularly shiny thanks to superstitious students giving it a rub before exams.

Off to the right, before leaving the quadrangle, is a rough-hewn granite bench. Here, A. Bartlett Giamatti, a former president of the college would sit, philosophizing about life and comparing it to a baseball game. His best loved essay, *Green Fields of the Mind*, is baseball-oriented.

So keen was he on baseball, America's favorite summer game, that he gave up academia to become the Commissioner for Baseball and run the professional sport. Sadly, he died soon after taking up the appointment.

▶ *Cross the quadrangle and exit onto High Street.*

SPECIAL TO...

Among the contributions Yale students have made to the world, nothing is quite as much fun as the Frisbee. Since 1947, students supposedly have whizzed flat aluminium pie dishes at one another across the Old Campus. When Wham-O, inventors of the hula-hoop, bought the patent for a plastic flier, they called it a Frisbee because those dishes came from Bridgeport's Frisbie Baking Company. Such major inventions are often in dispute: Middlebury College in Vermont (see page 117) also claims to be the home of the Frisbee.

The Old Campus at Yale is an architectural showpiece

FOR HISTORY BUFFS

Like its perennial rival Harvard, near Boston, Yale is one of America's Ivy League schools. Originally started by the Puritans in 1701 to train clergymen and administrators, the first Collegiate School moved to New Haven 15 years later, and changed its name to Yale in recognition of wealthy benefactor Elihu Yale. Students were nicknamed the "Elis" in honor of the English merchant, whose donation of books was sold to finance the institution. The roll call of famous Yale students ranges from dictionary compiler Noah Webster and architect Eero Saarinen to movie star Jodie Foster, Class of 1984. From the renowned graduate schools, especially the Law School, recent celebrities include former President Bill Clinton and his wife, Hillary, who first met here.

3 Saybrook College and the Harkness Tower

Above the elaborate wrought iron gate as you exit is an inscription: "For God, For Country and For Yale." The seal of the college has the Latin words *Lux et Veritas* (Light and Truth), but these jollier words are also the last lines of Yale's student song, *Bright College Years*, composed in 1888.

Across the street are the twin buildings of Saybrook and Branford Colleges, reminders of the school's locations before it moved to New Haven. Yale consists of a dozen separate and self-governing colleges. Their buildings were funded by the Harkness family, commemorated by the tall, dark, Gothic Harkness Tower that soars 221 feet (67m), and houses a 54-bell carillon, one of the largest in the world. Its partner, the Wrexham Tower, is modeled on the church steeple in Wrexham, Wales, where Elihu Yale is buried.

▶ *Turn left and continue on High Street.*

4 Skull and Bones Society

Just before walking under the arch, the windowless and ominous-looking stone building on the right is the Skull and Bones Society. Founded in 1832, it is Yale's oldest secret society. Although the membership is never publicized, it supposedly included former president George Bush, Snr. Among many "Bones" legends is one that the remains of the great Apache chief, Geronimo, are interred within its walls.

▶ *Pass under the arch and then turn right for the Yale University Art Gallery and Yale Center for British Art.*

5 Yale University Art Gallery

The nation's oldest college art gallery dates back to 1832 and is one of several fine museums here, some of which offer free admission. A replica of the original gallery is named for John Trumbull (1756–1843), the founder, and exhibits his work. This artist depicted major moments of the Revolution, such as the Battle of Bunker Hill in Boston, and the signing of the Declaration of Independence.

> **SPECIAL TO...**
>
> Call them secret societies or senior societies, only half a dozen of the most famous, such as Skull and Bones, are known. Each has only 15 members, all of them seniors who choose their successors from the junior class. Only members have keys to the unmarked windowless buildings where, rumor insists, Masonic-like rituals take place. Some clubhouses resemble grand English manor houses, others echo Greek mausoleums, giving rise to the nickname, "the tombs."

Today, the museum boasts an enormous international collection. From the past are Greek, Roman, Egyptian, and pre-Columbian antiquities. From 19th- and 20th-century Europe are paintings by Manet, Millet, Matisse and Magritte. Of the museum's two buildings, the 1953 addition is the work of architect Louis Kahn. He also designed the Yale Center for British Art, across Chapel Street.

▶ *Cross Chapel Street.*

6 Yale Center for British Art

The center's enormous collection, the gift of Paul Mellon in 1966, traces the development of British art over the centuries and includes a roll call of the great: Van Dyck, Gainsborough, Reynolds and Turner. For more specialist tastes are the works of visionary William Blake and animal painter George Stubbs (*A Lion Attacking a Horse*).

▶ *Continue on Chapel Street, passing the Atticus Bookstore.*

> **SPECIAL TO...**
>
> America's second-favorite fast-food is the pizza, and that, too, belongs to New Haven. In 1925, Italian immigrant Frank Pepe started selling his special "tomato pies" from a horse-drawn cart. As the pies' popularity grew, he opened Pepe Pizzeria on Worcester Street in New Haven's Little Italy. His trademark *focaccio*-like crust is still cooked in a brick oven, after almost 60 years.

> **SPECIAL TO...**
>
> "Bulldog, Bulldog, Bow wow wow. Eli Yale!" goes the chant. For over a century, the bulldog has been the mascot of Yale's sports teams. Some say an English student introduced the dog; others credit Professor Andrew Graves, whose pooch accompanied him everywhere. The dog was so clever, the story goes, that he barked whenever Yale scored in a football game. Since 1933, there has been a succession of bulldog mascots, each one called "Handsome Dan." The late Handsome Dan XV was Louis; number XVI is Mugsy.

Here browsers and buyers are joined by sippers of exotic teas and coffees served in the small café. Walk to the corner of Chapel and York streets.

7 Yale Repertory Theatre

Since 1966, a small professional company, boosted by students from the graduate school, has presented avant-garde, cutting-edge work in this 500-seat, converted Victorian gothic church.

▶ *Diagonally across from the theater on York Street is the Yale School of Architecture. What looks like nine stories on the outside actually hides 36 floors, and caused much discussion when it was put up in the 1960s. Turn right on York Street and walk to the University Theater, home of Yale's illustrious graduate schools.*

8 Yale School of Drama

Students who have attended a three-year course here include Paul Newman and Meryl Streep. Contrary to popular myth, Jodie Foster did not attend the Drama School: she was a liberal arts undergraduate.

▶ *Continue on York Street to Elm Street. Turn left, then veer right onto Broadway. Look up to the right.*

9 Payne Whitney Gymnasium

Dominating the skyline is the tower of what looks like a Gothic cathedral. Inside, however, are neither pillars nor pews but "Yalies" in sweat pants and sneakers. The Trophy Room contains memorabilia dating back to 1842. Although the university does not award athletics scholarships, sports facilities are as good as anywhere in the country, and "The Game," the annual football game against Harvard, is both a passionate match and a social occasion.

▶ *Return to York Street and turn left. Halfway down the block,*

The impressive Gothic-style Payne Whitney Gymnasium

at No. 300, is Toad's Place, well known to rock music fans. Next door is Mory's, one of the most popular spots in town.

10 Mory's

Today, Mory's is a private club for eating and drinking, but it started out as a bar and inspired a famous ballad, the Whiffenpoof song:

*"To the tables down at Mory's
To the place where Louis dwells ... "*

Louis Linder was the club's proprietor back in 1909 when four students, members of the Yale Glee Club singers, formed the barbershop-style Varsity Quartet. They took the name of the Whiffenpoof, a mythical half-bird, half-dragon that was a character in a contemporary Broadway show. Now, the 14-strong Whiffenpoofs are the oldest a cappella choir in the country, giving 150 concerts a year. They still meet at Mory's every week.

▶ *Turn right on Wall Street and walk to the corner of Wall and High streets to Beinecke Rare Books.*

11 Beinecke Rare Book and Manuscript Library

This three-star building alone is worth the journey to New Haven: the exterior, the most memorable of the university's modern buildings, looks like an unbroken cube of white Vermont marble supported at four corners by the lightest of steel pads. Even more memorable is the interior, glowing with bronze-hued light filtering through the translucent marble. The central stack is a six-story glass tower of rare books. On the mezzanine level are two large cases: one holds a rare 1455 Gutenberg Bible, one of only 22 known, the other a complete edition of *Birds of America* by naturalist John James Audubon (1785–1851).

▶ *Continue on Wall Street, to the corner of College Street.*

12 Scroll & Key

Enigmatic and bearing no name or sign, this stone building, with minarets and mystical carved figures, is home to another of the private secret societies.

▶ *Turn right on College Street, left on Elm Street, and return to the Green.*

FOR HISTORY BUFFS

Eli Whitney, the Yale graduate who became "father of mass production," made his name by inventing the cotton gin, which separated cotton fibers from the seeds. Although he patented the design in 1794, it was much-copied, so he did not make his deserved fortune. Next, his analytical brain turned to the making of guns. By standardizing components, he produced guns faster and cheaper in his factory than craftsmen could by traditional methods.

The Litchfield
Hills

1 DAY • 151½ MILES • 245KM

The rolling Litchfield Hills and the Housatonic River give a special character to the scattered villages that dot the peaceful northwest corner of Connecticut, among the thick woods.

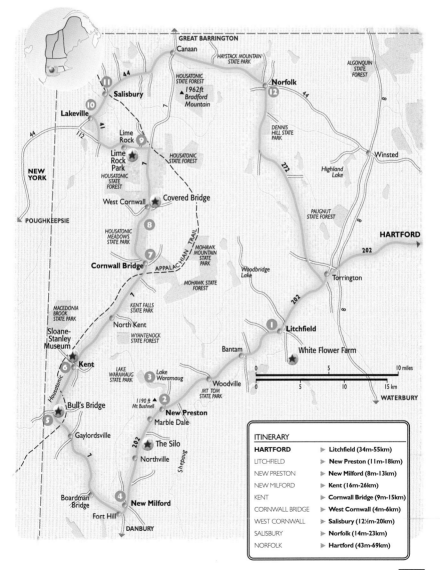

ITINERARY

HARTFORD	▶	**Litchfield (34m-55km)**
LITCHFIELD	▶	**New Preston (11m-18km)**
NEW PRESTON	▶	**New Milford (8m-13km)**
NEW MILFORD	▶	**Kent (16m-26km)**
KENT	▶	**Cornwall Bridge (9m-15km)**
CORNWALL BRIDGE	▶	**West Cornwall (4m-6km)**
WEST CORNWALL	▶	**Salisbury (12½m-20km)**
SALISBURY	▶	**Norfolk (14m-23km)**
NORFOLK	▶	**Hartford (43m-69km)**

The colored leaves of fall in the Litchfield Hills

ⓘ I Civic Center Plaza

▶ *Leave Hartford on **Route 44** west. After 16 miles (26km), **Route 202** branches off to Torrington. Continue through Torrington and drive 6 miles (10km) to Litchfield.*

❶ Litchfield

Rather as a judge surveys his court, so Litchfield dominates the local landscape. Appropriately, the Tapping Reeve House on South Street was owned by Judge Tapping Reeve, who had America's first law school built in the grounds. Opened in 1773, it produced judges by the score, as well as three justices of the U.S. Supreme Court, 28 senators, and two vice-presidents. Exhibits here relate the importance of the school and its students to the new nation. During that era, Litchfield was also famous for its leather goods, mills, and factories. Townspeople have proudly maintained their homes and the common to re-create the classic

The First Congregational Church

New England village seen today. The First Congregational Church, with its white columns, has a stately position at the head of the Green with North, South, East and West streets reaching out in their appropriate compass headings. North Street, often labeled one of the country's most beautiful, boasts textbook examples of late 1700s Georgian and Federal architecture, such as the Sheldon Tavern. The red-brick building at the corner of North

Grill is known for its celebrity customers, from politicians to movie stars.

☐i☐ *Litchfield Hills Information booth, The Green*

▶ *Drive west for 11 miles (18km) on* **Route 202**.

❷ New Preston
The road climbs abruptly to New Preston, alongside the tumbling waterfalls of the Aspetuck River, which give a clue to the town's industrial background. In the early 1800s, no less than 21 water-driven mills operated between New Preston and Marble Dale, barely a mile (1.5km) away. The mills did not survive the transition to steam power, but New Preston thrives on a new economy centered on its chic antiques shops.

▶ *Continue through New Preston to Lake Waramaug.*

❸ Lake Waramaug
To the Indians, Lake Waramaug was the "place of good fishing." Today, most visitors just come to catch the view, or to visit the Hopkins Vineyard, where the red-painted Yankee barn houses the winery and store.

SPECIAL TO...

Between Preston and New Milford, The Silo is an unusual combination of cooking school, art gallery, and gourmet kitchenware and food store. Set in former stables and a barn, The Silo is always associated with the late Skitch Henderson, the British-born broadway veteran and founder-director of The New York Pops. His Henderson American Music Archive is an important source for 20th-century American culture.

▶ *Return to New Preston and take* **Route 202** *south for 8 miles (19km) to New Milford.*

❹ New Milford
The Town Hall on The Green stands on the site of Roger Sherman's birthplace. He is the only native of Connecticut whose signature appears on all the significant documents concerning America's independence. Near the bandstand is a tank whose small scale and Victorian styling make it an unusually decorative armed forces memorial.

▶ *Drive through New Milford on* **Routes 202** *and* **67** *southwest, cross the Housatonic River bridge, turn right at the traffic lights onto* **Route 7** *north and continue through peaceful countryside to Bull's Bridge.*

❺ Bull's Bridge
Bull's Bridge, one of just two covered bridges in the state that still see daily use, is barely longer than a large car. Beneath, the Housatonic River rushes through a particularly rugged gorge. Raging waters and winter ice jams destroyed four successive bridges until the present one, which has lasted since 1842. Back in 1781, a horse in George Washington's party fell into this gorge while making the crossing. Washington's own financial accounts record "getting a horse out of Bull's Bridge falls, $215.00." The high price suggests that the horse was probably the general's.

▶ *Continue on* **Route 7** *to Kent.*

SCENIC ROUTES

From New Milford north to Canaan is one of Connecticut's prettiest drives. Running parallel to the Housatonic River the entire way, Route 7 is bordered by the Litchfield Hills to the east and the Taconic Mountains to the west. Housatonic is an Indian word meaning "place beyond the mountains," and it offers tempting photo opportunities.

SPECIAL TO...

White Flower Farm is an emporium of gardening located 3½ miles (5.6km) out of Litchfield via South Street (Route 63 South), Open from April to October, its 5 acres (2ha) are a technicolor extravaganza, with the begonia displays a high point. Its *Garden Book*, a weighty catalog published twice a year, offers a wealth of horticultural information.

---

and West streets was the Litchfield County Jail. Built in 1812, it was in use until the 1990s.

Also on North Street is a red saltbox house. On this site lived two 19th-century personalities: the charismatic preacher Rev. Henry Beecher and his sister, the author Harriet Beecher Stowe. The Litchfield History Museum on The Green has a fine collection of early paintings, decorative arts, and furniture, and The Green is lined with trendy shops, galleries and restaurants. The West Street

6 Kent

Just as Litchfield was once industrial, so Kent was known for its iron foundries. Where pig iron was smelted in the early 1800s, the Sloane-Stanley Museum and Kent Furnace now stands. A dedicated historian and fine artist, Sloane chronicled all aspects of early American life, from the building of barns to his favorite subject, the making and using of tools. The museum, housed in a big barn, includes a dog-powered butter churn, an authentic frontier cabin, and a re-creation of his art studio, right down to his paint-splattered telephone. Ruins of the furnace stand on the grounds, recalling a vanished local industry. Next door is the Connecticut Antique Machinery Association Museum, a mining museum, and an agricultural museum, with exhibitions on local traditions.

▶ *Stay on **Route 7** north for 5 miles (8km) to Kent Falls State Park. Continue to Cornwall Bridge.*

RECOMMENDED WALKS

Kent Falls State Park is one of a dozen or so state parks and forests in this corner of Connecticut. All are popular spots for picnics and hiking. Here, the special attraction is a broad view over Connecticut's wild terrain.
For a grand view, climb the steep 200-foot (60m) path beside the falls, which are often used for commercials and feature in the TV soap opera *The Guiding Light*.

7 Cornwall Bridge

From here north, the valley narrows and the hills steepen. Hardly more than an intersection and the bridge, the hub of this little community is Baird's General Store, a well-known stopping point for Appalachian Trail hikers. The "world's longest continuous footpath" stretches 2,175 miles (3,500km) from Georgia to northeast Maine. It crosses Route 7 only

SPECIAL TO...

You can visit the workshop of the Cornwall Bridge Pottery, south of Cornwall Bridge, to see the craftspeople at work and view the huge wood-fired kiln in which their stylish pots are fired. Seconds are on sale here; the main shop is in West Cornwall.

a few steps from the front porch where weary walkers stack their backpacks.

▶ *Cross the Housatonic again; bear right after the bridge and continue north to West Cornwall on **Route 7**.*

SPECIAL TO...

The only covered bridges for cars in the state are here: at West Cornwall and Bulls Bridge, Kent

Clarke's Outdoors, a log cabin on the left. Although U.S. Olympic teams may make this their home base, Clarke's also outfits day trips for recreational paddlers and provides a shuttle service to and from the entry/exit points. The favorite "playground" for the kayakers is beneath the covered bridge at West Cornwall, built in 1837.

▶ Stay on **Route 7** north for 4½ miles (7km), bearing left on **Route 112** for ¾ mile (1km) to Lime Rock Park.

9 Lime Rock Park
Deep in the rural idyll, the self-styled "Road Racing Center of the East" comes as a surprise. The deceptively simple 1½-mile (2.4km) track has tested the best from every category of motor-sport. Drivers from Formula 1 to NASCAR and sports car racing have all taken the wheel here. Among celebrity competitors often seen here are the actors Paul Newman and Tom Cruise.

▶ Continue west for 3¾ miles (6km) on **Route 112**. Climbing out of the Housatonic Valley, grand views open up of magnificent farms. To the north and west, the Berkshire Hills continue and blend into the Catskill Mountains of New York and the Green Mountains of Vermont. Turn north onto **Route 41** and drive for 1½ miles (2.4km) to Lakeville.

10 Lakeville
Two fascinating museums lie opposite each other at the heart of the Lakeville Historic District. The first is Holley-Williams House Museum, where costumed guides portray the everyday life of a late 19th-century family and highlight the social issues of the times. Among the household items here is an early vacuum cleaner, and you can view a seven-holer outhouse and learn about topics as diverse as pre-electric refrigeration and women's suffrage.

The Salisbury Cannon Museum is where weapons were made during the Revolutionary War. Children especially enjoy the hands-on experience, learning about important figures during the Revolution, and about Salisbury's ironmaking history.

▶ Continue north on **Routes 41** and **44** for 2 miles (3km) to Salisbury.

11 Salisbury
Salisbury is best know for having two prep schools, and the students add a buzz to the atmosphere of this pretty town. Nearby is the venerable Salisbury Ski Jump, where the annual winter festival in February brings competitors from as far as Norway. In summer, the population doubles with weekenders.

▶ Follow **Route 44** for 7 miles (11km) to Canaan and on for another 7 miles (11km) to Norfolk.

12 Norfolk
Connecticut's highest town, tucked away in the northwestern corner, has an elevation of 1,770 feet (540m). Here, the Battell Chapel, with its Tiffany glass windows, faces the central Green that sits atop the hill. Each summer, the Norfolk Chamber Music Festival, with the Yale Summer School of Music, attracts music fans as it has for almost a century. Rachmaninov, Caruso and Paderewski are among the legends who have performed during the season. Many of the town's street signs, painted by hand, have been brightened up with engaging pictures of animals.

▶ From The Green take the tranquil country drive back to Torrington on **Route 272**. This is a peaceful stretch of hilly evergreen and oak forest, dotted with lovely homes and farms. Return to Hartford.

Water tumbles down a 200-foot (60m) flight of natural steps in Kent Falls State Park

8 Cornwall Bridge to West Cornwall
This is one of the prettiest stretches of the Housatonic, known as a fly-fisherman's paradise. Throughout the summer, anglers come here to practice the elegant art of casting and placing the fly delicately on the water.

Somewhat rougher are the sports of white-water canoeing and kayaking. Paddlers meet at

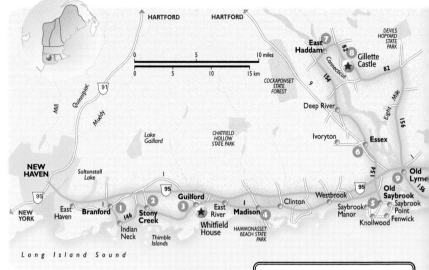

HARTFORD   HARTFORD

DEVILS
HOPYARD
STATE
PARK

East
Haddam ⑦
⑧ Gillette
Castle

Connecticut

82

0   5   10 miles

0   5   10   15 km

COCKAPONSET
STATE
FOREST

⑨

154

Eight Mile

156

Deep River

91

Quinnipiac

Mill

Muddy

Lake
Gaillard

CHATFIELD
HOLLOW
STATE PARK

Ivoryton

Essex

⑥

NEW
HAVEN

Saltonstall
Lake

95

154

Old
Lyme

95

Guilford

Westbrook

95

Old
Saybrook

95

158

NEW
YORK

East
Haven

Branford ①

② Stony
Creek

146

③

Guilford

East
River

Madison ④

Clinton

Saybrook
Manor

⑤

Saybrook
Point
Fenwick

Whitfield
House

HAMMONASSET
BEACH STATE
PARK

Knollwood

Indian
Neck

Thimble
Islands

Long   Island   Sound

The
Connecticut
Shore

2 DAYS • 158 MILES • 254KM

New Haven is a mixture of industry and academia. Some areas still recall the might of the Industrial Revolution that had its roots here; other areas are a delight, thanks to the ivied walls and grassy quadrangles of Yale University (see pages 66–70). East of New Haven, the Connecticut shore is dotted with some surprisingly sleepy villages, sheltered from traffic by I-95, the interstate highway that speeds traffic on its way and diverts it from the coast.

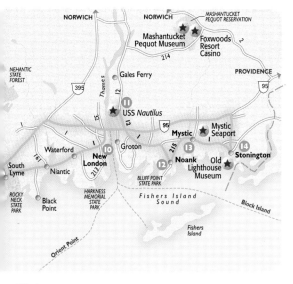

[i] *Corner of College and Chapel streets*

▶ *Start in New Haven on **Route 95** east. Take exit 53 and at the rotary take **Route 146** east to Branford (7 miles/11km).*

❶ Branford

The pleasant town of Branford has an old-fashioned green with an unusually opulent library, church and school nearby. The only historic mansion open to the public is the Nathaniel Harrison House on South Main Street, a restored 1724 saltbox with beautiful period furnishings and flower and herb gardens.

▶ *Stay on **Route 146** for 6 miles (10km), following the shoreline through Indian Neck to Stony Creek.*

❷ Stony Creek

Millions of Americans and foreigners have seen the pink granite produced from the local quarry: it was used in Grand Central Station and for the pedestal of the Statue of Liberty. Just off shore, the water is speckled by the tiny Thimble Islands. Called the "Hundred Islands" by the Colonists, there are actually over 300 of them scattered throughout Long Island Sound.

Some are barely big enough to accommodate the cottages built on them, often on stilts. With names like Treasure Island and Money Island, it is no surprise that the pirate Captain Kidd supposedly hid out here. Small boats are ready at Stony Creek harbor to give tours.

▶ *Continue on **Route 146** for 4 miles (6km) to Guilford.*

❸ Guilford

There is a particularly English feeling about this town, founded in 1639 and built around an unusually large green. Luckily, it escaped serious damage during the War of Independence, and around 80 pre-Revolutionary houses still stand.

The oldest, the 1639 Henry Whitfield State Museum, is also the oldest stone building in New England. Sitting on a slight rise in the middle of a large lot, this originally looked more like a fortified manor house, but the steeply pitched roof and small, leaded, lattice windows reflect its remarkable age.

Other homes with history include the 1660 red saltbox Hyland House, and the 1774 Thomas Griswold House, now a museum, occupied by Griswold descendants until 1958. Harriet

Beecher Stowe, who later wrote *Uncle Tom's Cabin*, stayed in Guilford on her grandmother's farm where she got to know the African American servants.

▶ *Continue on **Route 146** and turn onto **Route 1** east.*

❹ Madison

On the Green at the entrance to the town is the late 17th-century Deacon John Grave House, which has been a school, infirmary, arsenal, tavern and courtroom in its time. Madison also has one of the few beaches on this shore that is open to all. The 2 miles (3km) of sandy shore is in the enormous Hammonasset Beach State Park. The area also includes a nature reserve.

▶ *Continue on **Route 1** east, then turn right to Old Saybrook.*

❺ Old Saybrook

Though busy and commercially developed, Saybrook still has many fine Colonial homes, including the General William Hart House (1767), with its corner fireplaces and herb garden. Saybrook's most famous son is David Bushnell (1742–1824), credited with building the first "sub-marine" (see below).

▶ *Return north on **Route 154** and drive for 5 miles (8km) to Essex.*

FOR HISTORY BUFFS

In the 1770s, Yale student David Bushnell was fascinated by explosives. Tests of his limpet mine, in Otter Cove near Old Saybrook, impressed George Washington and renowned inventor Benjamin Franklin. But Bushnell's pride and joy was his *American Turtle*. Reconstructed at the Connecticut River Museum in Essex, this self-propelled underwater capsule is considered the first "sub-marine." It was lost in battle against the British.

Essex

In a 1996 book called *The 100 Best Small Towns in America*, Essex came out number one. Founded in 1648, it became quite wealthy due to the skill of its carpenters and shipwrights. The splendid Colonial, Georgian and Federal homes on Main Street were built by their bosses, the shipbuilders and sea captains. The town's social hub is the 200-year-old Griswold Inn. Here, collections of marine art and 19th-century firearms add to the atmosphere of "the 'Gris,'" a busy, though jolly, hotel-restaurant. At the end of the street, in an old warehouse on Steamboat Landing, is the Connecticut River Museum. This tells the story of Essex and of the Connecticut River, from its source in northeastern New Hampshire to the mouth. Star attraction is the reproduction of

Cruising on the Connecticut River near East Haddam

David Bushnell's remarkable underwater craft, *American Turtle*. A stone's-throw away, the keel was laid for the *Oliver Cromwell*, the colony's first custom-built warship, back in 1776. From then on, Essex was an important ship-building center. The tradition continues nearby at the Brewers Dauntless Shipyard, which produces sleek modern yachts. The 1732 Pratt

House Museum portrays an 1800s home with a herb garden.

▶ *Return to* **Route 154** *and drive north to* **Route 82** *east. Turn right and cross the Connecticut River on the turntable bridge to East Haddam.*

SCENIC ROUTES

The Essex Steam Train and Riverboat Ride is organized by the Valley Railroad Company, whose volunteers restore, maintain, and operate old steam engines and cars. They puff through the countryside for the hour-long trip up to Chester and then stop at Deep River to connect with a river boat for an hour-and-a-half-long cruise.

SPECIAL TO...

No prizes for guessing how Ivoryton, 2 miles (3km) west of Essex, got its name. In the old days, ivory from Africa was unloaded in Essex and driven here in horse-drawn carts. It was then cut and polished into piano keys, buttons and combs. Although a factory nearby is now the world's largest producer of piano and organ keyboards, ivory is no longer used. The hamlet itself is tranquil, with huge beech trees on its main street, a general store, and a summer theater.

BECKY THATCHER

7 East Haddam

Just at the end of the bridge, high above the river, stands the Goodspeed Opera House. This six-story, white "wedding cake" is a grand reminder of the late 19th century, when East Haddam was a resort town, used by Mr. William Goodspeed's very own steam ships. Restored in the 1960s, the house's specialty is musical comedies. It hosted pre-Broadway runs for brand-new shows such as *Man of La Mancha*, in 1966, and *Annie*, in 1977. Now, new musicals are presented in a second theater in Chester, while this house concentrates on revivals. Land for East Haddam's original 17th-century settlement was sold to the English by local Native Americans in exchange for 30 coats. The one-room school-house, where Nathan Hale once taught, is next to the church.

▶ *Continue on* **Route 82** *south to Gillette Castle.*

8 Gillette Castle

At the turn of the century, actor William Gillette (1853–1937) had superstar status, drawing huge audiences to see his 1,300 performances portraying Sherlock Holmes. By 1919, he had poured a million dollars into this extraordinary fake medieval stone castle. An amateur inventor with an odd sense of humor, he made many of the "puzzle locks" on its doors and designed a system of mirrors to be able to see who was visiting. After a major renovation, which included a new visitor center, the castle reopened in 2002. The 184-acre (74-ha) grounds make a fine picnic spot, high on the bank overlooking the Connecticut River.

▶ *Continue on* **Route 82** *for 5 miles (8km) to* **Route 156** *south. Drive to Old Lyme.*

9 Old Lyme

Old Lyme, one of America's first art colonies, is the unofficial home of American Impressionism, thanks to Florence Griswold. At the turn of the century, "Miss Florence" decided to take in boarders; first one, then more artists moved into her fine, late Georgian home, drawn by the light and the serenity of the surrounding beaches and marshes. Instead of signing the visitors book, guests such as Willard Metcalf, Childe Hassam, and William Chadwick painted scenes on their landlady's doors and wall panels. This 1817 house, in the heart of the Old Lyme Historic District, is now a museum; the Krieble Gallery, opened in 2002, has

Housefront in Essex

changing exhibitions from the collection. Next door, the Lyme Academy College of Fine Arts is one of America's leading art schools.

▶ *Leave town and follow* **Route 156** *east, crossing Niantic Bay, with a view of the Millstone Energy Center, a nuclear power plant. After 16 miles (26km), arrive in New London.*

SPECIAL TO...

Called the "Fresh River" by Dutch explorer Adriaen Block and the "Great River" by English settlers, the waterway for which Connecticut is named was always the Quinnetukut to the Native Americans. The name means "long river whose waters are driven by wind and tide." It starts in the three Connecticut lakes, up in the northeastern corner of New Hampshire, near the Canadian border.

⑩ New London

Although New London is slowly renewing its image, it still remains a working town, just as it has been for 300 years. While not as attractive as smaller, more gentrified places in New England, the history here is just as impressive. The deep harbor made this an important port in the early 18th century, and the Hempsted Houses offer an insight into the lives of seafarers' families in Colonial times.

During the American Revolution, New London was the headquarters of the patriots' naval resistance, which made it a target for the British Army. Later, the port became one of the world's biggest and busiest whaling ports, with as many as 80 ships in its fleet. Whale Oil Row has four splendid 1832 mansions, grandiose Greek Revival temples of affluence.

The town's nautical history was boosted further in 1876 when the U.S. Coast Guard Academy opened. Its 60-year-old German barque, the *Eagle*, was confiscated from Germany by the U.S. Navy after World War II. Now, this 295-foot (109m) long sail training ship welcomes visitors on Saturday afternoons when in port.

FOR CHILDREN

The 300-acre (120-hectare) Denison Pequotsepos Nature Center has been educating and entertaining children for some 50 years, with its wildlife sanctuary, nature trails and fun tree house.
For simply letting off steam, take them to Ocean Beach Park, where swimming pools, waterslides, mini-golf and a playground are among the attractions.

FOR HISTORY BUFFS

Benedict Arnold was a brilliant but vain American general who switched sides in the middle of the war. In 1781, he attacked New London with 1,700 British troops. Having grown up nearby, at Norwich, Arnold knew the area and the communication codes of the local militia. He caught the defenders off guard and burned New London. This was the final engagement of the war in New England. Discover more at Fort Griswold Battlefield State Park, Groton.

Near the Coast Guard Academy is the Lyman-Allyn Art Museum which offers something for everyone: toys and a dolls' house, Native American artifacts and paintings by Connecticut artists.

Playwright Eugene O'Neill spent unhappy boyhood summers at Monte Cristo Cottage, to the south on Pequot Avenue. Bleak family events there a century or more ago are recalled in three O'Neill plays, including *Long Day's Journey into Night*. On Route 213, 6 miles (10km) south, is the Eugene O'Neill Theater Center, known for presenting staged readings of new productions.

▶ Follow signs to I–95 east and cross the Thames river. Exit 86 leads north on **Route 12** to the Nautilus Memorial.

⑪ USS *Nautilus*

The USS *Nautilus*, dating from 1954, is the world's first nuclear-powered sub and the first to venture under the ice cap at the North Pole. Now open for visitors, it shows just how crowded conditions are when living underwater in a "sub."

▶ Return on **Route 12** and take **Route I** east. Turn right on **Route 215** for Noank.

⑫ Noank

Noank is as salty and undiscovered a town as there is on the Connecticut shoreline. A fishing and shipbuilding community in the past, it now looks as if every house might have a retired lobsterman or sea captain sitting out on the front porch. Pearl Street is the main thoroughfare and provides all the high points, from the Deacon Robert Palmer House with its whimsical gingerbread architecture and wild colors to Abbott's Lobster-in-the-Rough. This is a lobster house of the traditional sort found in Maine – informal, with picnic-style eating.

Monte Cristo Cottage, named after O'Neill's actor-father's greatest role

▶ Continue on **Route 215**, then **Route 1** to Mystic.

13 Mystic

The town itself is attractive, but often overlooked by the visitors who swarm to Mystic Seaport, the re-creation of a 19th-century fishing village. A mixture of real and replica, this is much more than a conventional open-air museum, with the largest and most complete maritime collection in the country. Taking full advantage of its waterside location, it has sailing vessels and models of every description and size on display.

The 1841 *Charles W. Morgan*, the last wooden whaling vessel ever to be built, and the *L. A. Dunton*, a sleek 123-foot (45.5m) Gloucester fishing schooner which looks more like an America's Cup race competitor, can be seen.

Every possible craft and trade associated with seafaring life can be found and studied somewhere on the 40-acre (16.6-ha) site. Active craftsmen re-create the workaday world of an early 19th-century fishing village. Nautical terms such as "sandbag-gers," "smacks," "chandlers," "coopers" and "cordage" are all explained. To understand how sailors used to navigate by the stars, take in one of the shows at the Planetarium. You can even board a steam-boat for a trip out onto the river.

Also in town is the Mystic Aquarium, its centerpiece a coral reef stocked with sharks, sting-rays and reef fish. You can learn about alligators and other swamp life, then watch Beluga whales in the Alaskan Coast exhibit. Undersea exploration, such as finding the *Titanic*, is the theme of Challenge of the Deep.

▶ Take **Route 1** toward Stonington. After 3 miles (5km), turn onto **Route 1A** for the village.

14 Stonington

Stonington Borough, a peninsula covered in old houses, remains peaceful and untouristy. The docks of this working fishing

Lobster shop in Noank

port, which has Connecticut's largest commercial fleet, provide an atmospheric place to stroll and watch the dragger fleet and lobster boats come in each afternoon. At the end of the long narrow main street is the Land Battery, with two of the cannons that helped repulse a British naval attack in the War of 1812. A few steps farther is the Old Lighthouse Museum (1823), the first Government-operated lighthouse in Connecticut with gear for whaling and "ice harvesting" displayed in the "pocket-size" lighthouse.

Guided tours are available at the home of Captain Nathaniel B. Palmer, who discovered Antarctica. Exhibits in the house cover his career and his family life.

▶ Return to **Route 1**, then join **I-95** west and return to New Haven.

THE MARITIME TRADITION

The Atlantic Ocean has had a profound affect on the development of New England. Five of the six states in the region are adjacent to the coastline, and the Europeans who first arrived all had to cross the stormy North Atlantic. Once they arrived, ships maintained the umbilical cord linking them with the Mother Countries, and permanent communities grew up around safe harbors. The abundance of fish offshore made fishing an easy and reliable means of finding food, and it became so vital to the early settlers that fishermen were exempt from military service.

Once the Colonies were established, shipping became an important part of the economy, though strict laws from London insisted that all manufactured goods had to be imported from England, alone. Enforcement was another matter, and not only were "illegal" cargoes landed, customs duties were, on occasion, evaded.

Ships were a necessity for England, and the navy increasingly relied on lumber from Maine. Soon, the boats themselves were being constructed in the Colonies, since shipbuilding costs were from 20 to 50 percent less than in the Mother Country. Shipbuilding thrived and by 1760, one-third of the total British merchant tonnage was produced in the American Colonies.

By this time, the patterns of triangular trade routes were established. Merchant ships sailed from New England with grain, timber and fish for the West Indies. These were traded for fruit, sugar, and molasses, which were taken on to England. There, the holds were loaded up with manufactured goods to be transported back home. Similar routes connected New England with Africa and the Mediterranean.

After years of lax enforcement, Britain decided to toughen up its policing of the trade laws in order to raise more revenue from the Colonies. Not only did this

hurt the New England economy, but it fostered anti-London feelings. The major ports of Boston and Portland, along with New York to the south, were targets before and during the Revolution.

Shipping again became a contentious issue during the Napoleonic Wars in Europe. Although the U.S. remained neutral, Britain interfered with American shipping, hoping to deprive the French of supplies. In addition, seamen were taken off captured ships and forced to sail for Britain. Eventually, these grievances led to the War of 1812.

From their early days, Colonists learned from the Native Americans how to catch whales when the mammals swam near shore, and towns such as New London and Mystic in Connecticut, and New Bedford and Provincetown in Massachusetts thrived at the expense of the whale. In 1774, 360 whaling ships sailed from Nantucket. Rhode Island developed a huge candle-making industry based on whale products. The oil was used to light streets and homes in Europe, while bones and baleen were used to make anything from umbrella spokes to corset stays. Only the discovery of oil (made into kerosene) in Pennsylvania, in 1859, ended the bloody trade. The business of whaling was epitomized in Herman Melville's novel, *Moby-Dick*,

Above: humpback whales can reach 40 to 50 feet (13 to 16m)

based on his own experiences aboard ship. Today, museums such as Nantucket's Whaling Museum, housed in a former whale oil refinery, record the exploits of American sailors who roamed the oceans in the early 19th century.

Apart from their heavy involvement in the slave trade, "Yankee traders" sailed round South America to do business with China and the Pacific islands, bringing back huge wealth to towns such as Boston, Salem and Portsmouth. Along the Maine coast, at Kennebunkport and Kittery, Bath, Camden and Belfast, shipbuilders continued traditions begun in 1607, when the *Virginia* was the first ship built in the Colonies, near Bath.

Today, New England's nautical traditions concentrate on the pleasure industry, with yachting keeping the shipbuilders and sail-makers of the region at the forefront of technology. For the first half of the 20th century,

Tall ships at Mystic Seaport

Newport rivalled Cowes (in England) as the sailing capital of the world. The rich and famous built ever-larger yachts and raced them. Battles in the wind-swept seas off Newport for the legendary America's Cup were a feature of the town between 1930 and 1983.

In Bristol, Rhode Island, the Herreshoff Marine Museum recalls the Herreshoff Company's contribution to sailing. Between 1893 and 1934, eight consecutive winners in the America's Cup competition were built on the site, as well as the first torpedo boats for the U.S. Navy. In Newport, the Naval War College Museum emphasizes America's rise to power as a world force on the high seas. Out at Fort Adams State Park, at the Museum of Yachting, the America's Cup Gallery traces 150 years of competition for the "Auld Mug."

"Windjammers," old sailing ships, are now a popular way of spending a vacation, afloat along the coast. In Maine, Rockland and Camden are the best-known centers, while summer festivals such as Windjammer Days in the Boothbays and the finish of the Great Schooner Race, at the Rockland Breakwater, celebrate the nautical tradition.

Nowhere records New England's tradition better than Mystic Seaport on the Mystic River in Connecticut. An American whaler, the *Charles W. Morgan*, built of wood in 1841, is one of several sailing vessels ready for visitors to explore.

83

RHODE ISLAND

Rhode Island, "Little Rhody," is the smallest state, yet it also boasts the longest name: officially, it is The State of Rhode Island and Providence Plantations. This densely populated and heavily industrialized state received its title back in 1644, when two colonies were combined. A mere 48 miles by 37 miles (77km by 59km), it is nicknamed the "Ocean State" because of its 400 miles (640km) of shoreline, which includes some 100 beaches with public access. Not all the coast runs along the Atlantic Ocean; it also borders Narragansett Bay, which bites into the southeast corner of the state and stretches 28 miles (45km) inland, to the capital city of Providence.

Although the Vikings may have visited North America in the 11th century, Giovanni da Verrazano, the Italian explorer, is on record for sailing past what is now Block Island in 1524. He named it after the Island of Rhodes in Greece. When Roger Williams and a band of followers fled the intolerance of the Puritan colony in Massachusetts in 1636, they settled in what is now Providence. Two years later, Anne Hutchinson was similarly banished, and led another group to Aquidneck Island, now better known for the town of Newport. Both communities believed in religious freedom, for Christians as well as non-Christians. The first synagogue in the U.S. was built in Newport, while the first Baptist church was founded in Providence.

The First Baptist Church, Eastside, Rhode Island

Rhode Island has been a holiday destination for almost two centuries. In the early 1800s, the seashore attracted wealthy Southerners, keen to escape the summer heat of the plantations. Families such as the Astors and Vanderbilts spent the summer social season in their "cottages," whose magnificence rivaled European palaces. Tennis, then the sport of the rich, made its American debut at the casino in Newport, and the International Tennis Hall of Fame now has its home here.

But it is sailing, rather than tennis, that is most associated with Newport. For some 50 years, the town hosted the America's Cup challenges, until 1983 when Australia broke the home team's winning streak and took the cup "down under." Nevertheless, Newport remains the sailing capital of the East Coast.

Tour 12

Providence, the capital of Rhode Island, is a gem of a city, all too often overlooked by visitors to New England. The riverfront and downtown area have been successfully restored and revitalized, while the historic district around Benefit Street is full of 18th- and 19th-century houses, now used for offices and museums, classrooms and private homes. Nearby is Brown University, the seventh oldest in the country, founded in 1764, and the Rhode Island School of Design, one of the country's leading art schools. Not surprisingly, this area is known as College Hill. Across the river is Federal Hill, where Little Italy is full of delicatessens and cafés. With its ethnic mix and large student population, Providence is a lively city, with a thriving music scene, art galleries and numerous restaurants. The *haute cuisine* is a by-product of Johnson and Wales University, which specializes in the culinary arts and hospitality business.

Tour 13

Newport is situated at the southern tip of an island, with a harbor on one side and beaches stretching along the other. This town of contrasts has its share of plain pre-Revolutionary houses as well as opulent summer homes, such as Château-sur-Mer and The Breakers. A century ago, entrance was only for the privileged few; today, visitors are welcome to see the priceless art and grandiose architecture.

Yachting is big on Rhode Island, and in Newport in particular

Sailing has long been popular here, with the most famous race of all, the America's Cup, a long tradition. Even though the cup has been lost to Australians, New Zealanders, and the Swiss, Narragansett Bay still brings in the sailing crowd.

Newport also attracts tennis fans, who visit the Hall of Fame. In summer, you can see one of the few professional tournaments outside the British Isles that is still played on grass. The town also draws music lovers. Since the first Newport Jazz Festival in 1954, the outdoor summer concerts have become important fixtures on the U.S. music calendar.

Providence

Providence, the third largest city in New England, is known as one of New England's most approachable destinations. It has fine examples of pre- and post-Revolutionary architecture, a lively and artistic student body as well as high-quality restaurants, thanks to the influence of one of America's leading culinary schools. It is compact and walkable, but has steep hills, so wear comfortable shoes.

HALF A DAY

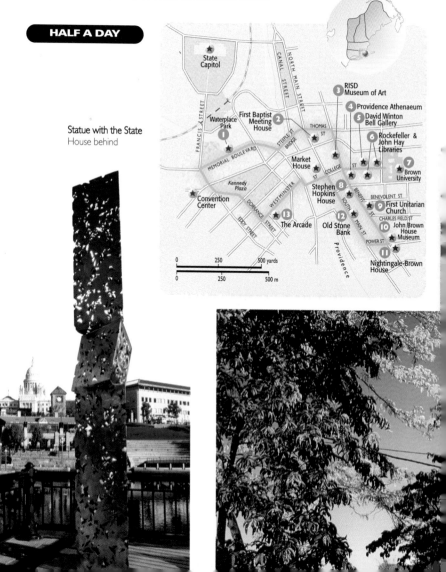

Statue with the State
House behind

State Capitol

RISD Museum of Art

Providence Athenaeum

David Winton Bell Gallery

Rockefeller & John Hay Libraries

Brown University

Waterplace Park

First Baptist Meeting House

THOMAS ST

Market House

Stephen Hopkins House

First Unitarian Church

Kennedy Plaza

Convention Center

The Arcade

Old Stone Bank

John Brown House Museum

Nightingale-Brown House

FRANCIS A STREET

CANAL STREET

NORTH MAIN STREET

STEEPLE ST

BRIDGE

MEMORIAL BOULEVARD

WESTMINSTER

DORRANCE STREET

EDDY STREET

COLLEGE ST

BENEFIT

SOUTH MAIN ST

BENEVOLENT ST

CHARLES FIELD ST

POWER ST

Providence

0   250   500 yards

0   250   500 m

ⓘ Convention Center, 1 West
Exchange Street

▶ Start at the Convention Center
(park here, or in one of the
public parking lots nearby).
Walk to Memorial Boulevard.

❶ Waterplace Park

This ambitious design is the
focal point of Providence's
extensive riverfront redevelopment. Cobbled walks, amphithe-
aters and bridges are part of the
backdrop for WaterFire
Providence, a summer spectacular with some 100 bonfires lighting up the river. This is the
perfect place to view the State
Capitol, sitting imperially on the
hill. Built in 1904 of Georgia
marble, its dome is the fourth
largest unsupported dome in the
world. On top, the gilded statue
Independent Man symbolizes the
free-thinking founders of Rhode
Island. Inside hangs one of the
most famous paintings in the

country: the full-length portrait
of George Washington, which
appears on dollar bills, painted
by Rhode Islander Gilbert
Stuart.

▶ Continue along Memorial
Boulevard, cross the
Providence River on Steeple
Street Bridge; follow Steeple
Street up the hill to No. 75
North Main Street.

❷ First Baptist Meeting House

Although Roger Williams
founded the Baptist congregation in 1638, the first church was
not built for 50 years. This house
of worship dates from 1775. A
plan for St. Martin-in-the-Fields
in London provided the inspiration for architect Joseph Brown,
but the ability of the 185-foot
steeple (56m) to withstand
storms was due to the carpenters' extensive shipbuilding
experience.

▶ Turn up Thomas Street to
Benefit Street. Turn right to
No. 224 Benefit Street..

❸ Rhode Island School of Design Museum of Art

Rhode Island School of Design,
always abbreviated to RISD
("Ris-dee") is one of America's
leading art schools. The modern
entrance to the school's museum
is in the Daphne Farago Wing
where the focus is *Mantled
Figure*, Howard Ben Tre's sculpture in solid cast glass. Works
by Monet and Picasso, an
Egyptian mummy and a 9-foot
(2.7m) tall Buddha, dating back
ten centuries, are among the
rich and varied 65,000-piece
collection. Must sees include the
costume and textile collection,
and the Pendleton House,
whose early American works
include paintings and the furniture of Townsend and Goddard.

▶ Continue along Benefit Street
to No. 251, on the corner of
College Street.

❹ Providence Athenaeum

In the old days, a club for
learned men was often called an
"athenaeum," in honor of
Athena, the goddess of wisdom.
This Greek Revival building
was finished in 1838, and its
stern exterior contrasts with the
warm intimacy of the main reading room, with its tiers of books.
Here, poet Edgar Allen Poe met
and wooed local widow Sarah
Whitman, who accepted, then
rejected him (she is thought
to have inspired his poem
Annabel Lee).

Today, anyone in need of
inspiration needs only to look up
to busts of the Greek historian
Homer, the English authors
Milton and Keats, and the
American statesman, Daniel
Webster.

▶ Walk up College Street. On
the left is the List Art Center
and the David Winton Bell
Gallery.

Attractive mansion house in the
College Hill district of Providence

5 David Winton Bell Gallery

A distinctive modernistic building on College Street houses the List Art Center and the David Winton Bell Gallery. The gallery has a permanent collecion of more than 4,000 works, from Rembrandt prints to contemporary pieces, and also stages a varied program of exhibitions.

▶ *Continue to the corner of College and Prospect streets.*

6 Libraries

This could be called "library corner." On the right is "the Rock," the bustling J. D. Rockefeller Library, open only to Brown students. Opposite is the "Hay," the hushed John Hay Library, where the public may explore the vast book collection and the small gallery in the lobby.

John Hay graduated from the university in 1858. A poet and

The famous *Brown Bear* statue at Brown University

historian, he was also the U.S. Secretary of State at the turn of the century.

▶ *Cross Prospect Street and enter the campus of Brown University.*

FOR HISTORY BUFFS

Roger Williams founded Providence, but the city's success in the late 18th and early 19th centuries followed the fortunes of the four Brown brothers.
John was a merchant. Joseph, the architect, designed the Market House, First Baptist Church, and a mansion for brother John. Moses founded the Providence Bank and financed the mill at Pawtucket, which started the Industrial Revolution in New England. Nicholas gave land and money to Rhode Island College, which was to be later renamed Brown University in 1804.

7 Brown University

The Van Wickle Gates, leading to the quadrangle, open just twice a year: to let new students in and graduates out. Founded in 1764, Brown is the seventh-oldest university in the country, and became co-ed in 1971. The main quadrangle boasts a variety of architecture. At the upper end of the college's grounds is the Carrie Tower, built by Paul Bajnotti of Turin in memory of his wife. It is inscribed: "Love is strong as death."

The oldest building, University Hall (1771), was used as a barracks by French and American troops during the Revolution. Behind is the larger-than-life bronze *Brown Bear* statue. Rearing up, with its rather kindly expression, it supposedly stands on a slate from the rock where Roger Williams first set foot on his arrival from Massachusetts in 1636.

▶ *Return down the hill on College Street and turn left on Benefit Street.*

FOR HISTORY BUFFS

Which Civil War general gave his name to a fashion trend? General Ambrose Burnside, whose statue stands in City Hall Park. So well-known were his side whiskers that the style became known as "sideburns." He went on to be governor and senator for Rhode Island, and lived at No. 314 Benefit Street.

8 Benefit Street

Originally known as Back Street, because it ran behind the houses facing the main street, Benefit Street was transformed from a path into a proper road in 1758 "for the common benefit of all." Now it is known as the "Mile of History," with its many 18th- and 19th-century houses: note details such as the old-fashioned street lights and boot scrapers.

At No. 43 Benefit Street, on the corner of Hopkins Street, stands the clapboard Governor

Brown University's first building, University Hall, is now a National Historic Landmark

Stephen Hopkins House. This delightful example of early 1700s architecture was the home of the ten-time Governor of the state and signatory of the Declaration of Independence.

▷ *Continue along Benefit Street.*

9 First Unitarian Church
John Holden Greene, the architect, rated this 1816 church his finest achievement. High in its steeple hangs the largest ever bell cast by the Paul Revere Foundry. Better known now as the messenger who rode from Boston to Lexington in 1775 to warn the Colonists that the British were approaching, Revere was a silversmith and bell-maker.

▷ *Continue on Benefit to the corner of Power Street.*

10 John Brown House Museum
John Brown was a successful merchant who opened up trade with China after the American Revolution. His brother, Joseph, designed this imposing brick house, whose entrance is at No. 52 Power Street. President John Quincy Adams once called it "the most magnificent and elegant mansion that I have ever seen on this continent." Filled with fine examples of Rhode

Island's furniture-making tradition, it exemplifies the gracious living of the 18th century.

▷ *Continue a few steps along Benefit Street to No. 357.*

11 Nightingale-Brown House
Supposedly the country's largest wood-frame house, this 200-year-old yellow and cream merchant's home has been restored so completely, it could have been built yesterday.

▷ *Return to Power Street and walk down the hill. Turn right on South Main Street; walk to No. 86, the Old Stone Bank, established in 1819.*

12 Old Stone Bank
After the geometric simplicity of most of the buildings on this walk, the art nouveau-style gilt and green dome seems extravagant.

▷ *Continue to Westminster Street, then cross the river to The Arcade.*

13 The Arcade
Shopaholics in the early 19th century had their own indoor shopping malls. This was the U.S.A.'s first, built back in 1828. The stores and goods may have

changed, but it is still popular with visitors as well as locals. The cantilevered stairways and ironwork are remarkable even today. The Greek Revival porticoes give this building the look of a bank or university library. Imagine teams of oxen dragging the 20-foot (6m) long columns from the granite quarry, 5 miles (8km) away in Johnston.

▷ *Continue on Westminster Street to Dorrance Street. Turn right, heading toward Kennedy Plaza and the Fleet Skating Center. Turn left and return to the Convention Center.*

SPECIAL TO...

Quahogs, often pronounced *ko-hogs* in Rhode Island, are the local clams. The shells were once used as *wampum*, or currency, by the Native Americans. Nowadays, big shells are often saved for a dish or ashtray. Baby quahogs, called cherrystones or littlenecks, are eaten raw, on the half shell, while mature quahogs are used in chowder.

Newport

The original settlement of Newport was founded on the principles of religious tolerance, attracting Jews, Quakers, Baptists and followers of the established Church of England. With its safe, deep-water harbor, it rivaled Boston and Philadelphia by the middle of the 18th century. The city tour route starts with a walk through the Newport of the early days, and finishes with a drive past the grand mansions of the late 19th century, referred to as the "Gilded Age." As well as fine museums, Newport offers wide, flat beaches, making this an appealing destination for families. **HALF A DAY**

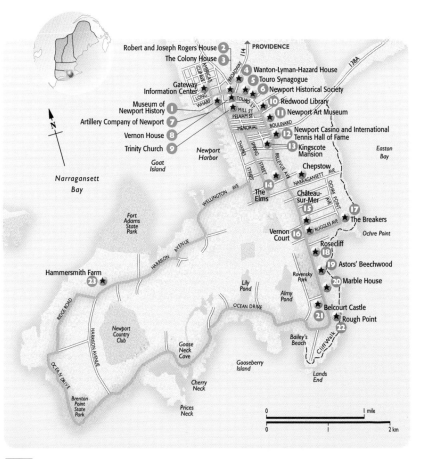

ⓘ *Gateway Information Center, 23 America's Cup Avenue (tickets for the mansions are sold here. Some visits by reservation only)*

▶ *Park in the parking lot behind the Information Center. Walk south along America's Cup Avenue for one block to Long Wharf. Cross the avenue and follow the sign to Washington Square Historic District.*

❶ Museum of Newport History

This handsome three-story building, erected in 1762, was the commercial hub of Colonial Newport. Its arches and columns were radical features in their day, marking a move away from the strictly geometric Georgian style. Now it is the Museum of Newport History, with furniture, tools, interactive computer displays, and the figurehead from the yacht *Aloha*.

In the triangular Washington Square, the statue of Oliver Hazard Perry is a reminder of the naval hero who grew up in Newport. Aged 28, he defeated the British on Lake Erie in what was an important battle during the War of 1812. "We have met the enemy and they are ours," was his victory message.

▶ *On the right is the Robert and Joseph Rogers House.*

❷ Robert and Joseph Rogers House

Now over 200 years old and still standing, this house displays the swells and bulges resulting from the settling of its foundations. The once rectangular windows have shifted into a curious variety of rhomboids and trapezoids. This is one of only a handful of Federal-style houses in Newport.

▶ *At the top of the square, on the left, you will reach The Colony House.*

❸ The Colony House

In a town constructed primarily of wood, this brick building would have looked even more imposing in the 18th century. The fourth-oldest capitol building in the country, it was the headquarters of government from 1739 until 1900, when the new State House was opened in Providence. Important announcements read from the central second-floor balcony range from the coronation of King George III in 1760, to the results of elections for Rhode Island governors.

FOR HISTORY BUFFS

"...Whereas George the Third ... forgetting his dignity ... instead of protecting is endeavoring to destroy the good people of this colony ..." Those words, read to a crowd waiting outside the Colony House, announced the repudiation of English authority in the colony of Rhode Island. The date was May 4, 1776. Two months later, on July 4, came the Declaration of Independence of all 13 colonies.

▶ *From the Colony House, exit the square and follow*

Newport is an attractive little town set dramatically against Narragansett Bay

Broadway to No. 17, the Wanton-Lyman-Hazard House. Tours start from the Museum of Newport History.

❹ Wanton-Lyman-Hazard House

When this house was built around 1697, it was one of more than 260 in a thriving village. Notice that the chimney stack is in the middle of the steep roof, but the front door is off-center; this style was known as the "Rhode Island floor plan." A century later, Tory-enthusiast Martin Howard lived here, but was forced to flee from an angry mob who were protesting against the Stamp Act.

▶ *Return to the square and turn left on Touro Street.*

❺ Touro Synagogue

"Erected 5603." That inscription celebrated the opening in 1763 of the second synagogue in the States, the oldest Jewish place of worship still standing in North America. A community of Sephardic Jews had been in Newport since 1658, led by the Reverend Isaac Touro. Like the Quakers, the Jews were important in building Newport's trading links and wealth. Architect Peter Harrison, who also designed the Brick Market and the Redwood Library, included 12 pillars to represent the 12 tribes of Israel in an interior that looks much like a classic New England meeting house.

▶ *Continue to the building next door.*

6 Newport Historical Society

The Newport Historical Society, a driving force behind the preservation of Newport's historic buildings, was established in 1853. The Seventh Day Baptist Meeting House, built in 1729, is the oldest in the country. It was moved here in 1887.

▶ *Return to Washington Square and turn left on Clarke Street. Walk halfway down this street of painted houses to Nos. 23–25, the Armory of the Artillery Company of Newport.*

The moon rises over white-steepled Trinity Church

7 Artillery Company of Newport

Uniforms worn by Field Marshall Montgomery, Prince Philip and President Anwar Sadat of Egypt are among the uniforms, flags, regalia and other artifacts in the museum

contained in this 1836 stone building. The "1741" over the door refers to the date of the artillery's charter, making this the oldest military organization in the country.

▶ *Walk to the corner of Clarke and Mary streets.*

8 Vernon House

In 1781, General Washington met with French Generals Lafayette and Rochambeau to decide tactics for the next stage of the war. Rochambeau, commander of the French troops quartered in Newport, lived in this house. If you look closely you will see that what appears to be weathered stone block is actually wood.

▶ *Continue up Mary Street, turn right on Spring Street and proceed to Trinity Church.*

9 Trinity Church

Since 1726, the tall white spire has been a landmark on the hill above the harbor. In the vestibule is the church's original bell, "probably the first bell that rang over a New England church." The church's organ, made by Richard Bridge, came from London in 1733 and may have been played by composer Friedrich Handel himself. On the main floor stand box pews, which were privately owned and could be bought and sold. Note the individually chosen cushions and elaborate needlepoint covers for the kneelers. The inscriptions on Pew 81 commemorate the most famous worshippers, from George Washington to Queen Elizabeth II and Archbishop Desmond Tutu of South Africa. Stained-glass windows by Tiffany stand out against a background of white walls and green-gray woodwork. They were paid for by wealthy summer residents such as Cornelius Vanderbilt.

▶ *The next left is Mill Street. Turn left, and walk up the hill past Touro Park and the mysterious Stone Tower. Legend says that it*

was erected by Vikings in the 11th century. More probably, it was a windmill belonging to Governor Benedict Arnold (great-grandfather of the Revolutionary traitor) who owned much of the land. Turn left and cross Bellvue Avenue.

10 Redwood Library

A £500 donation in 1746 bought the first books for what is the oldest continuously used library in the country. The benefactor was Abraham Redwood, a rich trader from the West Indies. The building is typical of the pre-Revolutionary era, with wood painted to look like stone. As well as books, there is a sculpture of Benjamin Franklin

by Jean-Antoine Houdin and paintings by Gilbert Stuart.

▶ *Walk next door.*

11 Newport Art Museum

Clipped gables, airy verandas, scroll-sawed trim and ornamental timbers, or "sticks," epitomize the "stick style" of 19th-century architecture.

Dating from 1864, this is the first of many buildings in Newport designed by Richard Morris Hunt, but it is vastly different from the extravaganzas that made him the defining architect of the later "Gilded Age."

▷ *Cross Bellevue to Touro Park and walk down Pelham Street to the harbor area. Along the way, you pass the tiny Arnold Burying Ground, where the stones date back to 1677. At the bottom, turn right and return to the Gateway Information Center. The rest of the route is followed by car. Drive up Memorial Boulevard and turn right on Bellevue Avenue and head for No. 194.*

for "little house." The first major commission for Stanford White and the McKim, Mead and White architectural firm, its "shingle" style was another popular Victorian trend. It spreads over almost a full city block; there are stores on the ground floor, with the ever-expanding International Tennis Hall of Fame above.

Outside are the world's oldest continuously used grass tennis courts, dating from 1881. (The All-England Club in the U.K. is older, but moved to its present Wimbledon site in 1922.) The annual professional tournament here is played each July, immediately after Wimbledon.

judge's view of two players volleying. If you feel so inclined, book time on one of the 13 courts and play where the U.S. Open Tennis Championships were born in 1881.

▷ *Drive along Bellevue Avenue. Single and multiple tickets for Preservation Society houses can be bought at all their properties.*

⓭ Kingscote Mansion
In 1841, the Bellevue Avenue area was only starting to develop as a residential neighborhood, and Kingscote Mansion looks positively simple compared to the grandiose designs of the 1890s. Typical of the Gothic

Moored boats at sunset in Newport's harbor

⓬ Newport Casino and the International Tennis Hall of Fame
The Casino, not a gambling casino but a gentlemen's club, was founded in 1880 as a rival to the Newport Reading Room. It takes its name from the Italian

On entering the main gate to the Hall of Fame, there is the distant roar of cheering tennis fans and the voice of an announcer calling a famous match from the past. The all-encompassing collection of tennis memorabilia includes an 1876 tennis racquet-bending machine, while state-of-the-art computer displays provide a net

Revival style are the elaborate barge-boards, lancet arch case-ment window, and sawn cornice trim. Designed by Richard Upjohn and built for George Noble Jones, some say that the expression "Keeping up with the Joneses" originated here.

▷ *Continue on along Bellevue Avenue.*

14 The Elms

When Pennsylvania coal baron Edward Berwind went to France, he was so impressed by the 18th-century Château d'Asnières, near Paris, that he made it the model for this house. The Elms, built in 1901, has furnishings that span the Louis XIV and XV styles, while the formal gardens have spacious terraces and lawns. At the top of the house, a hidden third story contains the servants' quarters.

▶ *Continue on Bellevue Avenue. To the left, on Narragansett Avenue, is Chepstow, an Italianate mansion built for a cousin of the Astors, with a fine collection of 19th-century American paintings.*

15 Château-sur-Mer

In 1857, William Wetmore invited 2,500 guests to a party in his five-year-old home. He paid for those festivities, and for this lavishly decorated mansion, with profits from trading with China. The grounds have some fine old trees, a Chinese moon gate and a Colonial Revival pavilion.

▶ *Continue on Bellevue Avenue.*

16 Vernon Court

Most of the mansions that are open to visitors are historic monuments; this grandiose version of a 17th-century French château is a private home. On the first floor is the National Museum of American Illustration, a pictorial history of American society from 1870 to 1965.

▶ *Turn left at Ruggles Avenue and follow the signs to The Breakers.*

17 The Breakers

This is the ultimate in extravagance and the most famous summer "cottage" of all. Two decades after Richard Morris Hunt renovated Château-sur-Mer, he created this mock 16th-century Italian palace for the railroad tycoon Cornelius Vanderbilt II. Hundreds of

craftsmen were employed, many brought over from Europe, but the grand salon was actually built in France, disassembled, shipped across the Atlantic, and reassembled by the same French craftsmen. In the dining room, a painted ceiling is two stories above the life-sized figures and gigantic marble columns. Although the kitchen is the size of an average house, it looks surprisingly simple and functional, hung with yard after yard of copper cooking pots and pans. The stables house a display of family items, including historic coaches.

▶ *Return to Bellevue Avenue and continue.*

18 Rosecliff

The Grand Trianon of Versailles was the inspiration for the summer home of Mrs. Hermann Oerlich. Soft-white tiles cover the outside; inside, the 80-foot (24m) long ballroom is all cream and gold. Elegant and refined, Rosecliff sits near the ocean and was used for shooting the 1974 movie, *The Great Gatsby* and, in 1994, *True Lies* with Arnold Schwarzenegger.

▶ *Continue along Bellevue Avenue.*

19 Astors' Beechwood

At the end of the 19th century, Caroline Astor was the reigning queen of American society. To be invited to her parties meant social acceptance. Her famous list of "The Top 400" people supposedly reflected the capacity of the ballroom in her New York City residence. Today, costumed guides play the parts of the Astors, their guests and their servants, bringing to life the heyday of the country house party.

▶ *Next door is Marble House.*

20 Marble House

Marble House is another Richard Morris Hunt creation, built in 1892 by William Vanderbilt, the brother of Cornelius. The overpowering entrance is covered in Italian marble, while the dining room boasts one-of-a-kind bronze Louis XIV chairs weighing 60 pounds (27kg) each. Most amazing of all is the ballroom, where "all that glisters" really is gold, or gilded. When Alva

Cornelius Vanderbilt's Breakers,
Newport's most splendid estate
Inset: the Newport coastline

23 Hammersmith Farm

This shingled 1888 beach house
was the location for the wedding
reception of Jacqueline Bouvier
and John F. Kennedy. From 1961
to 1963 it was also the "Summer
White House" for President
Kennedy. (Now private.)

Vanderbilt divorced her husband,
she took the house, then married
Perry Belmont (see below).

▶ *Proceed along Bellevue Avenue*
to Belcourt Castle.

21 Belcourt Castle

Alva Vanderbilt did not move far
after she divorced William K.
Vanderbilt and married his good
friend Perry Belmont. Where
Vanderbilt was keen on yachts,
Belmont followed horse-racing
and helped build the Belmont
Track in New York.

▶ *Opposite is Rough Point.*

22 Rough Point

Peek at the 1889 mansion built
for a Vanderbilt, then owned by
the Dukes. It remains a time
capsule, left just as it was when
the heiress, Doris Duke, lived
here. Admire works by Renoir,
Reynolds and Van Dyck.

▶ *Ocean Drive starts here and*
follows a scenic stretch of
shoreline, dotted by breath-
taking private homes. Bailey's
Beach, the first on the left, was
the beach favored by the
"400." Some 5 miles (8km)
farther, also on the left, is
Hammersmith Farm.

SCENIC ROUTES

The 3½-mile (5.6km) Cliff
Walk, starting at Cliff Walk
Manor on Memorial Boulevard
and ending at Bailey's Beach, is
an excellent way to see the
splendors of the mansions
from a different angle.

▶ *To return to the harbor area,*
follow Harrison, Halidon and
Wellington avenues to Thames
Street. Turn right, then left on
West Narragansett Avenue
and left on Spring Street to
Memorial Boulevard.

VERMONT

Vermont has been called "every American's second state" because of the small farms with red barns, and villages with white churches that make up the traditional image of "old-fashioned America." The most rural of all states, it has only one major town, Burlington, with 40,000 inhabitants. The remainder of the half million or so Vermonters are scattered throughout the rolling hills and valleys stretching north–south between Canada and the Massachusetts border.

Although Lake Champlain lies on its western flank and the Connecticut River forms the eastern border, Vermont is the only New England state with no access to the sea. What it does have is mountains. French explorer Samuel de Champlain first remarked on the *verts monts*, the green mountains, back in the 17th century. While still a colony, Vermonters argued over land ownership with neighboring New York; the Vermonters won. When the colonies threw off the yoke of the English crown, Vermont went its own way; from 1777 to 1791 it was a republic, minting its own coins and printing its own stamps.

View of the mountains surrounding Stowe, the area's main skiing and recreation center

The population has always been small. The roller-coaster landscape is difficult to farm, winters are bitter and summers are short. Despite that, Vermont has had its moments of affluence. Early in the 19th century, its wool was in demand world-wide. When that trade was lost, dairy farming took over. Although forests now cover acres of land once cleared for pasture, cattle remain a significant revenue earner. The sharp flavor of Vermont cheddar cheese is rated by gourmets, while a more recent dairy-related success is Ben and Jerry's Ice Cream. Other natural resources such as marble and granite provide a base to the economy, matched by furniture-making, paper production, and computers. Most important of all, however, is tourism.

Each autumn, "leaf peepers" by the millions invade the state, drawn by the natural phenomenon of the maple leaves turning to brilliant shades of red and gold. Since the first ski tow was set up in Woodstock in 1934, the winter season has attracted both downhill and cross-country skiers.

Tour 14

The southern Vermont town of Bennington rarely rates more than a few lines in the history books, yet it played its part in the Revolution, and a 306-foot (93m) high stone needle commemorates the 1777 battle. Nearby is the grave of one of the country's favorite poets, the 20th-century writer Robert Frost. Bennington's museum displays a fine collection of naive paintings by Grandma Moses. These, along with handsome old houses and business buildings, add up to a town that is worth exploring.

Tour 15

Southern Vermont looks softer than points farther north and is known for its photogenic farms and villages. Weston, set on a hilltop, preserves the atmosphere of a typical 19th-century Vermont village. Ludlow offers its own ski mountain; while the center of Grafton, known for its cheese, has been preserved, scrubbed clean, painted white, and seems suspended in time. The only crowded place is Manchester, full of shoppers hunting for bargains at the numerous factory outlet stores.

Tour 16

This part of Vermont is best known for the world-class ski resort of Killington. Apart from that, it is also another peaceful area where artists and craftspeople create minor masterpieces in small villages tucked away in the Green Mountains. Former U.S. president Calvin Coolidge is a local hero, his birthplace and homestead have become minor shrines. A few villages, such as Woodstock, have been deliberately "prettied up," but overall, the natural, unhustled pace of life will reward those looking for a relaxed vacation. Take time to bike the back roads.

Tour 17

Compared with the quieter regions to the south, the northern section is a bustling part of the state. Celebrities range from Ben and Jerry, whose ice creams have taken the world by storm, to the Von Trapp family of *Sound of Music* fame, who run an inn near Stowe. Teddy bears and Icelandic horses, a house with secret passages, and the Robert Frost Trail are some of the offbeat attractions. The Shelburne Museum is an outstanding collection of American folk art, housed in buildings that were moved here lock, stock and barrel from locations all over New England. The elongated Lake Champlain is fine for a ferry ride, water sports, or for those merely in search of quiet contemplation.

The first pumpkins of the season: they must be picked before the frosts arrive

TOUR
14

HALF A DAY

Bennington

Outside the state, Bennington is best known for Ethan Allen and his Green Mountain Boys. This group of feisty Vermonters not only had a grievance against the British, but also against the land-greedy "Yorkers" (New Yorkers) in the state next door. The historic district and its college make this an attractive small town.

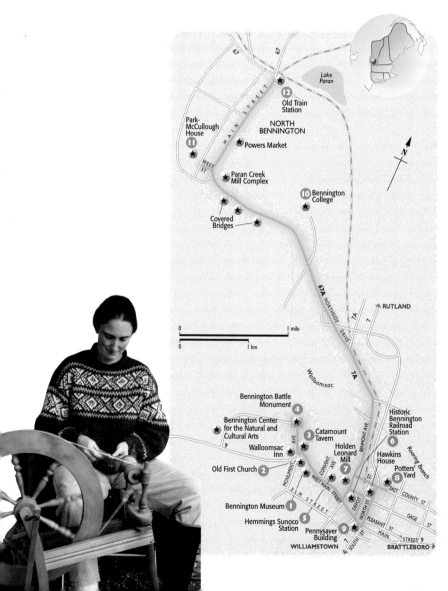

Route 7, north of downtown

▷ Park at the Bennington Museum to start the tour.

❶ Bennington Museum

Grandma Moses (1860–1961) was known as much for her longevity as for her "primitive" portrayals of rural life. This farmer's wife only started to paint when she turned 70, recording countryside activities such as haymaking and maple sugaring. Critical acclaim led to an exhibition at New York's Museum of Modern Art. Although she lived just across the state line, in Eagle Bridge, New York, this Vermont museum has the largest public collection of her work, with 30 paintings shown in a special gallery. A favorite picture, often used on greetings cards, is *Over the River*, which depicts the trip to Grandmother's house for Thanksgiving. Memorabilia are found in the old schoolhouse where she, her grandchildren, and her great-grandchildren all

studied. The museum also houses the 1777 Battle of Bennington flag, thought to be the oldest "Stars and Stripes" in existence. Look for the Bennington pottery and glass collection from the 19th century and the Bennington Wasp (1920s), the only automobile ever to be manufactured in Vermont.

▷ Walk up the hill to the small green in the center of Old Bennington. Look to your left.

The grave of Robert Frost, a simple memorial to the poet, lies in Bennington cemetery

❷ Old First Church

"And were an epitaph to be my story I'd have a short one ready for my own.
I would have written of me on my stone:
I had a lover's quarrel with the world."

The final line of Robert Frost's 1942 poem, *The Lesson for Today*, is engraved on the plain stone marking his grave in the cemetery. One of the best-loved poets of his time (1874–1963), he captured the essential sights, smells, and character of New England.

Also buried here are five Vermont governors and many patriots who fell in the Battle of Bennington. The original 1763

meeting house was replaced in 1805 by this handsome church, with its stylish belfry.

Less than a mile (1.5km) along Route 9 is the Bennington Center for the Arts. Watch a live performance or visit the Vermont Covered Bridge Museum, or see the galleries of Native American and Southwestern Art.

▷ Turn right on Monument Avenue and head toward the obelisk. Just on the right is a statue.

The observation platform on top of Bennington's Battle Monument gives excellent views over the city

3 Catamount Tavern

Looking ready to pounce on unwary passersby, this big bronze wild cat commemorates the site of the Catamount Tavern, which was built in 1767. It was the meeting place of Ethan Allen and the Green Mountain Boys. The catamount, or catamountain, is the state mascot of Vermont. It also goes by the names puma, cougar and lynx.

▶ *Walk to the top of Monument Avenue.*

4 Bennington Battle Monument

Confusingly, the Battle of Bennington took place in New York. In 1777, the British were running low on food and arms, so General Burgoyne sent troops to capture the American stores that were stashed in a depot in Bennington. Before the Redcoats could reach the town, they were intercepted and overpowered by the patriots led by General Stark and Colonel Seth Warner. This was a significant victory in a regional campaign that ended with the surrender of Burgoyne at Saratoga a few months later.

The statue of local hero, Colonel Seth Warner, stands before the simple monument on the site of the supply depot. Over a century old, the statue, built of locally quarried limestone, ranks as the tallest man-made structure in Vermont, soaring 306 feet (91.8m). Take the elevator to the observation levels for spectacular views of three states – New York, Massachusetts and Vermont. Each year, the important victory is celebrated in style on Bennington Battle Day Weekend, in mid-August.

▶ *Return down Monument Avenue, noting the fine examples of Federal and Georgian houses on either side. Turn left on West Main Street and head down the hill into the town. On the left is a service station.*

5 Hemmings Sunoco Station

You could be forgiven for thinking this is a museum of classic vehicles. Although it is a functioning Sunoco station, the owners are the publishers of *Hemmings Motor News*. The store is full of car books, models, toys and artwork, as well as Vermont products. Unusual classic cars, tractors, wreckers, steamrollers and panel trucks from the 1920s to the 1940s are often on display outside.

▶ *Walk on for a block, then turn left on Depot Street. Continue to the junction with River Street.*

6 Historic Bennington Railroad Station

The Bennington and Rutland Railroad was successful a century ago, when this temple of limestone and blue marble was built. However, passenger trains have not stopped here since 1933, although freight trundled through up to the 1950s. The handsome 1897 building survives.

▷ *Turn left on River Street, then right onto Benmont Avenue.*

7 Holden Leonard Mill
Back in the 19th century, Bennington was a manufacturing town, using the river to power grist and paper mills such as the Holden Leonard Mill. This massive building, with a central tower rising four stories high, has been converted to offices, but stands as a legacy to the industrial past.

▷ *Turn right on County Street. At the corner of North Street is the Hawkins House with its contemporary crafts. Cross North Street and continue to No. 324 County Street.*

8 Potters' Yard
In the 19th century, the town was known for its pottery, as the 4,000-piece collection in the museum shows. Today, around 40 potters still work in what was an old grist mill on County Street. This center was founded by David Gil, whose colorful splatterware has been popular since 1948. Although he died in 2002, the Bennington Potters continue to produce the jugs, pitchers and vases, and his dinner services are in great demand, both in restaurants and homes. Take a self-guided tour and watch potters in action (weekdays).

▷ *Return to North Street and turn left. This becomes South Street after the intersection with Main Street.*

9 Pennysaver Building
The houses and churches of 19th-century New England are familiar from postcards and calendars, but the commercial architecture can be just as fascinating. The former Putnam Hotel block curving round from South to Main and the Pennysaver Building at 107 South Street are typical. The

Pennysaver, a free newspaper, still occupies the premises. The huge, globular lights outside were originally gaslit.

▷ *Return to Main Street and turn back west, returning to the car. Drive to the main intersection and go north on **Route 7A**, then left on to Northside Drive (which becomes **Route 67A**). After 3 miles (5km) reach Bennington College.*

10 Bennington College
Founded in 1925 to offer further education to women, Bennington College is now co-ed. It was once the most expensive private college in America, and former students include actress Carol Channing and movie star Alan Arkin, as well as a host of artists. Known for its programs of fine arts, the campus is an attractive blend of mock Colonial and modern buildings in a rural setting.

▷ *Continue on **Route 67A** to North Bennington (2 miles/3km). Three covered bridges cross the river on the left: the Silk Road, Papermill Village and the Bert Henry Bridge on Murphy Road. On the right, entering the town, is a fine complex of water-driven mills on Paran Creek. This is a convenient place to park. Cross Main Street and bear left up West Street. At the corner of Park Street is the Park-McCullough House.*

11 Park-McCullough House
With its handsome curving veranda, this early example of an American Second Empire-style mansion (1875) gives some idea of the lifestyle of the wealthy in the second half of the 19th century. The name combines that of lawyer Trenor Park, who built the house, and his son-in-law, John McCullough, one of the two Vermont governors who lived here. The 35-room house contains furniture, clothing and toys, which are all displayed in the original family context. Out in the stables is a collection of old sleighs and carriages. Open to the public, there is a small replica of the mansion on the front lawn.

▷ *Return to Main Street and turn left up the hill, past the imposing Greek columns of Powers Market. It is no more than a country store inside, but at the top of the hill is the station.*

12 Old Train Station
North Bennington's Victorian railroad station, attractively decorated in shades of green and barn-red trim, dates back to 1880. These days, it functions as an office complex.

▷ *Return to the car at the bottom of the hill.*

Taking a quiet moment in Bennington, once a center of Revolutionary action

THE FALL

While most of the world experiences a dull, even sad end to the year, New England's landscape goes out in a blaze of glory. Due to a combination of soil and trees, sun and rain, the hillsides change from green to a tapestry of scarlet and gold, purple and orange. This is the "foliage season." Rudyard Kipling, who lived for a while in Vermont, felt almost powerless to depict the transformation. "No pen can describe the turning of the leaves – the insurrection of the tree people against the waning year. A little maple began it, flaming blood-red of a sudden where he stood against the dark green of a pine-belt. Next morning there was an answering signal from the swamp where the sumacs grow. Three days later, the hill-sides as far as the eye could range were afire, and the roads paved with crimson and gold." (*Leaves from a Winter Notebook*, 1900.)

in Vermont and New Hampshire. The Columbus Day holiday (second weekend of October) is the most crowded of the year in those tiny states. Hotels and inns tend to have "foliage season rates" that start in mid-September and carry on through mid-October. Of course, there is no promise from Mother Nature that she'll get her paint-brushes out at this time: a dry summer and the leaves could change earlier; a wet summer and the "foliage" could be delayed. To avoid the inevitable

Photographs cannot prepare you for your first sight of New England in September and October. Millions of visitors, "leaf peepers," visit the region every year, with cameras at the ready. Most go by car or on bus tours, but hot-air balloons and river cruise boats also provide a spectacular experience.

Science

Scientists have a clinical explana-tion for the changes. They say that sunny days, allied with chilly nights, stop the production of chlorophyll, the chemical that turns leaves green. This, in turn, allows other pigments such as anthocyanin (red) or carotenoids (orange, yellow) to show through in the leaves. The Native American explanation is far more entertaining: the Great Bear (in the sky) was killed in a hunt, and its blood dripped down onto the leaves. As for the yellow, that was attributed to the fat of the bear splashing out of the cooking pot.

The time

The leaves change color in a tide that sweeps down from north to south, usually starting in late September in Maine, northern Vermont and New Hampshire and reaching Connecticut in the south, around the middle of October. The most intense period is, by tradition, the first two weeks in October, especially

The beautiful colors of fall

crowds, a few visitors gamble and go north to Maine, where the weather might not be so gentle, but the roads are almost certainly quiet. Otherwise, the trick is stay off the main roads, and drift along the twisting country lanes which often have poor or even no signs at all. Take warm clothing; leaf watching is warm in the sun, but can turn chilly by the end of the day.

The trees

The dark green is usually provided by fir and spruce.
Scarlet and crimson: dogwood, red (or swamp) maple, sassafras and red oak.
Gold and yellow: poplar, elm, birch and gingko.
Orange: hickory, mountain maple and mountain ash.
Brown: oak.
Purple: sumac.

Hotlines

As well as information on the web, the New England states have special telephone numbers with up-to-date information on the progression of the color, and where to find it. It is also an indicator as to where the most "leaf peepers" are likely to be!

Connecticut (tel: 800/282-6863)
Maine (tel: 888/624-6345)
Massachusetts (tel: 800/227-6277)
New Hampshire (tel: 800/258-3608)
Rhode Island (tel: 401/222-2601)
Vermont (tel: 802/828–3239).

2 DAYS • 151 MILES • 244KM

Southern
Vermont

"The Switzerland of North America" was a British ambassador's description of Vermont, yet the southern part is softer than the rest of this rugged state, with hamlets and houses scattered across the landscape. Almost every village has a green, a white steepled church, and an inn and roadside stands selling maple syrup.

RUTLAND
3343ft
Okemo Mountain
Ludlow 9
GREEN
Proctorsville

100
Gassetts

8 **Weston**
Chester Depot

GREEN Mountains
GREEN
Peru 7
6
Chester 10
Brockways Mills Gorge

EMERALD LAKE STATE PARK

3301ft
Bear Mountain
Bromley Mountain ski area
Londonderry
35

3816ft
Mount Equinox
5 **Manchester Center**
2 **Manchester Village**
4 Manchester Depot
100
Grafton 11

NEW YORK
SKYLINE DRIVE
3 Hildene
MOUNTAIN
Cambridgeport

Batten Kill
1
Stratton Pond
3936ft
Stratton Mountain
35

Arlington
East Arlington

NATIONAL
Townshend

SHAFTSBURY STATE PARK
3748ft
Glastenbury Mountain
Somerset Reservoir
TOWNSHEND STATE PARK
30

Shaftsbury
APPALACHIAN TRAIL
3556ft
Mount Snow
12 **Newfane**
LEBANON

FOREST
West Dummerston
91

3420ft
Haystack Mountain

15
2410ft
Hogback Mountain
West Dummerston

ALBANY
BENNINGTON
Woodford
2767ft
Prospect Mountain
Wilmington
MOLLY STARK TRAIL
9
Marlboro 14
13 **Brattleboro**

7
9
Harriman Reservoir
MOLLY STARK STATE PARK
West Brattleboro
91

Connecticut

| 0 | 5 | 10 miles |
| 0 | 5 | 10 | 15 km |

i Route 7, 1 mile (1.5km) north
of downtown

▶ From Bennington drive north
on **Route 7A**. Robert Frost
lived at the Stone House in
Shaftsbury (open to the
public).

❶ Arlington

Illustrator Norman Rockwell,
famous for his *Saturday Evening
Post* magazine covers, spent the
middle part of his life here, from
1939 to 1953, using local people
as models for his countless views
of everyday life. Although the
most complete record of his
work is farther south in
Stockbridge, Massachusetts, the
Norman Rockwell exhibition,
in a former church, also has a
permanent record, though
these are all reproductions. The
country doctor who appeared in
a Rockwell picture popular in
many waiting rooms was one
Dr. Russell, whose vast collection of Vermontiana is housed
at the library.

Vermont's first grist mill was
built here in 1764 by the splen-
didly named Remember Baker.
Only a plaque remains to mark
the site.

▶ Proceed north on **Route 7A** for
4 miles (6km) to the foot of
Mount Equinox.

❷ **Mount Equinox**

The Carthusian order has a
monastery here on the 3,816-
foot (1,163m) Big Equinox peak,
the highest point in the Taconic
Range. The 5-mile (8km)
Skyline Drive toll road climbs
steeply to the top where memo-

SPECIAL TO...

Running parallel to Route 7A
is the Batten Kill River, one
of the world's great fly-fishing
streams, with 150 years of
tradition. Equally famous,
the Orvis Fishing Company
started making bamboo rods in
1886, in a small plant not far
from their current location in
Manchester. As well as exhibiting some 25,000 fishing flies,
the American Museum of Fly
Fishing nearby has rods
belonging to celebrities such as
Bing Crosby and baseball star
Babe Ruth.

Covered bridges are now recognized as historic landmarks. This
example is at West Arlington

rable views stretch across to Quebec, New York, New Hampshire, and Massachusetts. Cars are warned to have good "brakes, radiators and transmissions" before attempting the drive. Cyclists and sports-car racers frequently test themselves on "hill climbs." The record ascent is just over eight minutes by racing car.

▷ Continue on **Route 7A** to Hildene.

3 Hildene
Robert Todd Lincoln was the son of President Abraham Lincoln. As a child, he visited the Equinox Hotel with his mother, just before his father was assassinated, but only returned to the area many years later. Hildene, Lincoln's summer home, was built in 1904, and it was here that he died in 1926. Lincoln descendants lived here until 1975; the house is filled with authentic memorabilia of the Civil War leader, including Abe's "stovepipe" hat. The stately 24-room Georgian Revival home boasts a huge pipe organ and magnificent grounds. Polo matches are played on summer Sundays and, in winter, the former carriage house is a base for visitors who cross-country ski the 9 miles (14km) of trails. Take a picnic and enjoy the garden, farm and walks.

▷ Continue for 2 miles (3km) to Manchester Village.

SPECIAL TO...

Roadside stands and stores all sell maple syrup, a product synonymous with Vermont, even though the sticky, sweet liquid from the maple tree is made all over New England. Today, the traditional buckets and wooden sugar-houses of yesteryear have been replaced by plastic tubes inserted directly into the trees. Once the warm sun and cold nights of late winter/early spring cause the colorless liquid to rise, the sap is siphoned off. A good tree produces about 8 gallons (36 liters) per season. The sap is then boiled down to make the caramel-colored syrup. Anything from 30 to 50 gallons (135 to 225 liters) of sap is needed to make one gallon (4.5 liters) of syrup. Grade A, the most delicately colored and flavored, costs the most, while Grade D would do for baking.

---

4 Manchester Village
There are three Manchesters: Center, Depot, and the oldest and highest, the Village. This is where the rich and powerful summered, either in their own luxury mansions, or at the legendary resort hotel, the Equinox. Dating back to 1769, this splendid Victorian hotel has been expanded and renovated over the years and today has 183 rooms and the renowned par-71 Gleneagles golf course.

▷ Drive half a mile (800m) into Manchester Center.

5 Manchester Center
Nowadays Manchester is know for shopping, with bargain-hunters flocking to designer outlet stores such as Polo/Ralph Lauren. More peaceful is the Southern Vermont Arts Center, just outside town. Join an art class or view the galleries and sculpture gardens; or stroll through its 407 acres (165ha).

▷ Drive 2 miles (3km) and turn onto **Route 11** east.

6 Bromley Mountain
The road climbs steadily to Bromley ski area, a pioneer among ski resorts since 1937. Visitors come in summer to try out the alpine slide, the longest of its kind in Vermont.

▷ Continue on **Route 11** east, then turn off to Peru.

7 Peru
Peru, one of the state's little-known hamlets, was featured in the 1987 movie *Baby Boom*, with Diane Keaton. An old-fashioned grocery store shares the street with a church, an antiques shop and several lovely homes.

▷ Return to **Route 11**, east, and drive to Londonderry. Turn left onto **Route 100**, and go north for Weston.

8 Weston
Weston is well known, not only for its prettiness, but also for the two rival stores across the street from one another. The Vermont Country Store and the Weston Village Store both do everything

The Old Tavern Inn, in the pristine village of Grafton

pleasant stores and narrow green. In Chester Depot, the restored 1852 railroad station now welcomes the Green Mountain Flyer. This tourist train has been making the run from its home in Bellows Falls for some 20 years. Popular in summer, seats must be booked well in advance in September/October, when the fall color is spectacular, particularly in Brockway Mills Gorge.

⟩ *The Green (seasonal)*

▶ Take **Route 35** south for 7 miles (11km) to Grafton.

⓫ Grafton
In a state of many lovely villages, Grafton is probably the most photogenic of them all. It was once an affluent town on the Boston to Albany post road, with soapstone quarries and a thriving woolen industry, but after the Civil War, its economy collapsed. There was a revival in 1801, when the handsome Old Tavern was built with a California gold miner's money, but by the middle of the century, the village had all but died yet again. Help was at hand, however. In her will, Pauline Fisk instructed her nephews to use her fortune for a good cause of their choice. They came up with the idea of reviving Grafton.

In 1963, the Windham Foundation began the restoration of Grafton's historic charm that draws admiring visitors. For some, the houses are almost too pretty, too perfect for such a rural setting. The village has also revived a former industry: a nutty cheddar-style cheese, made by the Grafton Village Cheese Company. The tiny Grafton Grocery Market also has locally made preserves and hand-knits, and there is a working blacksmith's shop. Two covered bridges complete the scene. On Sunday evenings in summer, the cornet band plays on the green, a tradition dating back to 1867.

but bottle the nostalgia, and both offer an incredible variety of "country" and "Vermont" items that will bring visitors and their wallets to their knees. The circular town green, with its bandstand, inn and brick church on the hill above, is extremely photogenic. The Weston Playhouse is one of New England's oldest and most popular summer theaters.

Just north of the village is the Benedictine monks' religious community of Weston Priory, a tranquil place where visitors are welcome to join in services and walk around the grounds.

▶ Continue to Ludlow.

⑨ Ludlow
Where Weston is picture-perfect, Ludlow is full of character, though recent years have brought some gentrification to this former mill town on the banks of the Black River. Here, wool was recycled into inexpensive cloth called "shoddy," which has become a pejorative description for anything cheap.

The mill on Main Street is now a condo and the area has been revitalized. The Okemo Mountain Resort is widely acknowledged as having some of the best snow-making and grooming facilities in Vermont.

⟩ *Clocktower, Okemo Marketplace, Route 100/103*

▶ Take **Route 103** south for 13 miles (21km) to Chester.

⑩ Chester
Hidden away in the woods on the way to Chester was the home of Russian Nobel Prize-winner Alexander Solzhenitsyn. He lived here in isolation during his exile from the Soviet Union. The Stone Village on North Street, has, unusually for Vermont, some 30 cottages built of local stone. Dating from before the Civil War, these had hiding places for slaves escaping from the southern states on the so-called Underground Railroad to Canada.

The heart of Chester is the broad main street, with its inns,

▶ *Leave Grafton on **Route 35** south, which turns briefly into a dirt road after 6 miles (10km). At Townsend, take **Route 30** south for 5 miles (8km) to Newfane.*

12 Newfane

In summer, Newfane shows off its classic white Courthouse, church and inns, all of which have gleaming Greek Revival columns. The long-established air of the place is deceptive. Two hundred years ago, the buildings stood 2 miles (3km) away, on Newfane Hill. In 1825, the residents moved the town, using the slippery snow and ice of winter to slide the beams and boards to today's site. Jail accommodations were so comfortable and the food so palatable that paying guests were allowed in to enjoy "good pies and oyster soup" along with the inmates. Excellent fare is still a tradition, with both of the town's inns renowned for their cuisine. During the summer, everyone turns out for the free concerts on the green. Also popular are the flea markets held on Sundays; just outside the village on Route 30, this is one of Vermont's biggest and best.

The local museum, the Historical Society Museum of Windham County, is easy to spot, with its mid-19th-century bell standing outside. Inside are simple memorabilia from the area – Victorian dresses, old maps, and a variety of household items.

Beyond town, Route 30 runs parallel to the West River, where rafters and paddlers take up the challenge of high water in spring. In summer, the river is low, but fine for cooling off or "tubing," floating downstream in an inner tube.

▶ *Continue on **Route 30** to Brattleboro.*

13 Brattleboro

Fort Dummer, the first site in the state to be settled by Europeans, has now been covered by the waters of the nearby dam. Originally, this was the western frontier of the Bay Colony, used in defense against the French and the Native Americans.

Brattleboro is just down the road. In recent years, there has been a clean-up of the town's industrial infrastructure, centered around the main thoroughfare, Elliott Street. The former Union Railroad Station is now the Museum and Art Center, with five galleries. The focus here is on contemporary art and each year there is a different theme for the regularly changing exhibitions.

Just north of the town at Dummerston, in a house called Naulakha, author Rudyard Kipling lived and worked from 1892 to 1896, after marrying a local girl, Carrie Balestier. Books such as *Captains Courageous*, the *Jungle Books* and the *Just So Stories* were all written here. The house can be rented.

The notorious 19th-century swindler James Fisk, "Jubilee Jim," who once cornered the New York gold market, is buried in the cemetery, with a monument by local sculptor Larken Mead. Mead gained true recognition for his memorial honoring

a more reputable man: he carved the statue that graces Abraham Lincoln's tomb in Springfield, Illinois.

▶ Take **Route 9** west and start climbing into the hills. Pass Whetstone Valley Farm, known for maple sugaring in early spring, to Marlboro.

14 Marlboro

The countryside looks attractive today, but back in 1763 it must have been daunting for the European settlers. Two families

Newfane's County Courthouse

are credited with founding Marlboro, but neither pioneer family knew the other was nearby for over a year. The focus of town is Marlboro College, with its music school. The chamber music festival (mid-July to mid-August, weekend concerts) is a well established highlight, due to the long residency and efforts of cellist Pablo Casals in its early years.

▶ Continue west on **Route 9**. After 15 miles (24km), there is a panoramic view from one of the highest points on the road. Continue to Wilmington.

15 Wilmington and Woodford

The alpine-looking village of Wilmington is at the intersection with Route 100, the north–south route that winds its way through the villages and ski resorts of the Green Mountains. Haystack Mountain and Mount Snow are just to the north.

Route 9 climbs on into the Green Mountain National Forest, passing through Woodford, Vermont's highest village. Prospect Mountain offers hiking opportunities.

▶ Return to Bennington.

Central
Vermont.

The central part of the state gets busy in winter, due to the appeal of internationally known ski resorts such as Killington. In summer, attractions range from the Quechee Gorge, a sudden tear in the landscape, to Plymouth, the home of Calvin Coolidge. Rutland is nicknamed the "Marble City," because local quarries have provided floors and walls for many of America's grand civic buildings.

1 DAY • 109 MILES • 175KM

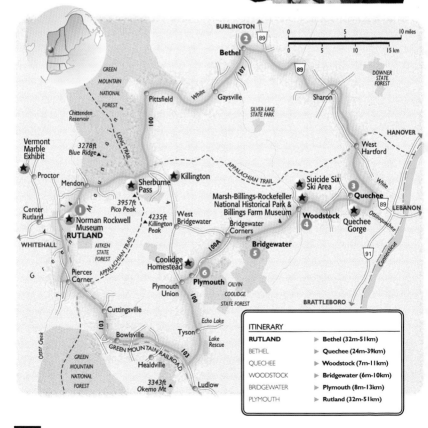

ITINERARY

RUTLAND	▶	**Bethel (32m-51km)**
BETHEL	▶	**Quechee (24m-39km)**
QUECHEE	▶	**Woodstock (7m-11km)**
WOODSTOCK	▶	**Bridgewater (6m-10km)**
BRIDGEWATER	▶	**Plymouth (8m-13km)**
PLYMOUTH	▶	**Rutland (32m-51km)**

[i] 256 North Main Street, also at junction of Routes 4 and 7 (seasonal)

▶ Leave Rutland on **Route 4** east. After 2 miles (3km) is the Norman Rockwell Museum on the right.

❶ Norman Rockwell Museum of Vermont

Better known collections of the popular illustrator's work can be found in Stockbridge (Massachusetts) and Arlington (Vermont), but you'll find 2,500 reproductions of well-loved covers from magazines such as *Saturday Evening Post*, *Life*, and *Literary Digest* here. There is enough to keep nostalgia hunters interested for an hour or so. After the museum, the road starts its long climb into the Green Mountains. Just before the Pico/Killington ski area, watch for hikers following the Appalachian Trail and Long Trail which crosses Route 4 but then splits, with the Appalachian Trail heading off to New Hampshire.

▶ Continue on **Route 4** over the Sherburne Pass, turn onto **Route 100** north, then take **Route 107** to Bethel.

❷ Bethel

Vermont Castings' popular wood-burning stoves, seemingly essential to any Vermont home, may be seen at Bethel's Brick Store on Main Street. A small exhibition at the White River National Fish Hatchery explains an ambitious project to bring back the Atlantic salmon to the Connecticut River. Abundant when the Colonists arrived, the fish had been virtually wiped out by dams, over-fishing and pollution.

▶ Follow **Route 107** and turn onto **I–89** south. After 18 miles (29km) take exit 1. **Route 4** leads to Quechee.

❸ Quechee and Quechee Gorge

Quechee (Kwee-chy) Gorge is 162 feet (49m) deep. Jagged

The Ottauquechee River runs wild as it cuts its way through the Quechee Gorge

chunks of schist rock protrude from the walls. While the best view of Vermont's "Little Grand Canyon" is from the old railroad bridge that spans the ravine, there is also a half-mile (800m) hike to the bottom. The Ottauquechee River that used to drive the woolen mills of Quechee now powers the converted Downer's Mill. It is here that Simon Pearce's well-known glass is made. Visitors can watch his craftsmen at work blowing glass. The Irishman opened his studios in 1981 and has since added a restaurant. All around the town are retirement communities.

RECOMMENDED WALKS

Two of the Northeast's most famous hiking trails part company near Pico Peak. The Long Trail runs the length of the state, some 260 miles (416km) from the Massachusetts line to Québec. This "Footpath in the Wilderness" opened in 1926. The southern part of it overlaps with the even longer Appalachian Trail, which runs from Maine down to Georgia. Be warned! These hikes are only for the hearty. They are administered by the Green Mountain Club, in Waterbury (tel: 802/244–7037) and have simple shelters on the trails.

▶ Continue on **Route 4** for another 7 miles (11km) to Woodstock.

FOR HISTORY BUFFS

Although Joseph Smith is always connected with Salt Lake City and Utah, the founder of the Mormons (Church of Jesus Christ of the Latter Day Saints) was actually born in 1805 on a farm near Sharon, 10 miles (16km) southeast of Bethel. His family left the state in 1816, but a huge granite monument at the top of a steep hill is a tribute to the prophet. Each foot of the 38½-foot (11.4m) high obelisk represents a year of his life.

From Thanksgiving to Christmas, 100,000 lights brighten the visitor center. Brigham Young, the other great Mormon leader, was another Vermonter, born in Whitingham, near the Massachusetts border.

4 Woodstock

This is New England as most people imagine it: a covered bridge, bandstand on the green, shuttered Colonial homes and an elegant inn. Regularly voted one of America's prettiest towns, Woodstock was one of the first in the state to develop as a two-season resort. In 1934 a Model T Ford car engine, set up at the bottom of a hill, was hooked up to a piece of cable on a wheel and Woodstock had the first ski tow in the U.S.A. The colorfully named Suicide Six Ski Area still tests even the most competent of skiers.

Woodstock has been a cultural center from its early days. One of the most intellectual of all its sons was George Marsh (1801–82), the lawyer, diplomat and fervent conservationist. His friend, Frederick Billings, promoted modern farming techniques.

The Marsh-Billings-Rockefeller National Historical Park is named in honor of the

SPECIAL TO...

Fans of birds of prey flock to see the snowy owls, peregrine falcons, red-tailed hawks, bald eagles and more at the VINS Nature Center. This 40-acre (16ha) attraction opened in 2004 between Quechee Gorge and Woodstock. It is as educational as it is fun, particularly if you join one of the naturalist-led walks.

two people who, along with Laurence and Mary Rockefeller, did so much to shape the landscape we see here today. Tours of the mansion show the countryside in art, with a fine collection of American landscapes, while tours of the surrounding forests interpret the way in which the estate has been carefully managed in order to balance the requirements of woodcrafts, recreation, education and ecology.

Everyday exhibits at the Billings Museum, Woodstock
Right: red barns and silos are a common sight in Vermont

The park is in partnership with Billings Farm and Museum, a working dairy farm where visitors can watch work in progress, including butter churning and ice-cream-making. An excellent introduction to both the park and the farm can be seen in the visitor center, where the Academy Award-nominated movie *A Place in the Land* is shown hourly.

Four bells cast by patriotic hero Paul Revere are at the Congregational Church.

▶ Continue for 6 miles (10km) to Bridgewater.

5 Bridgewater

Bridgewater and its namesakes farther upstream, West Bridgewater and Bridgewater Corners, were all mill towns. In Bridgewater itself, one old mill

One of the dozens of Victorian stained-glass windows in Wilson Castle, northwest of Rutland

has been turned into an outlet center for designer clothes, with a crafts center.

The Long Trail Brewing Company has a pub-style visitor center at Bridgewater Corners, where you can tour, taste and eat, either inside or on the deck overlooking the river.

▷ *Turn left on **Route 100A** south for Plymouth.*

6 Plymouth

Calvin Coolidge (1872–1933), the 30th president of the United States, was born here, the only president born on the Fourth of July. The five-room Coolidge Birthplace, his father's general store next door, the Coolidge Homestead, and the Wilder House, his mother's childhood home, have been kept much as they would have been when Coolidge was a boy. The summer White House, used in 1924 by Coolidge, has been re-created nearby. He and many other Coolidges are buried in Plymouth cemetery.

The President's father founded the Plymouth Cheese Company more than a century ago; in 1960, a descendant revived the tradition so, happily, the classic New England cheese lives on at Frog City Cheese.

▷ *Continue on **Route 100A**, then turn left on **Route 100** toward Ludlow, passing the Green Mountain Sugar House. Set on the shore of Lake Pauline, the Sugar House is a good place for maple-related products. Turn right on **Route 103** and return to Rutland.*

Northern
Vermont

In this sparsely populated part of the state, there are a surprising number of attractions.

2 DAYS • 134 MILES • 215KM

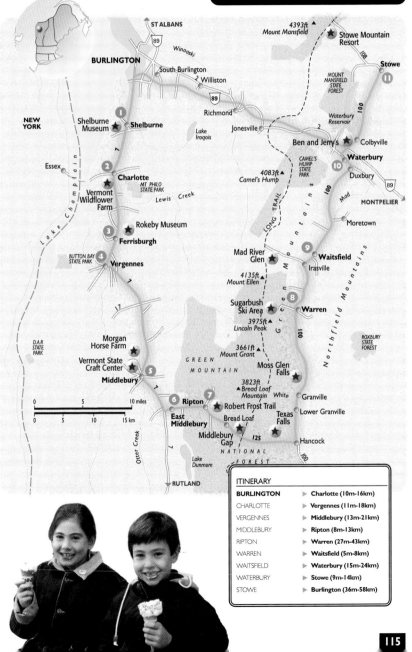

ST ALBANS

4393ft ▲
Mount Mansfield

Stowe Mountain
Resort

89

Winooski

BURLINGTON

South Burlington

Williston

Stowe

MOUNT
MANSFIELD
STATE
FOREST

89

Richmond

11

Jonesville

Waterbury
Reservoir

**NEW
YORK**

Shelburne
Museum ★ **Shelburne**

Lake
Iroqois

Ben and Jerry's ★ Colbyville

Waterbury

Essex

Charlotte

MT PHILO
STATE PARK

CAMEL'S
HUMP
STATE
PARK

10

Duxbury

Vermont
Wildflower
Farm

Lewis Creek

4083ft ▲
Camel's Hump

89

MONTPELIER

★ Rokeby Museum

Moretown

3

Ferrisburgh

BUTTON BAY
STATE PARK

4

Mad River
Glen

9 ★ **Waitsfield**

Irasville

Vergennes

4135ft ▲
Mount Ellen

8

D.A.R
STATE
PARK

Sugarbush
Ski Area

★ **Warren**

3975ft ▲
Lincoln Peak

ROXBURY
STATE
FOREST

Morgan
Horse Farm ★

3661ft ▲
Mount Grant

Moss Glen
Falls

Vermont State
Craft Center

GREEN
MOUNTAIN

5

Middlebury

3823ft
▲ Bread Loaf
Mountain

White

Granville

10 miles

6 ★ **Ripton**

7 ★ Robert Frost Trail

Lower Granville

0   5

15 km

**East
Middlebury**

Bread Loaf

Texas
Falls

Middlebury
Gap

125

Hancock

Lake
Dunmore

N A T I O N A L

F O R E S T

RUTLAND

ITINERARY		
BURLINGTON	▶	**Charlotte (10m-16km)**
CHARLOTTE	▶	**Vergennes (11m-18km)**
VERGENNES	▶	**Middlebury (13m-21km)**
MIDDLEBURY	▶	**Ripton (8m-13km)**
RIPTON	▶	**Warren (27m-43km)**
WARREN	▶	**Waitsfield (5m-8km)**
WAITSFIELD	▶	**Waterbury (15m-24km)**
WATERBURY	▶	**Stowe (9m-14km)**
STOWE	▶	**Burlington (36m-58km)**

[i] 60 Main Street

▶ From Burlington, take **Route 7**
south for 5 miles (8 km) and
turn right for Shelburne Farms.

❶ Shelburne

Most Vermont farms are humble
affairs, with red barns, a white
silo and a low-slung farmhouse.
Shelburne Farms is the opposite,
a millionaire's toy built in the
1880s and 1890s on a giant scale
and using all the latest technical
equipment available.

After William Webb married
Lila Vanderbilt, daughter of the
landscaped New York's Central
Park, to map out their property.
Like so many millionaires of the
late 19th century, the Webb's
"summer cottage" was extraordinary – a 110-room Queen
Anne-style manor house. It is
now the Inn at Shelburne
Farms. The farm continues to
be an experimental and working
farm, where visitors can watch
cheese- and butter-making, or
wool-spinning. Old-fashioned
pleasures such as hay rides will
entertain small children.

When J. Watson Webb, the
son of the Webbs of Shelburne

Fascinating exhibits of folk art in
the Shelburne Museum

railroad tycoon, they created a
European-style estate. The
Webbs called upon Frederick
Law Olmsted, the man who

FOR CHILDREN

Children (and lots of adults)
always love a boat trip, and
there are plenty of opportunities to cruise Lake Champlain.
One of the most popular trips
is from Burlington Boathouse
aboard the *Spirit of Ethan Allen
III*, a three-deck cruise ship
with narration and on-board
meals. Or you can go your own
way. Waterfront Boat Rentals in
Burlington rent canoes, kayaks
and motor boats.

SPECIAL TO...

Lake Champlain is shaped like a
sausage, 120 miles (192km)
long and anything from 400
yards (400m) to 12 miles
(19km) wide. Samuel de
Champlain, the 17th-century
French explorer, recorded see-
ing a 20-foot-long (6m) serpent
with a head like a horse, and
visitors have been trying to
spot "Champ" ever since. Lake
Champlain has four ferry services that cross from Vermont
to the New York shores: from
Grand Isle to Plattsburgh (12
minutes), from Burlington to
Port Kent (an hour), from
Charlotte to Essex (20
minutes) and from Shoreham
to Ticonderoga (6 minutes).

Farms, married Electra
Havemeyer, they began collect-
ing art objects, large and small,
and these now form the remarkable Shelburne Museum. The
37 buildings in which the quilts,
paintings, toys and farm equipment are displayed are themselves collector's items. These
buildings, each a historical landmark, have been rescued from
all over New England and
reassembled. You'll find a
schoolhouse, railroad station,
general store, barn, jailhouse and
inn, now serving as galleries.
Most arresting of all is a boat –
the 220-foot (66m) long side-
wheel steamer *Ticonderoga*. It
was hauled for 2 miles (3km)
from Lake Champlain to its final
landlocked berth here on the
farm. Although the folk art
collection is justifiably high-

houses in the historic district remain, along with three covered bridges.

Slightly farther along Route 7 is the Vermont Wildflower Farm with 6 acres (2.4 ha) of woodland and flower fields. Self-guiding trails explain the folklore of wildflowers and how Native Americans used them for herbal remedies. Visitors can also buy seeds. This stretch of Route 7 has magnificent views across Lake Champlain to the Adirondack Mountains.

▶ *Continue to Ferrisburgh. On a hill to the left is the Rokeby Museum.*

3 Ferrisburgh
One of the state's underrated museums is the Rokeby, home of the Robinson family for generations. Beautifully furnished, the house is a tribute to their own artistic talents, with portraits and landscapes they have personally painted lining the walls. Rokeby was also one of the last stops on the Underground Railroad, the escape route for slaves from the American South to Canada. It contains a secret passage and hiding room.

▶ *Continue south to Vergennes.*

4 Vergennes
Vergennes was named after France's foreign minister, a great supporter of the Americans in the Revolution. It is one of the smallest cities in the country, just one square mile (259 ha) with 2,700 inhabitants. On Basin Harbor Road, in a 19th-century stone schoolhouse, you'll find Lake Champlain Maritime Museum. During both the Revolution and the War of 1812, American and British warships battled for supremacy on this elongated strip of water. Benedict Arnold (see page 80), later a notorious traitor, delayed the British in 1776 with a series of clever ploys, as explained in the museum. A full-size floating

replica of his gunboat, the *Philadelphia II*, is the highlight.

▶ *Continue on **Route 7** south to Middlebury.*

5 Middlebury
Middlebury is best known for its college, founded in 1800. Visitors who come to visit old buildings such as Painter Hall and the Henry Sheldon Museum of Vermont History use it as a base. For more contemporary culture, the Vermont State Craft Center, in Frog Hollow, on Otter Creek Falls, is a modern showcase for the talents of some 250 artists and craftspeople from all over the state. (There are also branches in Manchester and Burlington.) Across the creek are the old marble works, filled with stores.

Middlebury College claims to be the birthplace of the Frisbee in 1938. Yale students may dispute this (see page 68), but the Vermonters have a handsome statue of a dog leaping to catch a flying disk. It was unveiled in front of Monroe Hall on what they insist was the 50th anniversary of spinning pie dishes at one another.

[i] *2 Court Street*

▶ *Follow **Route 7** south, then turn onto **Route 125** for East Middlebury.*

6 East Middlebury
Two hundred years ago the hamlet of East Middlebury was

lighted as one of the finest in the world, the Shelburne art collection is equally impressive. Pieces by American painters Andrew Wyeth and Winslow Homer are on display, as are European artists Rembrandt and Goya. You need a full day here to do justice to the museum.

The town of Shelburne has a more recent industry: the Vermont Teddy Bear Company, which exports its furry friends world-wide. Children can decorate and stuff "new born" bears.

▶ *Continue to Charlotte.*

2 Charlotte
Pronounced char-LOT, the town's heyday was in the early 19th century, when it was a stage-coach stop on the journey from Burlington to Troy. The old

---

RECOMMENDED WALKS

Split by the Mad River and the Moss Glen Falls, Granville Gulf State Reservation borders the eastern boundary of the Green Mountain National Forest. There is a 6-mile (10km) scenic drive, as well as two hiking trails. The easy 1-mile (1.6km) loop on the east side of the road contrasts with the shorter, but tougher half-mile (800m) hike to the west.

BACK TO NATURE

The Green Mountains, the backbone of Vermont, consist of more than one distinct range. The higher peaks are to the north, with Mount Mansfield (in Stowe), the highest in the state. About two-thirds of the mountains are protected by the Green Mountain National Forest, 370,000 acres (149,750 ha) devoted to maintaining scenic beauty and providing recreational opportunities. Some 500 miles (800km) of trails criss-cross the forests. The headquarters of the Green Mountain National Forest are in Rutland.

little more than a spot for stage coaches to Boston to change horses. In the 1980s television cameras arrived to film the hit TV comedy series *Newhart*, starring comedian Bob Newhart, at the Waybury Inn. Rooms in this quaint 1810 inn have been refurbished in period style.

▶ *Continue for 4 miles (6km) to Ripton on **Route 125**, the Robert Frost Memorial Drive.*

⑦ Ripton

The poet Robert Frost summered in the woods near Ripton for 23 years, and today the mountain to the north is named after him. Just after the

The densely wooded Green Mountains clothed in fall foliage

hamlet of Ripton is a picnic area on the left, and a rough track leading to his cabin. On the other side of the road is the Robert Frost Interpretive Trail, a 1¼-mile (2km) walk studded with plaques of quotes by the great man.

Seven miles (11km) after leaving Middlebury is the Bread Loaf Campus of Middlebury College. Once a hotel in the shadow of Bread Loaf Mountain, the campus is now well known for its summer writing schools and conferences. In winter it is a base for cross-country skiing.

▶ ***Route 125** climbs steadily, passing Bread Loaf and the Snow Bowl, a challenging ski area. Beyond the summit of Middlebury Gap the road*

drops down to Hancock, passing Texas Falls recreation area.
At Hancock, turn left on Route 100 north, alongside the White River. After 4 miles (6km) is Granville, and another 10 miles (16km) farther turn right to Warren and Mad River Valley.

8 Warren

Despite the popularity of the neighboring Sugarbush Resort ski area, Warren has changed little. The simple exterior of the Warren Store belies a sophisticated little emporium of gourmet foods and fine wines for the city folk who visit. Simpler pleasures survive, such as glider rides from the little airport.

Just north of Warren is the left turn for Sugarbush, the heart of one of Vermont's premier ski destinations. Opened in 1958, this affluent resort has expensive condominiums and a busy restaurant scene. Vermont's third highest peak, Mount Ellen (4,135 feet/1,260m), and Lincoln Peak (3,975 feet/1,211m) are the two mountains that provide the ski thrills. In summer, golfers test themselves on the course designed by Robert Trent Jones, Sr. There are also tennis courts.

▶ *Continue to Waitsfield.*

9 Waitsfield

The Mad River Glen Ski Resort is smaller, older and less formal than the nearby Sugarbush Resort, but it offers more challenging runs for the advanced skier. Mad River Valley also attracts cross-country enthusiasts, thanks to a total of four cross-country touring centers. As for Waitsfield, what was once a lumber and dairy town a long time ago is now a vacation destination both in winter and summer. First there are the stores selling the work of local artists and craftspeople; then there is the photogenic old covered bridge. Nearby, the Vermont Icelandic Horse Farm offers trail rides.

▶ *Take **Route 100** north to Waterbury (15miles/24km). Ben and Jerry's is 1 mile (1.6km) north of I–89.*

10 Waterbury

Waterbury means just one thing to ice cream aficionados: Ben and Jerry's. Ben Cohen and Jerry Greenfield's rags-to-riches story is the American dream, set deep in the Vermont countryside. In 1977, they started by producing home-made ice cream in Burlington, in a disused and dismantled service station. These days, the factory is in Waterbury, where tours with tastings are a constant draw. In summer, old-fashioned ice cream machines and real cows, ready for milking, keep children entertained.

Waterbury has expanded to include other tasty attractions: Lake Champlain Chocolates, the Cabot Annex Store for Cheese and the Cold Hollow Cider Mill, with its excellent pure pressed apple juices. The Green Mountain Club, half way to Stowe, administers the Long Trail and other outdoor activities.

▶ *Continue to Stowe, then follow **Route 108** to the Mount Mansfield Ski Area.*

11 Stowe

The Stowe Mountain Resort is one of New England's premier ski resorts, built on Mount Mansfield, Vermont's highest peak (4,393 feet/1,338m). In summer, a historic toll road, the Stowe Auto Road, leads to the summit, a 4¹/₂-mile (7km)

COLD HOLLOW CIDER MILL

Low mist over Stowe, the main skiing and recreation center for this popular area

journey. This steep route, with numerous tight curves, is a test of both car and driver. For a more relaxed journey use the Stowe Gondola, a half-hour scenic swing over the forested slopes. With tennis courts, a swimming pool and children's programs, this is a summer destination for the active.

Another attraction is the Trapp Family Lodge in Stowe, built by the real-life family of *The Sound of Music* fame. A new attraction is the Vermont Ski Museum, which traces the century-old history of the sport

in the state. Inside the 1818 Old Town Hall, Vermont's first single chair, double chair, quad chair and gondola hang from the ceiling, like a mobile, above old photos and memorabilia.

$\boxed{i}$ *Main Street, Stowe*

▶ *Return on **Route 100** to I–89 and drive northwest to Burlington.*

RECOMMENDED WALKS

The Stowe Recreation Path is a 5-mile (8km) trail alongside a mountain stream. Undulating gently, and carefully cleared in winter, this trail is used for walking, cross-country skiing and snowshoeing and is a tribute to the generosity of local residents, who have donated the right of way past meadows, woods, and cornfields for visitors to cross their land.

SPECIAL TO...

Justin Morgan was a Vermont teacher who created the country's first horse breed. A hardy colt called Figure was born in 1793, a mixture of Arabian and thoroughbred. The Morgan, as it became known, with its deep chest and powerful hindquarters, stands some 14 to 15 hands (1.42–1.52m) high. Usually long-lived, mildmannered, and bay in color, this multi-use equine was a boon to the army, who rode it and also used this hardy breed to pull guns and equipment. Now owned by the University of Vermont and open to the public, the Morgan Horse Farm is 2 miles (3km) north of Middlebury. The grounds are immaculate, with a slate-roofed 19th-century barn, lush meadows, and parade grounds, and is home to the 70 stallions, mares and foals.

FOR CHILDREN

Stowe is a wonderful area for children with an adventurous spirit. They can hurtle 2,300 feet (700m) down Spruce Peak on the Alpine Slide, for instance, or head off on two wheels into the countryside to explore the 70 plus miles (112km) of mountain bike trails in the area. As for younger children, they will love the public playground at the Stowe Elementary School. Local children raised the funds for it, including a donation from "Superman" (actor Christopher Reeve).

NEW HAMPSHIRE

New Hampshire's nickname is the "Granite State." Some say it refers to the rocky scenery, others maintain it describes the implacable nature of the residents. Certainly, the terrain is the very opposite of the English county that lent it its name. New Hampshire has only an 18-mile (29km) strip of Atlantic coastline, and a mere 80 miles (128km) away are the White Mountains, the tallest in New England. Hundreds of lakes, often bearing the Native American names given by earlier residents – Sunapee, Winnipesaukee and Squam – are scattered throughout the thick pine forests. Fifty four covered bridges stretch across tumbling streams.

The early settlers were "economic refugees," who had left Europe to make a better life rather than to find religious freedom. The land and climate made the early days a struggle. Later, the Scots-Irish added their resolute character to the New Hampshire persona. Today, car license plates bear the state motto: "Live Free or Die." The rest of this Revolutionary rallying cry is "death is not the worst of evils." The fiery words are attributed to farmer-turned-general, John Stark, one of the New Hampshire men who formed the backbone of the American troops in the early days of the Revolution.

The Kancamagus Highway, in the White Mountains, is famous for its fall foliage

Today, the politics in New Hampshire are notably "grass-roots," with the 234 towns and cities often regarded as "little republics." The state scorns income tax and sales tax, preferring to raise money by taxing liquor and betting. This tax – or lack of tax – structure has attracted businesses to move across the state line from Massachusetts. Shoppers also drive over the border from neighboring states to load up and save money. Since most of the one million inhabitants cluster near the Massachusetts border, the rest of the state seems sparsely populated. While agriculture has long been a mainstay of the economy, it has been the fast-flowing streams driving machinery that have benefited residents most. Towns like Manchester may not manufacture locomotives and fire engines any longer, but plastics, electronics, and paper products have successfully taken their place.

Tour 18

Portsmouth, New Hampshire's port, is wedged between Massachusetts and Maine. Forty years ago it was a rundown city, a place to escape rather than a tourist destination. However, the residents recognized the rich history beneath the dirt – instead of tearing down the old buildings, they started a major restoration project. Now the merchants' houses and warehouses, meeting houses and bankers' offices are the attractive heart of the city and a source of civic pride. Small parks and museums reflect Portsmouth's role as a ship-building center, others are filled with fine antique American furniture. Best known is Strawbery Banke, a collection of houses that show what everyday life was like over a period of four centuries.

Above: Strawbery Banke
Below: The Flume, a giant chasm where a mountain stream tumbles in a series of waterfalls

Tour 19

The White Mountains are a popular destination all year round. The focus is Mount Washington, first climbed by a European 350 years ago. It is now deluged by 250,000 enthusiastic tourists every summer. A cog railroad crawls its way up to the top. Those wanting to avoid the "madding crowds" can explore the numerous well-marked trails throughout the mountains, either for a day hike or a longer trek. In winter, "the Whites" attract both downhill and cross-country skiers. The spectacular scenery on this route includes "the Kanc," the famous Kancamagus Highway, one of America's prettiest drives.

Tour 20

Since 1981, Squam Lake has become a "must see" for fans of the film *On Golden Pond*. Nearby, larger Lake Winnipesaukee has long been a popular destination for summer visitors wishing to escape the heat and humidity of Boston. The western shore has become over-popular and built-up, but for the most part, this is a peaceful drive, with villages, craft shops, and museums en route. Anyone interested in top-quality crafts should plan to spend time in Center Sandwich, while Meredith is best known for its dolls.

Portsmouth

Portsmouth has one of New England's finest natural harbors and became wealthy on the lumber trade, exporting to Britain and the West Indies. Huge fortunes were made and spent on grandiose mansions, many of which still stand. A massive preservation program over recent decades has saved numerous fine buildings, making this a city for anyone interested in the architecture and craftsmanship of 18th- and 19th-century America.

HALF A DAY

☐ *500 Market Street*

▶ *Start at Market Square, the heart of the city.*

❶ Market Square

The lottery may seem a new idea but it has long been a means of raising money. Back in 1762, the militia's training ground was paved with funds from a public lottery. The Athenaeum, at No. 9, was originally the headquarters of a fire and marine insurance company, but became a private library in 1823. The classic pointed spire of North Church can be seen from anywhere in the downtown area, especially when it is illuminated at night. On the east side of the square stands the impressive wall of Bankers Row, the guardians of civic wealth for

The John Paul Jones House, where the Scots-born navy officer lived

nearly 200 years. No. 24/26 is thought to be the oldest bank in America, and it was extensively rebuilt in 1904.

▶ *Leave Market Square, heading south on Pleasant Street. Turn right on State Street.*

❷ State Street

Contrasting with the elegant white spire of North Church is the squat tower of South Church, at No. 292. This solid-looking granite building dates from 1826 and is still used for worship by the Unitarian Universalists. Nearby was the starting point of the 1813 fire, which blazed toward the waterfront. Some houses survived, only to be lost to a 1950s urban planning project. Still standing is the Abraham Shaw House (1810) at No. 379. A few doors farther on is the Rockingham Hotel (No. 401), whose lions

RECOMMENDED TRIP

Just off the coast are nine islands, the Isles of Shoals, partly in Maine, partly in New Hampshire. Take a picnic on the delightful one-hour boat ride. Visit Star, an island used as a church retreat which also has the Vaughn Cottage Memorial and Celia Turner Museum, or Appledore, once an artists' colony.

became the personal emblem of Frank Jones, a flamboyant brewer and entrepreneur whose bust is on the right. He turned the hotel into "the most elegant and superbly furnished establishment ... outside of Boston."

▶ *At the corner of State and Middle streets is Haymarket Square, with its enclave of elegant homes. At No. 43 Middle Street is the John Paul Jones House.*

❸ John Paul Jones House

Scottish-born John Paul Jones is known as the "father of the U.S. Navy." He did not own this handsome clapboard house, but rented rooms from Mrs. Sarah Purcell. The naval hero was in Portsmouth in 1777 to supervise the fitting out of the *Ranger*, and once again in 1781, for the building of the *America*. The house is now the headquarters of the local historical society.

▶ *Turn south on Middle Street. Cross the square to No. 18 Court Street.*

❹ John Peirce Mansion

This is "the best" of the city's 19th-century houses, according to some critics. No expense was spared when Peirce built this home in 1799. It was handed down through the family for generations until 1955, when the Baptist Church bought the property.

▶ *Two blocks farther along Middle Street is No. 364.*

5 Rundlet-May House
James Rundlet started out as a farm boy but ended up a wealthy man. With the money he made from importing textiles and wallpaper, he built this mansion in 1807. The garden, pet cemetery, and stables add an extra dimension to the period furniture.

▶ Retrace your steps to Court Street; bear right and walk two blocks to Pleasant Street. On the corner of Pleasant and Court streets is No. 93 Pleasant Street.

6 Ann Treadwell Mansion
This house was built to comply with the 1814 law specifying that structures of more than one story had to be made of brick. The previous year, yet another fire had taken its toll, this time along Court Street, with hundreds of houses ruined.

▶ Retrace your steps. Cross Court Street, then go south on Pleasant Street to No. 143.

7 Governor Langdon House
John Langdon was one of New Hampshire's founding fathers who made his money in ship-building and buying and selling goods captured from the British.

Langdon became President of the Senate, delegate to the Constitutional Convention of 1787, and finally state governor for three terms. He built this mansion, one of the finest in New England, and the garden to impress, and it still does today. Note the exquisitely carved pale green fireplace in the drawing-room, where Langdon hosted parties. One guest was President George Washington, who commented that, among the town's houses "Col. Langdon's may be esteemed the finest."

▶ Walk next door to No. 145.

8 Thomas Thompson House
Portsmouth's importance to the New Hampshire economy is reflected in the state seal and flag, which show shipbuilders at work on a frigate. The first frigate was the *Raleigh*, often called the "first ship in the U.S. Navy." Its owner, Thomas Thompson, erected this house in 1784, and his business partner, John Langdon, put up his mansion next door a year later.

▶ Continue on Pleasant Street, then bear left on Gates Street.

Inside one of the many houses that make up Strawbery Banke

9 Gates Street
James T. Fields (1817–81), the publisher of *The Atlantic Monthly* magazine, gave American writers a boost onto the world literary stage. He was born and lived in the house at 83/85 Gates Street. A few doors down, No. 130 is another fine old place, built as early as 1731 by the Peirce family. This street was one of the first to be saved back in the 1960s rebirth of Portsmouth.

▶ Turn right on Manning Street, then left at the Children's Museum. Cross Marcy Street to Hunking Street. Turn left on Mechanic Street and walk to No. 50.

FOR CHILDREN

Portsmouth has a long history of building warships. At Albacore Park, there is a rare chance to explore a submarine, the 205-foot (61m) long USS *Albacore*. The cramped space did not allow room for beds for each of the crew, so, men "hot bunked": when one shift finished, they slept in the bunks of those going on duty. The submarine never fired a shot in anger.

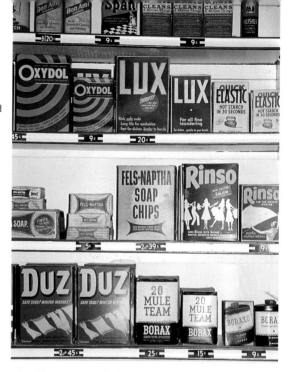

10 Wentworth Gardner House

Tiled fireplaces, fine carving, and paneling make this a "must" for those interested in 18th-century craftsmanship. The owner, Thomas Wentworth, was the younger brother of the last royal governor of New Hampshire.

▶ *Continue on Mechanic Street, which bears left; turn right on Marcy Street.*

11 Liberty Pole

Colonials showed dissent by putting up a liberty pole on their village or town green. The residents of Portsmouth first did this in 1766, to protest against the infamous Stamp Act. The pole became a permanent reminder of that feisty spirit in 1824. Each season, the gardens in Prescott Park are planted with varieties developed by botanists from the University of New Hampshire.

▶ *Across from the liberty pole is Strawbery Banke.*

12 Strawbery Banke

Close to the waterfront, the site of the original 1630 settlement is now one of America's finest outdoor museums. Some 40 buildings, examples of Portsmouth's architecture from 1695 to World War II, stand on this 10-acre (4-ha) site, once a slum. It all comes colorfully to life, with the potter and cooper working at their trades. A favorite spot is the 1766 William Pitt Tavern, which shows the

role of the pub in everyday life. The newest building is Abbott's Store (1943), complete with products on the shelves from that era.

▶ *Continue on Marcy Street to the end. Turn left, then right across the parking lot to No. 150 Daniel Street.*

13 Warner House

The oldest brick house in town was once part of a row of splendid brick mansions built around 1716. The museum-quality furniture behind the 18-inch (45cm) walls was used by the same family for two centuries, while the hall staircase is covered with extensive murals. These murals, possibly the oldest in the country, date from 1720, and include biblical scenes and portraits of two members of the Mohawk tribe. A lightning conductor set into the west wall was supposedly installed by the inventor Benjamin Franklin.

▶ *Turn right on Chapel Street.*

14 St. John's Church

Designed by Alexander Parris to replace a church burned in the fire of 1806, St. John's boasts America's oldest working organ,

The Old Country Store at Strawbery Banke

the 1708 Brattle Organ, as well as splendid *trompe-l'oeil* paintings of biblical scenes.

▶ *Continue on Chapel Street to Bow Street. Turn left, then right on Ceres Street. At the end, take the steps to No. 154 Market Street.*

15 Moffatt-Ladd House

Little imagination is needed here to visualize the life of a wealthy Portsmouth family. The Moffatts built their home in 1763 directly across from their warehouses. The counting house next door, with its wall safe, was a more recent addition – in 1830. Now a museum, family mementos range from wedding dresses and portraits, to jewelry and silver. Two inventories of household goods in the late 18th century provided the curators with the details to re-create the Moffatt home, where the family lived until 1913. The beautiful gardens are a highlight: the plan is 18th-century but the interpretation is 19th-century.

▶ *Return to Market Square via Market Street.*

The White
Mountains

Weekend hikers and serious climbers come to test themselves against the mountains, of which Mount Washington is only one of 86 named peaks.

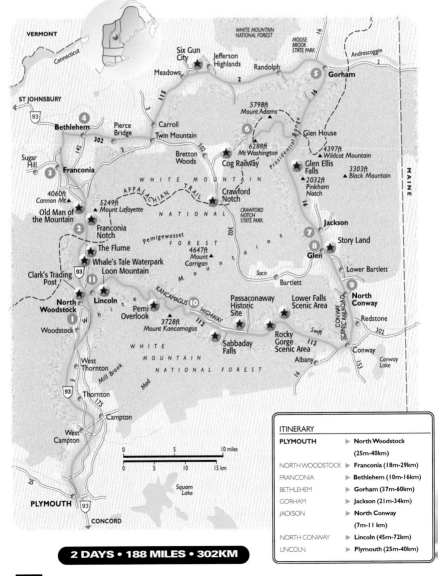

2 DAYS • 188 MILES • 302KM

ITINERARY		
PLYMOUTH	►	**North Woodstock** (25m-40km)
NORTH WOODSTOCK	►	Franconia (18m-29km)
FRANCONIA	►	Bethlehem (10m-16km)
BETHLEHEM	►	Gorham (37m-60km)
GORHAM	►	Jackson (21m-34km)
JACKSON	►	**North Conway** (7m-11 km)
NORTH CONWAY	►	Lincoln (45m-72km)
LINCOLN	►	Plymouth (25m-40km)

i *Chamber of Commerce, exit 28, off I–93*

▶ *Starting in Plymouth, proceed north on I–93, noting the frequency of the "moose crossing" signs and warnings. After 25 miles (40km), exit 32 heads off for North Woodstock and Lincoln.*

❶ North Woodstock

With storefronts that look like movie sets for Hollywood westerns, North Woodstock is not your typical New England village. The main attraction is Clark's Trading Post, a theme park from the days before theme parks were a "dime-a-dozen." Florence Clark took the unlikely title of "first woman to reach the summit of Mount Washington using a dog sled." The Clark family still runs the show after 70 years. The attraction, which began as a dog ranch, now features performing bears, Merlin's Mystical Mansion, a garage from yesteryear, an old fire station, and other eccentric and eclectic Americana. Clark's

Trading Post also claims to have the world's last remaining Howetruss railroad bridge in the world, a covered, 120-foot (36m) long affair.

▶ *At this point I–93 becomes the Franconia Notch State Parkway. Continue north to The Flume and Franconia Notch Pass.*

❷ Franconia Notch

The Notch is the best-known high pass in New England. Ever since the first Europeans saw its towering granite walls 200 years ago, tourists have come to admire the pass, formed by a massive prehistoric glacier. Preserved and protected in their own privately funded State Park, these natural wonders are easily accessible and the park is geared for those who wish to see the sights without much effort. The Flume Visitor Center has information on all the attractions in the Notch, as well as a shuttle bus to the Flume itself. Gravel paths and wooden walkways lead through a narrow gorge, 800 feet (240m) long. Its sheer walls stretch 90 feet (27m) straight up on both sides. Through the Notch, the Flume Brook bounces down the side of Mount Liberty and into the glacial pool.

Farther along the road is the viewpoint for the Old Man of

Clark's Trading Post includes a reconstructed New England street

the Mountain, also called the Great Stone Face or Profile. Until 2003, five ledges of granite towering above Profile Lake looked like the silhouette of a man's face. Now it has collapsed (see Special to…)

About a half mile (800m) along is the Cannon Mountain Aerial Tramway II. Gondolas whisk 80 passengers at a time up to the top of Cannon Mountain (4,180feet/1,275m), climbing some 2,022 feet (616m) in just 7½ minutes. The view is well worth the fee, and there are plentiful marked walks around the Summit Observatory Platform. Refreshments are available here.

FOR HISTORY BUFFS

New Hampshire claims many firsts in skiing: the first ski club, in Berlin in 1872; the first ski school, in Sugar Hill, in 1929; the first overhead cable ski tow, at Black Mountain, in 1935; and the first trail cut for skiing, right here on Cannon Mountain, in 1930. These historic moments are all described at the New England Ski Museum.

Seats are limited on the Mount
Washington Cog Railway, so
reservations are recommended

Next to the base of the
tramway is the New England
Ski Museum. Echo Lake, a little
farther on, is a natural mirror,
reflecting Cannon Mountain and
Mount Lafayette in its still
waters. The energetic can cycle
through the Notch on the 8-mile
(13km) bike path which passes
most of the attractions.

▶ Continue on Franconia Notch
State Parkway, which becomes
I–93 again. Take exit 38 for
Franconia.

❽ Franconia

Once a flourishing resort,
Franconia has seemingly gone
back to sleep. It has been over-
taken by the more ambitious
towns south of the Notch.
Poetry lovers drop by the Robert
Frost Place, the 150-year-old,
white clapboard hillside farmhouse to which Frost returned in
1915, upon his homecoming
from England. Aged 40 and still
virtually unknown, he farmed
the land, wrote three books of
verse and won a Pulitzer prize,
all in the next five years. Visitors
can see his writing desk, signed
first editions and a rare collection of his Christmas card

SCENIC ROUTES

On Route 302, toward Bretton Woods, is the Mount Washington Cog Railway, the most popular way to reach the top of New England's highest peak. Open year round. On Mount Washington's western slope is the world's first mountain-climbing railroad, a miracle of engineering. Built in 1869 at a cost of $139,500, and powered by a roaring coal-fired steam locomotive, it is still the second steepest of its kind in the world, and uses a toothed wheel-and-ratchet mechanism designed by Herrick and Walter Aiken and Sylvester March. The round trip takes three hours, grinding along at about 4mph (6km/h), up gradients of 37 percent at their steepest.

---

5 Gorham

Gorham is a useful stop for those who are keen on wildlife. At dawn and dusk, guides take visitors on a 3-hour explanatory Moose Tour in search of these big beasts, which are abundant in the woods.

▷ *Leave town on Route 16 south to Glen House, at the foot of Mount Washington.*

FOR CHILDREN

Six Gun City, well signposted between Routes 115 and 2, is a theme park dedicated to the Wild West. It has a dozen rides, including the Tomahawk Run Waterslide. Youngsters can see the usual cowboy riding stunts, help the sheriff to capture outlaws, and have fun in Fort Splash water play area.
Nearby is Santa's Village, which promotes Christmas in high summer with themed rides, such as the Yule Log Flume and Santa's Express Train, as well as seasonal shows.

---

poems. In summer, there are readings by a poet in residence and a Festival of Poetry in late July and early August. A half-mile (800m) nature trail, highlighted with plaques along the way, presents 15 of Frost's favorite poems.

▷ *Return to I–93 and drive 6 miles (10km) to exit 40 for Bethlehem. Turn on to Route 302 east.*

4 Bethlehem

The little town of Bethlehem is more Victorian-looking than Colonial, reflecting its heyday as a vacation destination a century

Inset: a young moose

ago. Back then, thousands flocked here by train. The air was so clean and clear of pollution that the National Hay Fever Relief Association was started here in the 1920s. Now, apart from its antiques shops, Bethlehem is a base for touring and hiking.

▷ *Stay on Route 302 east for 8 miles (13km) to Twin Mountain. Turn left onto Route 3. At Carroll, take the 115 through Meadows, then join Route 2 and head east to Gorham.*

6 Mount Washington

Mount Washington is the tallest mountain in the East, at 6,288 feet (1,916m). A road and railroad allow visitors access to the bare granite summit. On the eastern face of the mountain, at Glen House, about 8 miles (13km) south of Gorham, is the start of the 8-mile (13km) toll road to the top and an audio tour, on CD or cassette, gives you an in-car commentary. Built back in 1861, the road is advertised as America's first man-made attraction. Six horses used to pull a wagon full of tourists up the grade, which still averages 12 percent. Today, large vans provide the same service. Bolder folk drive up, a test of their automobiles and their nerve.

The top is surprisingly busy with radio and TV transmitters, an observatory and the Summit Building, with its glassed-in viewing area. At the peak is the old Tip Top House, a hotel built in 1853. There is also a museum of mountain memorabilia and local wildlife.

the SnowCoach trip up the mountain.

▶ Continue for 13 miles (21km), then take the left-hand turn on **Route 16A** to detour into the town of Jackson.

7 Jackson

Always labeled a "classic White Mountain village," Jackson (population 700) lives up to expectations, with its covered

> ### SPECIAL TO...
>
> The Jackson Ski Touring Foundation is dedicated to cross-country skiers. An unusual co-operative effort by the towns of Jackson and Bartlett has produced a network of some 100 miles (160km). The Ellis River Trail (5 miles/8km) is ideally flat for beginners. By contrast, the Wildcat ski area offers 11 miles (18km) of expert cross-country runs.

and Cranmore mountains offer more than 100 trails, enough to satisfy all levels of ability from mogul masters to modest beginners. Strict controls on building have kept this a picturesque village, with an emphasis on lodging and dining, rather than motels and fast food.

▶ Continue south to Glen.

8 Glen

The resort town of Glen has a popular attraction. Story Land, a well thought-out theme park, is aimed at a younger audience with re-creations of fairy-tales, and rides and flumes.

▶ Continue to North Conway.

9 North Conway

With no sales tax and an outlet strip mall 3 miles (5km) long, shopping is the number one sport in this popular small town. It's all a far cry from the days when artists would flock to paint Thompson's Falls. The 1874 railroad station, North Conway

Summer skiers willing to endure the tough hike can test themselves on the dangerous chutes and headwall of the Tuckerman's Ravine nearby. Skiing on July 4 is a traditional challenge among the hard-core skiers. At the base of the mountain is the Great Glen Trails Outlook Center, with a vast trail system for mountain-biking and hiking. In winter, there is cross-country skiing, snowshoeing and

Fun and fantasy at Story Land

bridges, white steepled churches, high mountains and rolling farmland. It could not be prettier. In summer, this is a perfect base for hiking, biking, canoeing, kayaking, or just relaxing by mountain streams. Seasonal festivals add to the fun. In winter, the town offers skiing – downhill and cross-country. The Attitash, Black, Wildcat,

Depot, has survived with much of its Victorian ambience, including the wind-up brass clock, the Telegraph Office, and the separate men's and women's waiting rooms. Now the Conway Scenic Railroad, with its Pullman carriages, runs from here for 11 miles (18km) alongside the Saco River to Conway or through spectacular Crawford Notch. A little way north of the village, the Weather Discovery Center, run by the Mount Washington Observatory, is another attraction. Computer-based interactive displays and audio-visual presentations give a fun insight into the laws of meteorology and how weather affects us.

▶ *Continue south and turn west onto **Route 112**, the 37-mile (59km) long Kancamagus Highway to Lincoln.*

Kancamagus Highway

Following alongside the rushing Swift River, "the Kanc" is one of America's National Scenic Byways – there are no private homes, service stations, or other encroachments to spoil the views. The 34.5-mile (55km) stretch of road, from Conway to the Pemigewasset River, climbs to 3,000 feet (900m) on the way, and honors New Hampshire's legendary Native American chief Kancamagus. He was the grandson of Passaconaway, who united and ruled the local tribes from 1627 to 1669. All along the road are Scenic Areas where you can stop. The best known spots include Sabbaday Falls, a short walk from the highway, and the Lower Falls and Rocky Gorge, where you can bathe in the pools and sunbathe on the small beaches.

Lincoln

The ski resort of Loon Mountain has transformed Lincoln into a busy year-round resort. The skyride, with its four-passenger gondola, is as attractive in summer as in winter, gliding to the summit where there are walking trails and glacial caves. Other popular attractions include the Whale's Tale Waterpark, with its variety of rides on land and in water, and the less frantic Hobo Railroad, which trundles through the Pemi River Valley for some 15 miles (24km).

▶ *Return on **I-93** south, 25 miles (40km) to Plymouth.*

The Kancamagus Highway

SPECIAL TO...

Mount Washington has a meteorological record to rival the North Pole. Nowhere in the world that is visited by as many as 250,000 people a year has such terrible weather. The highest wind speed ever recorded in the world was here, in April, 1934. Scientists clocked gusts of 231mph (370km/h). Year round, the average temperature at the summit is below freezing: fog is common.

1 DAY • 106 MILES • 169KM

Around Lake
Winnipesaukee

Lake Winnipesaukee is huge, the sixth largest body of water inside the country. The Native American name is "The Smile of the Great Spirit," though some experts prefer the more prosaic translation of "Beautiful Water in a High Place."

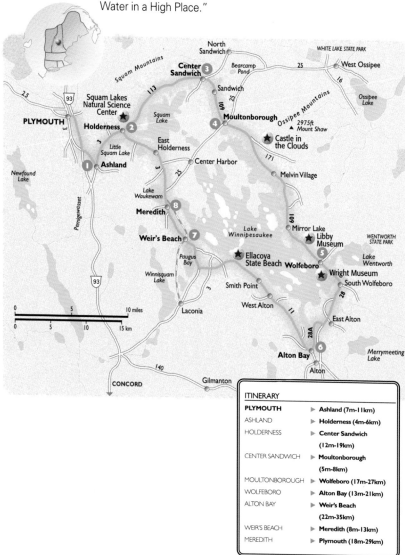

Lakes Region Association, exit 23, off I-93

▶ *Start in Plymouth and take I–93 south to exit 24 for Ashland.*

❶ Ashland

The small town of Ashland, once an important stop on the old Boston, Concord and Montreal Railroad line, retains the character of an old mill town. The Ashland Historical Society is based in the former home of Dr. George Whipple, the pathologist who won the Nobel prize for medicine in 1934. Next door, the Pauline Glidden Toy Museum has more than 1,000 early toys. A local resident, the late Milton Graton, was one of New England's experts on the restoration and building of covered bridges. His last was built here in his home town, where his son Arnold continues the tradition.

▶ *Continue on **Route 3** to Holderness.*

❷ Holderness

Holderness sits on Little Squam Lake; to the east is the much larger Squam Lake. The Academy Award-winning 1981 movie *On Golden Pond*, starring Katherine Hepburn and Henry Fonda, was filmed here, catapulting Squam Lake to fame, even though the movie was supposedly set in Maine. Small boats cruise the peaceful lake and delight in showing visitors where the scenes were shot. It is a favorite nesting place for loons.

▶ *Follow **Route 113** for Center Sandwich (12 miles/19km). Pass Squam Lake.*

❸ Center Sandwich

Sitting between the Squam Mountains and Squam Lake, this is one of several Sandwich villages in the area. New England poet John Greenleaf Whittier (1807–92) spent time in Center Sandwich. This crusading Quaker championed the anti-slavery cause and used poetry in his emotional campaigns:
"What! mothers from their children riven!
What! God's own image bought and sold!
Americans to market driven,
And bartered as the brute for gold!"
   Whittier wrote *Sunset* on the Bearcamp, the river that runs through Bearcamp Pond between Center Sandwich and North Sandwich. The Whittier covered bridge crosses the river in West Ossipee.

SPECIAL TO...

Peace and quiet attracted artists to the rural community of Center Sandwich. Sandwich Home Industries, an early collective, opened in 1926 with the aim of helping local craftspeople supplement their incomes. This lead to the founding of the League of New Hampshire Craftsmen, known for its seven stores in the state and an annual fair, the oldest in the country, held in August at Mount Sunapee.

BACK TO NATURE

The Squam Lakes Natural Science Center is just to the east of Holderness and enables visitors to observe wild animals such as otters, deer, bears and various birds of prey. All are unable to live in their natural habitats, due to injury. You can follow the ¾-mile (1.2km) nature trail, try hands-on puzzles, or take a boat trip.

Aerial view of the turreted hilltop Castle in the Clouds

▶ *Drive south on* **Route 109** *for 5 miles (8km) to Moultonborough.*

❹ Moultonborough

This typical New England village has the bonus of the lake as a backdrop. Apart from its idyllic setting, the big attraction is "Castle in the Clouds," a reminder of the astonishing wealth garnered a century ago. Set 750 feet (225m) up in the Ossipee Mountains, this mock castle and its extensive estate offers spectacular views. Millionaire Thomas Plant, who made his money from shoes, designed the $7 million house himself, which explains the variety of architectural styles, from Swiss chalet to Norman castle. A touch of English Tudor is the *coup de grâce*. It was built by hundreds of craftsmen, including Italian stonemasons brought over from Europe. Water from a spring on the grounds is bottled commercially. The nearby Loon Center and Markus Wildlife

Sanctuary specializes in New Hampshire's ecology.

▶ *Continue south on* **Route 109** *for 17 miles (27km) to*

SPECIAL TO...

West of Alton Bay on Route 140 (12miles/19km) is the town that shocked America in 1956. Gilmanton was the home of *Peyton Place* author Grace Metalious. This high-school teacher's wife had been unable to achieve success with her writing ... until her account of life and love in small town America topped the best-seller lists. Today, the town shows no signs of the steamy passions described in the book, movie and TV series. "You live in a small town and there are patterns you are a freak," she said, "I wrote a book and that made me a freak." She died, aged 39, in 1964.

Seaplane on Lake Winnipesaukee

Wolfeboro. The route passes through Melvin Village, known for its antiques shops. Continue along the shores of Winnipesaukee, through Mirror Lake.

❺ Wolfeboro

Just before Wolfeboro, on the edge of Mirror Lake, is the Libby Museum, with its eclectic collection. America's oldest resort began back in 1768, when Massachusetts Governor John Wentworth ordered a summer house here. To reach the house from Portsmouth, he even had the "Governor's Road" built. The retreat burned down in 1820, and people now come to swim and picnic in Wentworth State Park, 6 miles (10km) east of town.

The Wright Museum, in Wolfeboro, charts the story of America during World War II. In addition to its collection of military vehicles, the museum

reflects life back home, with room settings, costumes and other period items.

▶ Take **Routes 28** and **28A** south for 13 miles (21km) to Alton Bay, right at the foot of Lake Winnipesaukee.

6 Alton Bay

The little town of Alton Bay has much of the appearance it must have enjoyed in its summer heydays. There is a floating bandstand out in the bay, and the railroad station has been spruced up. Scenic lake cruises depart from the docks.

▶ Follow **Route 11** northwest. This side of the lake is much more open, affording great views of the water and to the White Mountains in the north. Weir's Beach is 22 miles (35km) farther on via the Ellacoya State Park, where you get a sense of how large Lake Winnipesaukee really is. Continue to Weir's Beach.

7 Weir's Beach

Weir's Beach is the Coney Island of the region with amusement parks, crowded boardwalks, beaches and a weekly fireworks display. One of New England's last drive-in movie theaters is here too. It is especially busy when the annual motorcycle races take place for one week in June in nearby Loudon. Weir's Beach has two waterslide parks, but tamer rides are also available, such as the scenic railroad along the lakeshore. Another good way to beat the crowds is to take a cruise on the lake, either for its simple scenic value, or to appreciate the wildlife on a special nature cruise.

▶ Take **Route 3** north to Meredith (8 miles/13km).

8 Meredith

Quieter than Weir's Beach, with pretty docks and landings on the lake, Meredith is the home of the popular felt Annalee Dolls. Annalee Davis Thorndike created these cutesy dolls in 1934 and now the factory is a major local employer. The dolls are bought by fans and collectors

SCENIC RIDES

Apart from the antique speedboat *Millie-B*, based in Wolfeboro, there are several passenger boats that run out of Weir's Beach. The venerable 1,250 passenger M/S *Mount Washington*, popular for dinner cruises and moonlight cruises, is the largest. Depending on the day, the *Washington* runs across to Wolfeboro, to Meredith, up to Center Harbor or down to Alton Bay. The M/V *Sophie C* doubles as a mailman, delivering mail to the island communities. The Winnipesaukee Railroad is another railroad nostalgia trip, conjuring up the 1920s and 1930s, and runs from Weir's Beach to Meredith.

FOR HISTORY BUFFS

Sport is a high-profile, major ingredient of today's U.S. college life. The first inter-collgiate sporting event, however, was very low key. It took place in 1852, at Center Harbor on Lake Winnipesaukee. Harvard took on Yale in a rowing race over "two miles to windward and straight away," and beat them by two lengths. The ten-minute duel began a rivalry that remains intense more than 150 years later.

from all over the world. There is also a museum dedicated to them, which includes the first doll and some valuable pre-war models.

▶ Return to Plymouth via **Route 3** through Holderness and I–93.

Delivering the mail by boat

MAINE

The Algonquin tribe called this region the "Land of the Frozen Ground" and the summer season is certainly the shortest here in New England, barely covering June through September. No-one knows how or why Maine received its present name. What is known is that it could swallow up the rest of the New England states. One single county, Aroostook, is bigger than the states of Connecticut and Rhode Island combined. Yet the population of Maine is only 1.3 million, mostly in the south and along the coast.

Residents and visitors alike come to Maine to enjoy the unspoiled natural beauty. Geographers estimate that the 230-mile (368km) long coastline would stretch to 3,500 miles (5,600km) if every cove and inlet were measured. Drive down the fingers of land that jut into the sea to find old fishing villages, quiet inlets and rocky cliffs. Offshore lie around 2,000 islands, some linked to the mainland by ferry, the majority barely habitable, and all surrounded by treacherous rocks and ice-cold water.

View over Camden Harbor

The coast is the biggest draw and some parts, such as Oqunquit and Boothbay Harbor, become quite crowded in season. Getting away from it all, however, is easy since 90 percent of the state is wilderness and forest. Maine attracts hikers and canoeists into its hinterland with 32,000 miles (51,200km) of river and 6,000 ponds and lakes dotted around. There are few people, but thousands of moose.

Although many experts assume that the Vikings could have paid a visit a thousand years ago, it was the French and English who first settled here. In 1677, the territory was assigned to Massachusetts, but in the early 19th century, when that state began to struggle economically, it cut the ties and Maine became a state in its own right.

Maine's nickname, the "Pine Tree State," is appropriate. Not only is the coastline wooded, there are vast forests inland. The tall, strong pines once provided masts for the British Navy; now, they are made into paper and pulp. Shipbuilding started in 1607, in Bath, and continues there today.

Lighthouses stand as symbols of New England's maritime history
Left: L. L. Bean, Freeport

galleries. Much of the handsome brick and granite architecture post-dates the devastating fire of 1866, and some earlier buildings remain. Included among these is the home of the writer Henry Wadsworth Longfellow, dating back to 1785. Do take time to explore the myriad islands of Casco Bay, using the regular ferry or mail boat. Take the morning boat, hop off at Chebeague Island, rent a bike and explore.

Tour 23

Getting away from it all is easy when you head for the lakes and mountains of Maine. This long drive explores the state's remote beauty, while also passing through some charming villages. The famous Shaker religious community lives in a village at Sabbathday Lake. Their pious faith still arouses admiration, even though only a handful of the sect survives. By contrast, the nearby Sunday River ski area is one of the liveliest in Maine. Winter temperatures will test a visitor's fortitude. Rangeley is not only the mid-point of this drive, but the town also boasts being precisely halfway between the North Pole and the equator.

Tour 21

For many, the "real Maine" begins north of Portland. Here, the coastline breaks up into long skeletal fingers of granite, pointing out to form bays dotted with pine-covered islands. The sea has always been the focus of this region and the earliest Europeans who spent time here were transient fisher folk. Seafaring and boat-building are long traditions that have continued with the U.S. Navy in Brunswick, the huge shipyard in Bath, and numerous smaller boat-builders and museums. Although tourism is a major

industry, towns such as Camden, Wiscasset, and Damariscotta have been able to retain their charm.

Tour 22

Portland is often rated as one of the best cities in which to live: small enough to feel friendly, but with a lively cultural scene and innovative restaurants. In recent years, it has made a conscious and successful effort to brighten up its downtown and old harbor by recycling historic buildings and employing novel methods of attracting locals to the stores and

The Mid-Coast
of Maine

2 DAYS • 260 MILES • 418KM

Rocky bays, cliff-top lighthouses, and peaceful harbors give the mid-coast of Maine its character. This route leads to busy towns and quiet hamlets, past historic houses and old forts. Artists and craftspeople have long been attracted by the area, so there are festivals and fine art galleries as well.

TED

ITINERARY

PORTLAND	▶ **Brunswick (27m-44km)**
BRUNSWICK	▶ **Bath (8m-13km)**
BATH	▶ **Wiscasset (10m-16km)**
WISCASSET	▶ **Damariscotta (7m-11km)**
DAMARISCOTTA	▶ **Pemaquid Point**
	(17m-27km)
PEMAQUID POINT	▶ **Thomaston (35m-56km)**
THOMASTON	▶ **Camden (12m-19km)**
CAMDEN	▶ **Belfast (19m-31km)**
BELFAST	▶ **Portland (125m-201km)**

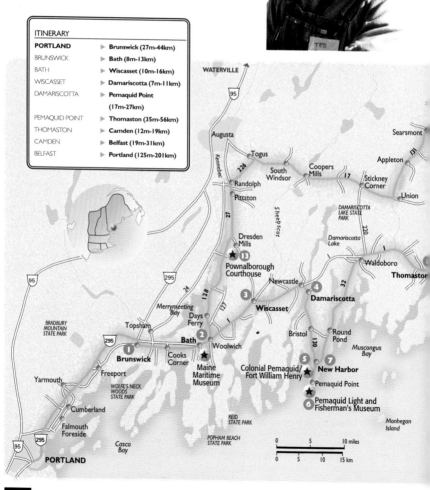

i 245 Commercial Street

▶ *Leave Portland on I–295 north, which becomes I–95. Take exit 22 for* **Coastal Route 1** *to downtown Brunswick. Turn right on Maine Street, then left on* **Route 24** *to Brunswick.*

❶ Brunswick

Brunswick is an attractive town, centered on Bowdoin College. Originally founded in 1794 as a men's college, Bowdoin has admitted women since the 1960s. Famous graduates range from 19th-century authors Nathaniel Hawthorne and Henry Wadsworth Longfellow to explorers Robert Peary, the first man to reach the North Pole, in 1909, and his colleague Donald MacMillan.

Memorabilia from their expeditions is the focus of the Peary-MacMillan Arctic Museum in Hubbard Hall, decorated with the only gargoyle in the whole of Maine (spot it on the left side of the building). The Museum of Art, located in the imposing Walker Art Building, has a varied collection including Gilbert Stuart's familiar portrait of Thomas Jefferson, author of the Declaration of Independence, and third President of the United States.

i 59 Pleasant Street

▶ *Leave the campus and turn right on* **Route 24** *north. Continue to Cooks Corner and rejoin* **Route 1** *north. Drive 5 miles (8km) to Bath.*

❷ Bath

The town may be 18 miles (29km) from the Atlantic Ocean, but boats have been launched on the deep Kennebec River since 1607. Bath's glory days were in the 19th century, when sailing ships made fortunes for the merchants, many of whose graceful homes still line Washington Street in the Historic District. Since 1891, the Bath Iron Works and Shipyard, the largest civilian employer in Maine, has built ships for the U.S. Navy. Right on the river, with the tallest crane (400 feet/120m) on the East Coast, it's impossible to miss.

Downriver from the shipyard is the Maine Maritime Museum, a collection of buildings with seafaring memorabilia and hands-on exhibitions. This is the place to learn the history of lobstering, and to understand how the many-masted schooners were constructed. You can watch a demonstration of sailors' skills, or perhaps take a narrated cruise down the Kennebec and Sasanoa rivers, either to look at lighthouses or the wildlife.

i Route 1 North, just south of Bath (seasonal)

▶ *Leave Bath on* **Route 1** *northeast and continue for 10 miles (16km) to Wiscasset.*

❸ Wiscasset

The Native American name means "coming out of the harbor but you don't see where." Today, "the Prettiest Village in Maine" is found easily by visitors, who flock to the antiques shops, historic houses, and quirky museums. Wiscasset is the seat of Lincoln County, which once stretched to the Canadian border. Throughout the original colonies, towns pride themselves on the fact that "George Washington slept here." Here, the claim is that General

Lafayette of France ate ice cream at the apothecary store, one of the first places in the U.S. to make the delicacy. That was in 1824, long after Lafayette had helped the Americans during the Revolution.

On High Street is the Musical Wonder House. This is the private collection of Danilo Konvalinka, who calls it "the world's finest museum of restored international antique music boxes and mechanical instruments." The full tour is fascinating, though expensive; but it costs little to wander round the front hall and look at the 19th-century coin-operated music boxes, hurdy gurdies and perforated metal disc players.

At the end of High Street, in a commanding position above the harbor and Sheepscot River, stands Castle Tucker. Built in 1807, it was bought by Captain Tucker in 1858, after he retired from the sea and settled down to married life. From its free-standing switchback staircase to the dramatic southeast façade with

its huge windows, the house is one of a kind, and remains much as Captain Tucker left it. The wallpaper is original, as are the furnishings. A descendant of the captain still lives here.

The Nickels-Sortwell House, on the corner of Route 1 and Federal Street, is another ship-captain's home. Built in the same year as Castle Tucker, it exemplifies the Federal period. Just along Federal Street is Lincoln County Museum and Old Jail. This large and foreboding granite building served as the county jail from 1811 to 1953. Below the tiny barred windows, the cold walls, 41 inches (105cm) thick in places, are covered with graffiti, such as the painstakingly detailed schooner under full sail.

▶ Continue on **Route 1** northeast to Newcastle and turn right for Damariscotta.

❹ **Damariscotta**
This attractive yet unpretentious riverside community has

plenty of old wood-frame and brick homes. The restored 1754 Chapman-Hall House on Main and Church streets is the oldest in the region. In summer, guides in period dress conduct you round the 18th-century kitchen and herb garden.

▐i▌ *Damariscotta Region Chamber of Commerce, 2 Courtyard Street*

▶ Leave town on **Route 130** south for 11 miles (18km). Turn right on Huddle Road at signs for Historic Pemaquid and Pemaquid Point. Service stations are few and far between off the main highways, so be sure to fill up before heading down any of the numerous peninsulas.

❺ **Colonial Pemaquid/Fort William Henry**
The re-creation of Fort William Henry stands guard over the

Typical wood-frame house, near the township of Damariscotta

Pemaquid Point Lighthouse juts out on rocky ledges carved by ancient glaciers

FOR HISTORY BUFFS

"Damariscotta" means "the meeting place of alewives." This has nothing to do with women involved in brewing. It refers to a member of the herring family that was popular with Native Americans. They also relished the local oysters and would congregate for "oyster festivals," leaving heaps of shells behind on the banks of the Damariscotta River. These "middens," an Old English word for rubbish dumps, contain shells as large as plates. Ask at the Damariscotta Region Information Bureau for maps of trails leading to the sites.

water, as did four earlier fortresses, and it now houses a museum of artifacts found on the site. Nearby, an on-going archeological dig has uncovered a 17th-century British settlement of houses plus a tavern, jail, burying ground and customs house. It is thought to have been one of the first European settlements in the New World. Although fishing and trapping were productive in the area, raids by the French and their Native American allies, and long, hard winters took their toll.

▶ *Follow Snowball Hill Road to* **Route 130** *and drive south to Pemaquid Point.*

❻ Pemaquid Light and Fisherman's Museum

Maine is famous for its lighthouses. There are 64 lighthouses in the state, but this is one of the most romantic and most photographed. From sundown to sunrise, the Fourth-Order light flashes its warning every six seconds. From as far as 14 nautical miles away, ships take note and adjust their course accordingly. The memorabilia in the small museum gives an insight

into the fishing industry of yesterday and today. The layers of rock show the geological formation of this distinctive coastline. When climbing upon the rocks near the ocean, be careful. The waters are dangerous; the undertow is strong, too.

▶ *Take* **Route 130** *north, then turn onto* **Route 32** *to New Harbor.*

❼ New Harbor

New Harbor is a truly picturesque and unspoiled Maine fishing village. A memorial here honors Chief Samoset of the local Pemaquid tribe. The chief learned English from British fishermen, and had traveled south to explore the Massachusetts coast in March, 1621, where he discovered the Pilgrim community. Imagine their surprise when he greeted them with the words "Welcome Englishmen."

▶ *Continue on* **Route 32** *north to Waldoboro (20 miles/ 32km). Turn onto* **Route 1**

FOR HISTORY BUFFS

Just off Route 32 is Round Pond, another fishing harbor. This once supposedly hid the notorious Captain Kidd, who buried treasure under a huge boulder on a nearby island. Some say it was on Devil's Oven, others on Otter Island. The mystery remains.

RECOMMENDED TRIPS

From New Harbor, take a daytrip out to tiny Monhegan Island, only 1½ miles (2.5km) across at its widest, with the highest cliffs on the East Coast. The energetic can hike through a wildlife sanctuary with hundreds of species of wildflowers and birds, while the less energetic can visit the artists' studios. There are also cruises for watching seals and Atlantic puffins, now a protected species.

*northeast and drive for
about 12 miles (19km) to
Thomaston.*

❽ Thomaston

This is another ship captain and ship owners' town, although Montpelier, the most imposing house in Thomaston was built by a general, Henry Knox. He was an important figure in the Revolution and the country's first Secretary of War. He retired here in 1795 and built Montpelier, a mansion high on a hill overlooking the town.

The house was torn down in 1871 but, thanks to the enthusiasm of locals, it was rebuilt in the early 1920s, and is now the General Knox Museum. Original records and descriptions penned by visitors were used to re-create the mansion, which even has many of the original furnishings. Note that the white-painted façade and its two-story bay looks very much like the south front of the White House in Washington D.C., designed in 1792.

▶ *Continue on **Route 1** to Rockland.*

❾ Rockland

This is the "Lobster Capital of the World" (though Shediac, north across the Canadian border in New Brunswick, also claims this title). It also boasts a gem of a museum, the result of a 1935 legacy left by an eccentric 96-year-old. The William A. Farnsworth Art Museum specializes in American painters from the 18th, 19th, and 20th centuries, and highlights Maine's role in American art.

The Wyeth Centre, in a historic church near the museum, houses the collection of Andrew and Betsy Wyeth. The new Maine Discovery Center is also home to the Maine Lighthouse Museum, as well as the local information center.

⌷ *2 Park Drive*

▶ *Follow **Route 1** north to Rockport.*

10 Rockport

The village of Rockport has a tiny harbor with lots of cultural activities. The musically minded make reservations for chamber music and jazz concerts at the opera house. Photographers head for the internationally known Maine Photographic Workshop, while the work of local artists and craftsmen is displayed in galleries such as the Center for Maine Contemporary Art, specializing in upcoming contemporary artists.

In the little park down by the

Below: yachts at rest in Camden Harbor
Right: lobsters at Boothbay Harbor

harbor is a statue of André the Seal. A children's book and movie were based on the story of André, who summered here for 20 years.

▶ Leave Rockport on scenic Russell Avenue, going north, with sudden glimpses of the Camden Hills and Penobscot Bay. This becomes Chestnut Street in Camden.

11 Camden

"*All I could see from where I stood Was three long mountains and a wood;
I turned and looked another way, and saw three islands in a bay.*"
The panorama from the top

of Mount Battie inspired Maine poet Edna St. Vincent Millay to compose this poem in 1917. The views today are still the same of the Camden Hills, Penobscot Bay, and, on a clear day, Monhegan Island.

In the town, below the hill, Millay's statue stands by the harbor in what is, arguably, the state's most popular year-round resort. Conway Homestead, dating from 1770, is one of the oldest houses in the area. It is now a museum that includes the house, barn, smithy, maple sugar house and modern museum building.

$\boxed{i}$ Public Landing

SPECIAL TO...

Lobsters, the specialty of Maine, are caught in the millions of traps set in the cold waters offshore. Traditionally, these box-like contraptions consist of an oak frame with cotton netting. Many visitors take them as souvenirs. However, don't be tempted to pick up any washed on to a beach by the tide: that counts as "molesting a trap" and carries a fine. Buy one from a road-side stand or, better still, stop at a fishing village, look for a pile on the dock or by a house, and make an offer to the owner.

▶ Follow **Route 1** north 6 miles (10km) to Lincolnville, then on 13 miles (21km) to Belfast.

12 Belfast

Belfast or Londonderry? A flip of a coin decided the name back in 1765. As usual in New England, a town's name pinpoints the home in the Old World. In this case, the Scots-Irish had come from what is now Northern Ireland. Over the centuries, Belfast has produced ships, axes, pantaloons, sarsaparilla, chickens, rum and shoes. The town has experienced a resurgence as the headquarters of the MBNA credit card.

_i_ *Main Street*

▶ *The rest of this route is rural and scenic. Take **Route 3** west to Belmont Corner for 6 miles (10km), then **Route 131** south through scenic farmland, past stone walls and hilly vistas. Pass through Searsmont, Appleton and Union. Take **Route 17** west, then before Togus, turn onto **Route 226** south to Randolph. Follow **Route 126**, then turn onto **Route 27** south. This passes a cluster of privately owned white houses moved here from various parts of the state. Turn right on **Route 128**, an old Native American trail that follows the bay. Continue on **Route 128**.*

13 Pownalborough Courthouse

Now a museum, this is one of only a dozen surviving pre-Revolutionary courthouses in the country. Here, a judge could dispense justice in the court on the middle floor, walk downstairs to quaff ale in the tavern, and retire to his bed on the top floor.

▶ *Join **Route 127** south at the pretty village of Days Ferry (the original river crossing) and continue to **Route 1** southwest at Woolwich by the Bath bridge. Return to Portland.*

Portland Head Light, dating from 1791

Portland

Portland aptly deserves its symbol, the phoenix, as well as its motto, *Resurgam*, "I shall rise again." In fact, the city has arisen nearly as often as the sun. Dating back to a settlement called Falmouth, it was virtually destroyed by Native American raids in 1676. After rebuilding, the community flourished until an English fleet bombarded the town in 1775, as punishment for supporting the independence movement. Once again restored, and renamed Portland in 1786, the port buzzed with business and finance, until the Great Fire of July 4, 1866. Again, it was rebuilt, and this tour reflects the development of Portland and the contributions made by prominent citizens to the arts, business and city life.

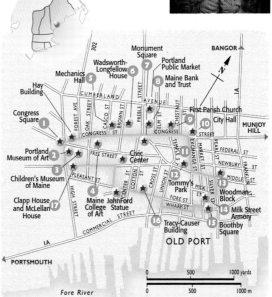

The Wadsworth-Longfellow House was the first brick house to be built in Portland

i *Convention and Visitors Bureau of Greater Portland, 245 Commercial Street*

▶ *Start at Congress Square.*

❶ Congress Square
This busy five-street intersection is the scene of many summer events, including concerts. On the corner of Congress and Free streets is the Hay Building, described as a flatiron building because of its wedge-shape. Built in 1826, it is one of the recognized icons of Portland.

❷ Portland Museum of Art
The I. M. Pei firm's brick colonnaded building (1983), right on the square, makes an impressive addition to the L. D. M. Sweat Memorial Galleries and rotunda, built in 1911. It houses one of New England's finest art collections and contains pieces by well-known Maine and American painters such as Winslow Homer, Rockwell Kent, Andrew Wyeth and John Singer Sargent. You will also find the Joan Whitney Payson Collection of Impressionist and Postimpressionist works here. One of the best known is Auguste Renoir's *Confidences*. A romantic tête-à-tête, this is a sensitive portrait of one of his favorite models, Margot Legrand.

❸ Children's Museum of Maine
Next door to the art museum, in a former Greek Revival church, is one of the best museums of its kind in New England. The Children's Museum of Maine really is for all ages. Even toddlers have their own play area, and older children can play at pretend in "Our Town," with its market, fire truck, lobster boat, bank, farm and animal hospital. For the technically minded, there are lots of

interactive exhibits and other things to fire the imagination, including the star lab, space shuttle and TV studio.

A wonder from the 19th century is a camera obscura, one of only seven in the world. A camera obscura is a dark room where images of objects from outside are projected onto a wall. It may sound simplistic in these days of "virtual reality," but this effective, primitive use of light and lens led to still and motion picture cameras.

▶ *Leave Congress Square and walk north on Congress Street to No. 522.*

❹ Maine College of Art
On the outside, the 1904 Porteous, Mitchell & Braun Building is a beaux arts classic, complete with cherubs. Inside is the Maine College of Art and the ICA, the Institute of Contemporary Art.

▶ *Look across Congress Street.*

❺ Mechanics Hall
This impressive, Italianate, granite-fronted building, with its statues of Archimedes and Vulcan, is the home of the Maine Charitable Mechanic

Association. Dedicated in 1851 to "informing and cultivating the mind and training up a race of mechanics (skilled workmen) of sound moral principle and intellectual power."

▶ *Continue along Congress Street to No. 489.*

❻ Wadsworth-Longfellow House
Three generations of one of the city's most distinguished familes lived here, behind the wrought-iron fence. In 1785, General Peleg Wadsworth, a hero of the Revolution and state senator, built this house, now the oldest surviving residence in Portland, and the first to be constructed of brick. The bricks were shipped in from Philadelphia.

Wadsworth's grandson, the poet Henry Wadsworth Longfellow, grew up here. His childhood flute is on show, and the house is furnished much as he would have remembered it as an adult. "Often I think of the beautiful town that is seated by the sea; often in thought go up and down the pleasant streets of that dear old town, and my youth comes back to me." Next door, the Maine Historical Society Museum has changing exhibitions about the state.

SPECIAL TO...

Henry Wadsworth Longfellow (1807–82) is America's best-loved 19th-century poet. *The Battle of Lovell's Pond*, his first published verses, appeared in the *Portland Gazette* when he was only 12 years old. His best-known works tell all-American tales such as *The Song of Hiawatha* and *Paul Revere's Ride*, but his popularity was not limited to the United States. He had a following in England that included Queen Victoria and, after his death, he was the first American to be commemorated with a bust in Poet's Corner at Westminster Abbey.

Portland's impressive City Hall

▶ *Continue on Congress Street.*

7 Monument Square

This space, originally the town's Market Square, is named for Our Lady of Victories Monument. The monument is a Civil War memorial that was built in 1891, with money raised by local soldiers and sailors. In recent years, the farmers' market has been revived, with stands set out on Wednesdays in the summer and fall. Summer brings concerts; in December, the city's Christmas tree lights up the square and on New Year's Eve, crowds gather here to watch the fireworks.

▶ *Look across Congress Street.*

8 Maine Bank and Trust

Portland's first skyscraper, built in 1910 in the beaux arts style, was at that time New England's tallest building. Unlike traditional structures of the period, where the exterior walls supported the building, this was constructed with a steel skeleton, allowing the building to achieve a greater height. Inside, the marble lobby soars to a ceiling at least three stories high.

The impression is of solidity and security – perfect for a bank building.

▶ *Continue on Congress Street to No. 425.*

SPECIAL TO...

Congress Street leads to Munjoy Hill, perhaps a derivation of the French *Mont Joie*. Here, the 221-foot (67m) high Portland Observatory was erected in 1807, as a signal tower. Communication by flags announced the identity of approaching merchant ships and enabled the docks to be prepared for their arrival. Views from the top are spectacular.

Nearby is the Eastern Promenade. Turn right for the bandstand. Here, the panorama encompasses Portland Harbor, the best deep-water port north of New Jersey. Watch for an oil tanker or a cruise ferry coming from Nova Scotia. Don't try to count the islands in Casco Bay; supposedly, there are 365 of them, hence the name, the Calendar Islands.

9 First Parish Church

Founded in 1674, this church predates any other house of worship in Portland. The second building on the site took several hits during the British bombardment of the town in 1775. Evidence of the conflict remains inside, where a cannon ball still lodges within the chain supporting the magnificent 600-pound (273kg) cut-glass chandelier. The 1794 clock and 1804 bell were saved and incorporated into the present building, which dates from a reconstruction using granite in 1826.

▶ *Continue on Congress Street.*

10 City Hall

The granite used to build the City Hall was quarried locally in Maine, but the architecture is based on the classic French *hôtel-de-ville*. Within the building is a 1,900-seat auditorium, where the Portland Symphony Orchestra often gives concerts. This is the third municipal headquarters to have been located on this site: the first was destroyed by the Great Fire of 1866, and its successor succumbed to another blaze in 1908.

▶ *Turn right on Exchange Street.*

⑪ Exchange Street

Exchange Street leads into the six-square-block Old Port Exchange area, the oldest part of the city. Warehouses and offices have now become boutiques, art galleries and ethnic restaurants. Look closely and you'll see another reminder of British shelling in 1775: the cannon ball embedded in the Coles-worth building, on the right, just past the entry to the parking garage.

▶ *Continue to the intersection with Middle Street.*

⑫ Tommy's Park

The *trompe-l'oeil* by two Portland artists on the wall represents architectural elements of the 19th-century marble post office that once stood across the street in what is now the postage-stamp size Post Office Park. In this sunny spot, the granite boulders represent the many islands of Casco Bay, just outside Portland Harbor.

▶ *Turn left on Middle Street and walk two blocks to the intersection with Pearl Street.*

⑬ Woodman Block

This was one of the first buildings put up after the Great Fire of 1866. Like its two neighbors with decorative cast iron, it was designed by George Harding. Look for the architect's autograph on the base of the left corner pilaster, on the Middle Street side.

▶ *Continue toward the harbor on Pearl Street. After a block, turn right on cobblestoned Milk Street. Straight ahead is the Regency Hotel.*

⑭ Milk Street Armory

It is no coincidence that the Regency Hotel, between Silver and Market streets, resembles a fortress. This was originally the armory, and was very active in the late 19th to mid-20th centuries. It also had a tradition of hospitality, as it was the site of musical events and impressive balls. The contemporary dolphin fountain was originally offered to, and rejected by, the city fathers. Shunted around town, it stood on a variety of sites until it was finally bought by the hotel.

▶ *Turn left on Silver Street.*

⑮ Boothby Square

At the intersection of Silver and Fore streets is Boothby Square. Directly in front is a row of old buildings, including the 1792 Sam Butts House and Store. It is the second-oldest surviving post-revolutionary house in Portland.

On your left is the 1868 granite U.S. Customs House. In the impressive interior, it is easy to imagine merchants sitting down to negotiate the tariffs on a cargo of molasses being unloaded at the wharf, just down the street.

▶ *Turn right on Fore Street, pass the granite-fronted 1828 Mariner's Church and turn left immediately onto cobbled Moulton Street. Turn right on Wharf Street, go right on Union Street, then left at the*

light on Fore Street. On the corner of Cotton Street is the Tracy-Causer Building.

16 Tracy-Causer Building

Note the old street sign on this building, one of the few survivors of the Great Fire of 1866. The city's Landmarks Association successfully campaigned for its preservation and restoration in 1996. On the harbor side stand some of the few remaining warehouses from the "Golden Age" of the 19th and early 20th centuries. Straight ahead is Portland's second flat-iron building, now full of artists' studios, used and rare book stores, and the Danforth Gallery, exhibiting alternative art.

At the five-street intersection known as Gorham's Corner is a seated statue of John Ford, complete with pipe. He grew up in Portland and the pub owned by this famous Hollywood director's father was here.

▶ *Continue through the five-street intersection onto Pleasant Street. Immediately past the first parking garage, turn right and go up the alley and stairs to Spring Street. On the right is the Civic Center. Cross the street and turn left.*

17 Clapp House and McLellan House

The Great Fire did not reach this area, so these two impressive merchants' homes still stand. The Maine College of Art has offices in Clapp House, a Greek Revival mansion. Major Hugh McLellan's grand Federal house was given to the Portland Society of Art, in 1908, by Mrs. Lorenzo de Medici Sweat, along with funds to build a "proper" art museum.

▶ *Turn right on High Street. Across the street is another Federal brick residence, now a private club, built by McLellan's brother, also a successful merchant and auctioneer. Return to Congress Square, at the end of the block.*

RECOMMENDED TRIPS

Portland's waterfront is busy with both working fishermen and pleasure boats. In summer, as many as 50 trips go out each day to whale watch or bird watch, to poke around the islands of Casco Bay, or to visit explorer Admiral Peary's former home on Eagle Island. Ferries run a regular service up to Nova Scotia in Canada.

The Portland skyline in the evening

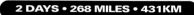

2 DAYS • 268 MILES • 431KM

Mountains &
Lakes of Maine

Nature lovers and sports fans head for the lakes and mountains, just as vacationers did 150 years ago when they came by railroad to escape the summer heat of more southerly states. Winter also brings visitors, such as downhill and cross-country skiers.

ITINERARY

i 245 Commercial Street

▶ *Leave Portland on **I–95** (the Maine Turnpike), turning off on Exit 63 at Gray (18m/29km). Follow **Route 26** north for 8 miles (13km) to Sabbathday Lake.*

BACK TO NATURE

North of Gray is the Maine Wildlife Park. For those who are not heading out into the wilderness areas of the state, this is a wonderful place to get a close look at moose, bears, deer and porcupines. This is not a zoo; the animals brought here were orphaned or injured.

---

❶ Sabbathday Lake

A cluster of white buildings plus a large red-brick house mark Sabbathday Lake Village, the home of the Shakers, the religious community founded in 1782 by Mother Ann Lee, who voyaged from Manchester, England. Some 30 years later, the Shaker movement had grown to around 7,000, with settlements in New England, Ohio, and Kentucky.

This is the last remaining group. Fewer than a dozen men and women live here, following the credo "Put your hands to work and your heart to God." They aim for self-sufficiency through farming, tending the orchards, knitting and printing. During the summer, outsiders are invited to join the Sunday services at 10am in the Meeting House, with its plain wooden benches. On other days, visitors can tour some of the buildings, including the museum, with examples of ingenious labor-saving inventions.

▶ *Follow **Route 26** to Poland Spring.*

❷ Poland Spring

The popularity of bottled mineral waters may seem a recent phenomenon but Poland Spring water has been prized for more than a century. When its "healing" powers became known, the spring attracted visitors, a hotel was built, and the area developed into a summer resort. The hotel is long gone but its "library" building remains. This is now the State of Maine Building from the Chicago Expo in 1893, moved and reconstructed here as an attraction for visitors. In Poland Spring Preservation Park, the 1907 bottling plant now houses interactive science displays and memorabilia. The visitor center and café are set on 100 acres (40 hectares) of woods with 4 miles (7km) of nature trails.

▶ *Continue on **Route 26** north for 17 miles (27km) through South Paris, where the Celebration Barn Theater puts on vaudeville, mime and juggling in the summer. Turn right to Paris.*

❸ Paris

Few Americans remember Hannibal Hamlin, Vice-President during Abraham Lincoln's first term. His home is the most impressive structure in this cluster of pristine white Federal and Victorian houses on the summit of a hill. Admire the vistas across the valley and to the White Mountains to the west, then tour the tiny library in the former jail. Built in 1822, it is constructed entirely of granite, including the floors. Ask to see the jail door keys, and to hear how a fat prisoner became stuck while trying to escape.

▶ *Continue and rejoin **Route 26** and drive north to the junction of **Routes 26** and **219**. On the east side of the road is a turn-off for Snow Falls Gorge, where there is a picturesque waterfall, picnic tables and nature trails.*

❹ Trap Corner

"Rockhounds" and gemologists from all over New England know Oxford County because it is rich in minerals and gemstones such as tourmaline, amethyst and quartz.

At the junction of Routes 26 and 219 is Perham's of West Paris, a landmark since 1919. As well as a shop selling local finds, and the museum, this is where modern-day prospectors can get maps of nearby quarries and information about panning for gold in the Rangeley area.

▶ *Continue on **Route 26**.*

❺ Bryant Pond

The people of Maine are renowned for their stubbornness. This town enjoyed making telephone calls the old-fashioned way, and made national headlines with its campaign to keep its hand-cranked phone system, the last one in the country. They lost their battle in 1983, but the

Reflections at Bryant Pond

antiquated telephone technology is the focus of what must be one of the smallest museums in New England.

▶ Take **Route 26** to Bethel.

⑥ Bethel

Founded on the Androscoggin River, the community nearly died after the Revolution. Railroads brought revitalization in the mid-19th century. As well as benefiting agriculture and lumber businesses, the trains

Main picture: the covered bridge at Newry
Inset: one of Bethel's attractive houses; blueberry leaves in Acadia National Park

carried tourists. Now, vacationers come by car to what is a four-season resort. In winter, cross-country and downhill skiers head for Mount Abram and Sunday River, with its 127-trail network over eight different peaks. The chairlift up the slope provides bird's-eye views of the White Mountains. In summer, the area offers a range of outdoor activities: camping, canoeing, mountain biking, fishing, golf and swimming.

⃞i Bethel Train Station, 8 Station Place

▶ Leave Bethel on **Routes 26 and 2**, and drive 5 miles (8km) north to Newry.

SCENIC ROUTES

About 10m (16km) northwest of Newry is Grafton Notch State Park, where the park road has been designated a "Maine Scenic Byway." Moose can be sighted during dawn and dusk hours, while views of Bald Pate Mountain, plus Screw Augur Falls, epitomize the beauties of the region. The Appalachian Trail crosses the road here. This hiking route starts in Georgia and follows the Appalachian Mountains all the way to Mount Katahdin in northeast Maine.

7 Newry

Just off the road is the Artist's Covered Bridge, much painted and photographed long before the movie *The Bridges of Madison County* lent cachet to similar bridges in Iowa. This one was built in 1872, over the Sunday River. More than just a scenic spot, it has popular swimming holes as well.

▷ *Continue on scenic **Route 2** north to the papermill town of Rumford and cross the river at the mighty Pennacook Falls to Mexico, where much of the country's paper for books is made. Take **Route 17** north toward Oquossoc, then turn east on **Route 4** to Rangeley.*

8 Rangeley

Wilderness and isolation are the hallmarks of the Rangeley region, surrounded by mountains and punctuated by more than 40 bodies of water. The village boasts of being midway between the North Pole and the equator, but there is nothing midway about the winters. A dog-sled mail service used to deliver letters to households cut off by snow; now, snowmobiles provide access to homes and businesses, but they are also raced for fun.

Other winter sports include snowshoeing, dog-sledding and ice-fishing, as well as cross-country and downhill skiing. The slopes here are less crowded than at most other resorts. When summer comes, there is fishing for landlocked salmon and trout, canoeing, hiking and golfing.

There are also two museums. The Rangeley Historical Society Museum, once a jail, recalls the 19th-century era of lake steamers and lodges that catered to New Yorkers escaping the heat of the city. More unusual is the Wilhelm Reich Museum, the home of the controversial Austrian psychoanalyst who studied with, then broke from, Sigmund Freud. Reich emigrated to the U.S.A. and eventually settled in Rangeley, to pursue "orgonomy, the science of the life energy." His

writings and inventions were all to do with sexual energy and personality analysis. In 1956, he was found guilty of violating Food and Drug Administration laws. He died, in prison, a year later. A museum preserves his library, memorabilia and surviving inventions.

i *Rangeley Lakes Region Chamber of Commerce, 6 Park Road*

▶ *Leave Rangeley via* **Route 4** *south. Note that Smalls Falls, in the Sandy River Gorge, has a good swimming hole, plus a waterfall, picnic site, and hiking trails. At Phillips, take* **Route 142** *northeast to Kingfield.*

9 Kingfield
What do violins, automobiles and cameras all have in common? They fascinated the ingenious minds of F. O. and F. E. Stanley, twin brothers who

lived here a century ago. Their most profitable discovery was a photographic process which they sold to a company that later became Kodak. Car fans know them for their Stanley Steamers, made by the Stanley Motor Carriage Company. One of their racing cars set a speed record of 127.66mph (204.3km/h) in 1906, and it remained unbroken for many years. The brothers also made fine violins. The Stanley Museum tells their story and displays their inventions, along with photographs taken by their sister, Chansonetta Stanley Emmons.

▶ *Take* **Route 27** *south through New Portland, stopping to see the amazing 1841 Fireproof Wire Bridge, suspended across the Carrabassett River. Rejoin* **Route 4** *and head for Farmington.*

10 Farmington
It is hard to imagine that this agricultural valley produced an international opera star. A simple farmhouse, just outside Farmington, was the birthplace in 1857 of Lillian Norton. As Madame Nordica, she triumphed in Europe and was the first American woman to take Wagnerian roles at the Bayreuth Festival. Returning to the States, her "liquid purity, exceptional range, and magnificent power" charmed New York critics during numerous seasons at the Metropolitan Opera House. The Nordica Memorial Homestead displays her costumes, annotated scores and other memorabilia.

A branch of the University of Maine is here, continuing a tradition of education dating back to 1864 when the school was founded, the first public college in Maine.

i *Franklin County Chamber of Commerce, 407 Wilton Road*

▶ *Continue on* **Route 4**, *which leads through Dryden, Jay and Livermore Falls, recognized long before arriving by the*

View over Step Falls, Grafton Notch State Park

sulphurous smell of the papermills. Take **Route 108** *east for the Washburn-Norlands Living History Center.*

11 Washburn-Norlands Living History Center
Step into the past at the former home of one of the most fascinating and influential families of 19th-century Maine. The seven Washburn sons included diplomats, congressmen, journalists, businessmen and a navy captain, yet the family exemplifies the thrifty lifestyle considered to be typical of New England.

On the hour-and-a-half-long guided tour, you learn the ways of farmers in the 19th century and see the 1828 church, the family's 1867 mansion, the library, farmhouse and barn on what is now a 445-acre (180-ha) estate.

Special activities include "Sugaring Days" in March. You have breakfast, with pancakes and farm-produced maple syrup, then watch the syrup being made.

▶ *Follow* **Route 4** *to Auburn and then take* **I-95** *south (Maine Turnpike) for the return to Portland.*

GETTING AROUND

Whether in your own car or a rental car, driving is the best way to see New England. The forested hills, winding river valleys, and historic towns and villages are most accessible and best appreciated at moderate speed on secondary roads (see **Motoring**, pages 159–60). But other means of transportation are available as well.

By Car

Within New England, you'll normally drive only an hour or two to your next destination. From Boston, it's only an hour's drive to Providence, Plymouth, Manchester or Portsmouth; about two hours to Hartford, Portland, Mystic or Cape Cod; about three hours to New Haven, the Berkshires, southern Vermont, Boothbay Harbor or New Hampshire's White Mountains; and only about four hours to central Vermont. Five hours takes you from Boston to the resort and national park at Bar Harbor, Maine.

By Recreational Vehicle

Among the most pleasant ways to tour the country is in an RV (motor home). These usually sleep four to six people comfortably, include a full kitchen (with cooking range, refrigerator and running water), and air conditioning; some have a shower.

Hundreds of campgrounds in New England can provide electrical, water and sewer hookups for $15 to $20 per night. Some RVs can operate for several days without hookups. In an RV, you're completely independent, and for families with young children it can be a very cost-effective way to tour New England.

Renting an RV has its disadvantages too. Rentals are fairly expensive and fuel consumption is high, so compare the cost of a trip in an RV to using a rental car and hotels before making your decision.

During the summer months, many of New England's choicest campgrounds fill up early in the day. You may have to make a reservation, which takes some of the fun out of footloose travel. Going the RV route would also mean you miss out on staying in New England's delightful country inns.

For more information on RVs, contact the Recreation Vehicle Industry Association, 1896 Preston White Drive, PO Box 2999, Reston, Virginia 20195-0999 (tel: 703/620-6003; fax 703/620-5071; www.rvia.org) or the Recreation Vehicle Rental Association, 3930 University Drive, Fairfax, Virginia 22030 (tel: 703/591-7130; www.rvra.org). RV America has a comprehensive website (www.rvamerica.com), as does Go Camping America (www.gocampingamerica.com).

By Plane

Larger cities, such as Boston, Providence, Hartford, Portland and Burlington, all have good air service provided by the larger domestic airlines. Numerous regional "feeder" airlines fly between the larger and smaller cities, and many regional carriers connect to New York City.

Almost all the small regional airlines operate in conjunction with larger national and international airlines (see www.flynewengland.com for information). The regional airlines' flights are included in the flight schedules of such airlines as American, Delta, Continental, United and USAir.

By Train

Amtrak (tel:1–800/USA–RAIL; www.amtrak.com) trains link Boston with Springfield and Pittsfield, Massachusetts, and Albany, New York; Hartford, New Haven, New London, and Mystic, Connecticut; Providence, Rhode Island; and Brattleboro, White River

Junction, and Montpelier, Vermont. The Downeaster from Boston goes to Portland, Maine, and there's the high-speed Acela service to New York City and Washington D.C.

Routes between Boston and points south and west are fast and frequent, but connections are not so good to Vermont.

By Bus

Bus services are quite good in New England.

Bonanza Bus Lines (tel: 401/751–8800 or 888/751-8800; www.bonanzabus.com), South Station Transportation Center, 700 Atlantic Avenue, runs from Boston to Cape Cod (Falmouth and Woods Hole) and Fall River (Massachusetts), and Newport and Providence (Rhode Island). Other routes run from Providence to central and western Connecticut and Massachusetts' Berkshires, and from Providence to Cape Cod.

Concord Trailways (tel: 603/228-3300 or 1-800/639-3317) is the line to take to New Hampshire. Buses start at Boston's Logan Airport and South Station, then go north to North Conway, Concord, Plymouth, and Franconia, as well as Meredith and Center Harbor.

Greyhound (tel: 800/231-2222; www.greyhound.com), at South Station and Boston University, 775 Commonwealth Avenue, operates many long-distance routes in New England, and connects the region with the rest of the US .

Peter Pan Bus Lines (tel: 617/526-1801 or 800/343-9999; www.peterpanbus.com), at South Station, runs between Boston and Albany, Amherst, Bridgeport, Danbury, Hartford, Holyoke, Lee, Middletown, New Britain, New Haven, New York City, Northampton, Pittsfield, Springfield, Waterbury, and Worcester. Other routes connect Springfield with Hartford, Connecticut.

Plymouth & Brockton Street Railway Co. (tel: 508/746-0378; www.p-b.com), South Station, is the one to take from Boston to Plymouth, Sagamore, Hyannis, Barnstable, and Provincetown on Cape Cod.

Vermont Transit Lines (tel: 802/864-9681, or 800/451-3292 in Vermont; www.vermont transit.com), South Station, has a comprehensive network.

HEALTH SERVICES

All New England cities have hospitals; blue signs bearing a white H mark the way. Boston is one of the most renowned medical centers, with dozens of hospitals and medical facilities.

To use most of these facilities, however, you'll need health insurance, since prices for treatments are astronomical.

HITCHHIKING

Hitchhiking is not a good way to get around New England, either within cities or between cities and towns. It's illegal to hitchhike on expressways. Incidents of robbery and violence by driver or hitcher, though few in number, mean most motorists won't stop.

HOLIDAYS

(LWE = long weekend, including Monday)
1 January – New Year's Day;
Third Monday in January – Martin Luther King Day (LWE);
Second weekend in February – Lincoln's Birthday (LWE);
Third weekend in February – Washington's Birthday (LWE);
(Presidents Week, linking the two weekends, is often a school holiday);
First Tuesday in March – Town Meeting Day (Vermont);
Third Monday in April – Patriots' Day (Massachusetts and Maine, LWE);
Easter;
Last weekend in May – Memorial Day (LWE);
4 July – Independence Day;
Second Monday in August – Victory Day (Rhode I, LWE);

16 August – Bennington Battle Day (Vermont);
First Monday in September – Labor Day (LWE);
Second Monday in October – Columbus Day (LWE);
First Tuesday in November – Election Day (some states);
11 November – Veteran's Day;
Fourth Thursday in November – Thanksgiving Day;
25 December – Christmas Day.

LIQUOR LAWS

The minimum age for drinking varies by state, but in most it's 21 years. A few towns in New England are "dry" (no store, restaurant or hotel may sell liquor, but it's not illegal to bring your own and serve yourself). Restaurants have either a full license (liquor, wine and beer), a wine and beer license, or no license. Some unlicensed restaurants let you bring your own. It's illegal to drink alcohol in public areas. Drink/driving laws are very strict.

MOTORING
Driving

In many places outside major cities, cars are permitted to turn right on a red light after stopping, if it is safe to do so.

Freeways and toll roads make travel easy, whereas side roads are often narrow and winding. Use particular care in winter.

You should always have your driver's license with you.

Speed limits, licensing of drivers, and all other rules governing automobile use are set by each state's legislature.

Car Rental

To rent a car in New York or New England, you must be at least 21 years of age (though at most major agencies it's 25) and have a valid driver's license. A credit or charge card is almost always a necessity.

Some companies may insist that non-U.S. residents have an International Drivers Permit.

If your own auto insurance covers damage to a rental car, you may not need to purchase Collision Damage Waiver

(CDW) or Loss Damage Waiver (LDW). Check with your insurer.

The major New England airports have national car rental chains:
Alamo (tel: 800/GO ALAMO)
Avis (tel: 800/230-4898)
Budget (tel: 800/527-0700)
Dollar (tel: 800/800-3665)
Hertz (tel: 800/654-3131)
National (tel: 800/227-7368)
Thrifty (tel: 800/847-4389).

Breakdowns

Car rental companies will advise drivers of what to do in the case of a breakdown. The American Automobile Association has reciprocal arrangements with many other motoring organizations around the world, so it is worth checking with your own association before leaving home. The AAA nationwide, toll-free number is 800-AAA-HELP. In case of a breakdown, lift up the hood, as a signal, and remain in the car. Only open doors and windows to police in a patrol car.

Accidents

All accidents should be reported to the police. Exchange names, addresses, driver's license number, and insurance details.

Non-U.S. residents who have caused, or are held responsible for, an injury, should insist on contacting their embassy or consulate.

Safety Belts

The use of safety belts is required by law. Throughout the United States, infants and small children (under 5) are required by law to be placed in child safety seats (available from car-rental firms at a small extra charge) secured by seat belts.

Speed Limits

The speed limit on New England highways is generally 55 to 65mph (88 to 105km/h). In cities and built-up areas, it is 20 to 40mph (32 to 64km/h), 20mph (32km/h) in school zones.

Speed limits are strictly enforced. When a school bus

stops, all traffic must stop too.

Police use radar to detect speeding drivers.

Road Maps
New England maps are sold in the region's bookstores and gas stations. State maps with greater detail are available, sometimes free, from official state tourism departments by mail, or from information centers on major highways near state borders.

For addresses of the state tourism offices, see **Visitor Information** below.

NEWSPAPERS/ MAGAZINES
Each of the larger cities in New England has its own daily newspaper. The *Boston Globe* and the *Boston Herald* are distributed throughout New England, as is the *New York Times*, and, in most cities, the *Washington Post*.

PERSONAL SAFETY
Whenever you're traveling in an unfamiliar city or country, stay alert and keep a close eye on your possessions.

POST OFFICES
Most post offices are open Monday through Friday from 8am to 5pm and Saturday from 8am to noon or 2pm. A few major post offices stay open until 5.30 or 6pm, and the post office at Boston's Logan Airport stays open until around 8pm.

TAXES
Taxes on hotel rooms, restaurant meals, some transportation, and purchases in general are levied by each state and by some cities. Taxes on rooms, meals, and other purchases (which can be as high as 11 or 12 per cent) are not included in the price. Sales tax on general goods and clothing varies from state to state, but will be between 5 and 7 per cent.

TIPS FOR SPECIAL TRAVELERS
Families
Museums, amusement attractions, whale-watching trips, and

the majority of other sights offer reduced admission for children or good-value family tickets.

Some attractions (outdoor concerts, state parks, beaches, and so forth) charge admission "per car," so families can pay as little as solo travelers.

A good source of information for family travel is *Frommer's Unofficial Guide to New England* and *New York with Kids*.

Seniors
Senior discounts are available throughout New England at museums, parks, attractions, and some hotels and on Amtrak trains, so carry some convincing form of photo identification.

It's best to request discounts on hotel rates, train and plane fares, and rental-car fees when making reservations, not when you're paying for the services.

For more information about senior discounts, contact the American Association of Retired Persons (AARP), 601 E Street, NW, Washington, D.C. 20049 (tel: 1-888/687-2277; www.aarp.org).

Travelers with Disabilities
All of New England's major hotels and most museums, stores, and other large institutions, have, by law, to be accessible to visitors in wheelchairs or on crutches. However, many small country inns and bed-and-breakfasts are not accessible or not fully accessible. Always call ahead to check whether the level of accessibility is sufficient.

For comprehensive information and useful contacts, go to www.discovernewengland.org and click on Visitor Info A–Z. Once in New England, information centers can advise about accessibility.

Amtrak trains are accessible to travelers with disabilities, but not all Amtrak stations are; ask about this when you make your reservations, and also inquire about help with your baggage, special seating, and other assistance. Amtrak grants discounts of 15 per cent (off the normal coach fare) to adult disabled

travelers and 50 per cent (off normal children's fares) to disabled travelers aged 2 to 15. For full information, obtain Amtrak's annual Travel Planner from Amtrak, National Railroad Passenger Corp., 400 N. Capitol Street NW, Washington, D.C. 20001 (tel: 800/USA-RAIL).

VISITOR INFORMATION
State tourism offices:

Connecticut Commission on Culture and Tourism, 1 Financial Plaza, 755 Main Street, Hartford, CT 06106 (tel: 860/270-8080; www.ctbound.org)

Maine Office of Tourism, State House Station 59, Augusta, ME 04333 (tel: 207/287-5711 or 888/624-6345; www.visitmaine.com)

Massachusetts Office of Travel & Tourism, 10 Park Plaza, Suite 4510, Boston, MA 02116 (tel: 617/973-8500 or 800/227-MASS; www.massvacation.com)

New Hampshire Division of Travel & Tourism, 172 Pembroke Road (P.O. Box 1856), Concord, New Hampshire 03302 (tel: 603/271-2665; www.visitnh.gov)

Rhode Island Tourism Division, 1 West Exchange Street, Providence, Rhode Island 02903 (tel: 401/222-2601 or 800/556-2484; www.visitrhodeisland.com)

Vermont Department of Tourism and Marketing, National Life Building, 6th Floor, Drawer 20, Montpelier, Vermont 05620 (tel: 802/828-3676; www.vermontvacation.com)

Discover New England. The official tourism website (www.discovernewengland.org) has a wide range of information on New England as well as links to the individual states.

WHEN TO GO
Climate
Without doubt, the best times to tour New England are summer (June through August), and fall (September and October), unless you're coming for winter skiing.

ACCOMMODATIONS AND RESTAURANTS

Following is a selection of hotels and bed-and-breakfasts (🏨) which can be found along the routes of each tour, together with suggestions for restaurants (🍴) where you can take a break.

Accommodations prices
Accommodations are divided into four price bands, based on the cost of a double room per night. Where hotels are also identified as a restaurant, prices are in relation to the cost of the bedrooms:

$	under $70
$$	$70–$110
$$$	$110–$150
$$$$	over $150

Restaurant prices
Restaurants are divided into three price categories based on the cost of a three-course meal for one, excluding drink:

$	under $20
$$	$20–$40
$$$	over $40

TOUR I
CONCORD
🏨 **Best Western at Historic Concord $$$**
740 Elm Street, Concord, MA 01742. Tel: 978/369-6100 or 800/937-8376.
105 rooms.

🏨 🍴 **Colonial Inn $$–$$$$**
48 Monument Square, Concord, MA 01742. Tel: 978/369-9200 or 800/370-9200.
56 rooms.

🍴 **Walden Grille $–$$**
24 Walden Street, Concord, MA. Tel: 978/371-2233. *Modern American cuisine.*

WEST CONCORD
🍴 **Nashoba Brook Bakery and Café $–$$**
152 Commonwealth Avenue, West Concord, MA. Tel: 978/318-1999. *Soups, salads, artisan breads.*

SUDBURY
🏨 **Longfellow's Wayside Inn $$$–$$$$**
72 Wayside Inn Road, Sudbury, MA. Tel: 978/443-1776.
10 rooms.

TOUR 2
MARBLEHEAD
🏨 **Harbor Light Inn $$$–$$$$**
58 Washington Street, Marblehead, MA. Tel: 781/631-2186.
21 rooms.

🍴 **The Barnacle $$**
141 Front Street, Marblehead, MA. Tel: 781/631-4236. *Fresh seafood in a restaurant overlooking the harbor.*

SALEM
🏨 **Coach House Inn $$–$$$$**
284 Lafayette Street, Salem, MA. Tel: 978/744-4092.
11 rooms.

🍴 **Red's Restaurant $**
15 Central Street, Salem, MA. Tel: 978/745-3527. *Big breakfasts, burgers, sandwiches.*

GLOUCESTER
🏨 **Atlantis Oceanfront Motor Inn $$–$$$$**
125 Atlantic Road, Gloucester, MA 90130. Tel: 978/283-0014.
40 rooms.

🍴 **Franklin Cape Ann $$–$$$**
118 Main Street, Gloucester, MA. Tel: 978/283-7888. *Contemporary American food in a bistro setting.*

ROCKPORT
🍴 **Grand Café $$**
Emerson Inn, I Cathedral Avenue, Rockport, MA. Tel: 978/546-6321. *Modern versions of New England dishes.*

ESSEX
🍴 **Tom Shea's $–$$**
122 Main Street, Essex, MA. Tel: 978/768-6931. *Seafood; good sea views.*

IPSWICH
🏨 **Inn at Castle Hill $$$$**
280 Argilla Road, Ipswich, MA 01938. Tel: 978/412-2555.
10 rooms.

NEWBURYPORT
🏨 **Clark Currier Inn $$–$$$$**
45 Green Street, Newburyport, MA 01950. Tel: 978/465-8363.
8 rooms.

TOUR 3
SANDWICH
🏨 **Dan'l Webster Inn $$$–$$$$**
149 Main Street, Sandwich, MA 02563. Tel: 508/888-3622.
53 rooms.

🍴 **The Belfry Bistro $$–$$$**
8 Jarves Street, Sandwich, MA. Tel: 508/888-8550. *New American; great desserts.*

BARNSTABLE
🍴 **Mattakeese Wharf $$–$$$**
271 Mill Way, Barnstable, MA. Tel: 508/362-4511. *Seafood and sunsets.*

DENNIS
🏨 **Isaiah Hall B&B Inn $$$–$$$$**
152 Whig Street, Dennis, MA 02638. Tel: 508/385-9928.
10 rooms.

🍴 **Gina's by the Sea $–$$**
134 Taunton Avenue, West Dennis, MA. Tel: 508/385-3213. *Italian favorites.*

EASTHAM
🏨 **Whalewalk Inn $$$$**
220 Bridge Road, Eastham, MA 02642. Tel: 508/255-0617 or 800/440-1281.
16 rooms.

PROVINCETOWN
🏨 **Carpe Diem Guesthouse $$–$$$$**
12 Johnson Street, Provincetown, MA 02657. Tel: 508/487-4242.
14 rooms.

The Masthead $$–$$$
31–41 Commercial Street,
Provincetown, MA.
Tel: 508/487-0523.
21 rooms.

The Commons Bistro and Bar $–$$
386 Commercial Street,
Provincetown, MA.
Tel: 508/487-7800. *Stop by for coffee and pastries or fill up on a gourmet pizza.*

Front Street $$–$$$
230 Commercial Street,
Provincetown, MA.
Tel: 508/487-9715.
Mediterranean fusion.

Ross' Grill $$
Whalers' Wharf, Commerical
Street, Provincetown, MA.
Tel: 508/487-8878. *Bar/bistro on water. Closed Tue.*

CHATHAM
Chatham Wayside Inn $$$$
512 Main Street, Chatham, MA.
Tel: 508/945-5550.
56 rooms.

Christian's $$
443 Main Street, Chatham, MA.
Tel: 508/945-3362. *Seafood.*

TOUR 4
GREAT BARRINGTON
Castle Street Café $$
10 Castle Street, Great
Barrington, MA. Tel: 413/528-
5244. *New American; good wine list.*

STOCKBRIDGE
Red Lion $$$–$$$$
30 Main Street, Stockbridge,
MA 01262. Tel: 413/298-5545.
108 rooms.

LENOX
Apple Tree Inn $$$–$$$$
10 Richmond Mountain Road,
Lenox, MA 01240. Tel: 413/
637-1477.
34 rooms.

Church Street Café $$
65 Church Street, Lenox, MA.
Tel: 413/637-2745. *Eclectic American cuisine. Book ahead.*

Dish $$–$$$
37 Church Street, Lenox, MA.
Tel: 413/637-1800. *Creative cooking; small premises so book ahead.*

NORTH ADAMS
The Porches Inn at MASSMoCA $$$$
231 River Street, North Adams,
MA 01247. Tel: 413/664-0400.
47 rooms.

Café Latino $$
Building 11, MASS MoCA,
Marshall Street, North Adams
MA. Tel: 413/662-2004. *Latin American cuisine.*

DEERFIELD
Deerfield Inn $$$$
81 Old Main Street, Deerfield,
MA 01342. Tel: 413/774-5587
or 800/926-3865.
23 rooms.

TOURS 5 and 6
BOSTON
Harborside Inn $$$
185 State Street, Boston, MA
02109. Tel: 617/723-7500 or
888/723-7565.
54 rooms.

Midtown Hotel $$–$$$
220 Huntington Avenue, Boston,
MA 02115. Tel: 617/262-1000.
159 rooms.

Newbury Guesthouse $$$–$$$$
261 Newbury Street, Boston,
MA 02116. Tel: 617/437-7666.
32 rooms.

Ritz-Carlton, Boston Common $$$$
10 Avery Street, Boston
Common, MA 02111. Tel:
617/574-7100 or 800/241-3333.
193 rooms.

Westin Copley Plaza $$$$
10 Huntington Avenue, Boston,
MA 02116. Tel: 617/262-9600 or
888/625-5144.
803 rooms.

Antico Forno $–$$
93 Salem Street, Boston, MA.
Tel: 617/723-6733. *Rustic Italian cuisine.*

Figs $–$$
42 Charles Street, Boston, MA.
Tel: 617/742-3447. *Italian food, including specialty pizza.*

Legal Seafoods $–$$
100 Huntington Avenue,
Copley Place, Boston, MA.
Tel: 617/266-7775. *Seafood. Several branches.*

Sel de la Terre $$–$$$
255 State Street, Boston, MA.
Tel: 617/720-1300. *Provençal cuisine.*

TOUR 7
CAMBRIDGE
Inn at Harvard $$$–$$$$
1201 Massachusetts Avenue,
Cambridge, MA 02138. Tel:
617/491-2222 or 800/458-5886.
112 rooms.

Sheraton Commander Hotel $$$–$$$$
16 Garden Street, Cambridge,
MA 02138. Tel: 617/547-4800 or
800/325-3535.
175 rooms.

East Coast Grille $$–$$$
1271 Cambridge Street,
Cambridge, MA. Tel: 617/491-
6568. *Fish and BBQ. Closed lunch Mon–Sat.*

Rialto $$$
Charles Hotel, 1 Bennett Street,
Cambridge, MA. Tel: 617/661-
5050. *Eclectic; top chef. Closed lunch.*

TOUR 8
HARTFORD
Goodwin Hotel $$$$
1 Haynes Street, Hartford,
CT 06103. Tel: 860/246-7500
or 800/922-5006.
124 rooms.

Residence Inn by Marriott $$$–$$$$
942 Main Street, Hartford,
CT 06103. Tel: 860/524-5550.
122 rooms.

Max Downtown $$–$$$
185 Asylum Street, Hartford,
CT. Tel: 860/522-2530. *Stylish, contemporary cooking.*

Trumbull Kitchen $$
150 Trumbull Street, Hartford,
CT. Tel: 860/493-7417. *Fusion.*

TOUR 9
NEW HAVEN
New Haven Hotel $$$
229 George Street, New Haven,
CT 06510. Tel: 203/498-3100 or
800/644-6835.
92 rooms.

Three Chimneys $$$$
1201 Chapel Street, New
Haven, CT 06511. Tel:
203/789-1201 or 800/443-1554.
11 rooms.

**Three Judges Motor
Lodge $**
1560 Whalley Avenue, New
Haven, CT 06515.
Tel: 203/389-2161.
34 rooms.

Frank Pepe $
157 Wooster Street, New
Haven, CT. Tel: 203/865-5762.
*Perhaps America's first pizza
parlor.*

Louis' Lunch $
261–263 Crown Street, New
Haven, CT. Tel: 203/562-5507.
*Famous as the home of America's
first hamburger.*

Roomba $$
1044 Chapel Street, New
Haven, CT. Tel: 203/562-7666.
Nuevo Latino cuisine.

TOUR 10
LITCHFIELD
**Tollgate Hill Inn
$$–$$$$**
Route 202, Litchfield, CT
06759. Tel: 860/567-1233.
20 rooms.

West Street Grill $$–$$$
43 West Street, Litchfield, CT.
Tel: 860/567-3885.
*Contemporary American cuisine;
seafood. Trendy, expensive. Closed
Mon, Tue.*

NEW PRESTON
Hopkins Inn $$–$$$
22 Hopkins Road, New Preston,
CT 06777. Tel: 860/868-7295.
13 rooms.

KENT
Bull's Bridge Inn $$
333 Kent Road, Kent, CT.
Tel: 860/927-1000. *Diverse menu
including classic grills.*

SALISBURY
**Earl Grey B&B at
Chittenden House $$$$**
Routes 41 and 44, Salisbury,
CT 06068. Tel: 860/435-1007.
2 rooms.

White Hart $$
Village Green, Salisbury, CT.
Tel: 860/435-0030. *Modern New
England cooking.*

NORFOLK
Manor House $$$
69 Maple Avenue, Norfolk,
CT 06058. Tel: 860/542-5690.
9 rooms.

TOUR 11
MADISON
Inn at Lafayette $$–$$$
725 Boston Post Road, Madison,
CT 06443. Tel: 203/245-7773.
5 rooms.

OLD SAYBROOK
Old Saybrook Diner $$
809 Boston Post Road, Old
Saybrook, CT. Tel: 860/395-
1079. *Classic diner.*

ESSEX
Griswold Inn $$$–$$$$
36 Main Street, Essex, CT
06425. Tel: 860/767-1776.
31 rooms.

IVORYTON
Copper Beech Inn $$$$
46 Main Street, Ivoryton, CT
06442. Tel: 860/767-0330.
13 rooms.

OLD LYME
Bee & Thistle Inn $$$–$$$$
100 Lyme Street, Old Lyme,
CT 06371. Tel: 860/434-1667 or
800/622-4946.
11 rooms.

Old Lyme Inn $$–$$$
85 Lyme Street, Old Lyme, CT.
Tel: 860/434-2600. *American
cooking.*

NOANK
**Abbott's Lobster in the
Rough $–$$**
117 Pearl Street, Noank, CT.
Tel: 860/536-7719. *Lobster dishes.
Seasonal specialties.*

MYSTIC
Old Mystic Inn $$$–$$$$
52 Main Street, Old Mystic,
CT 06372. Tel: 860/572-9422.
8 rooms.

Taber Inne $$–$$$
66 Williams Avenue, Route 1,
Mystic, CT 06355.
Tel: 860/536-4904.
34 rooms.

TOUR 12
PROVIDENCE
Old Court $$$–$$$$
144 Benefit Street, Providence,
RI 02903. Tel: 401/751-2002.
10 rooms.

**Providence Biltmore
$$$**
11 Dorrance Street, Providence,
RI 02303. Tel: 401/421-0700 or
800/294-7709.
288 rooms.

**Radisson Hotel on the
Harbor $$$–$$$$**
220 India Street, Providence,
RI 02903. Tel: 401/272-5577.
136 rooms.

The Gatehouse $$–$$$
4 Richmond Square,
Providence, RI. Tel: 401/521-
9229. *Seafood. Wood-fired grill.*

Mill's Tavern $$–$$$
101 North Main Street,
Providence, RI. Tel: 401/272-
3331. *New-wave American.*

XO Café $$
125 North Main Street,
Providence, RI. Tel: 401/273-
9090. *Fusion cuisine. Closed for
lunch.*

TOUR 13
NEWPORT
Adele Turner Inn $$$–$$$$
93 Pelham Street, Newport,
RI 02840. Tel: 401/848-8011 or
800/845-1811.
13 rooms.

🏨 Cliffside Inn $$$$
2 Seaview Avenue, Newport, RI 02840. Tel: 401/847-1811 or 800/845-1811.
16 rooms.

🏨 Francis Malbone House $$$–$$$$
392 Thames Street, Newport, RI 02840. Tel: 401/846-0392 or 800/846-0392.
25 rooms

🏨 ¶¶ Hotel Viking $$–$$$
1 Bellevue Avenue, Newport, RI 02840. Tel: 401/847-3300.
237 rooms.

🏨 Mill Street Inn $$–$$$$
75 Mill Street, Newport, RI 02840. Tel: 401/849-9500.
23 rooms.

¶¶ Black Pearl $$–$$$
30 Bannister's Wharf, Newport, RI. Tel: 401/846-5264. *Informal tavern; posh Commodore's Room. Seafood.*

¶¶ Clarke Cooke House $$–$$$
Bannister's Wharf, Newport, RI. Tel: 401/849-2900. *On the harbor, with three floors; three places to eat.*

¶¶ Tucker's Bistro $$
150 Broadway, Newport, RI. Tel: 401/846-3449. *Modern American.*

¶¶ White Horse Tavern $$$
26 Marlborough Street, Newport, RI. Tel: 401/849-3600. *America's oldest pub. Seafood a specialty.*

TOUR 14
BENNINGTON
🏨 South Shire Inn $$$–$$$$
124 Elm Street, Bennington, VT 05201. Tel: 802/447-3839.
9 rooms.

🏨 ¶¶ Four Chimneys Inn $$$
21 West Road, Bennington, VT. Tel: 802/447-3500.
11 rooms.

¶¶ Blue Benn $–$$
102 Hunt Street, Bennington, VT. Tel: 802/442-5140. *American/vegetarian. Diner.*

TOUR 15
ARLINGTON
🏨 ¶¶ Arlington Inn $$–$$$
Historic Route 7A, Arlington, VT. Tel: 802/375-6532.
18 rooms.

MANCHESTER
🏨 Barnstead Inn $$–$$$
Bonnet Street, Manchester Center, VT. Tel: 802/362-1619.
14 rooms.

🏨 ¶¶ The Equinox Resort and Marsh Tavern $$$–$$$$
3567 Main Street, Manchester Village, VT 05254. Tel: 802/362-4700. *Regional cuisine.*
183 rooms.

🏨 Manchester Highlands Inn $$$–$$$$
216 Highland Avenue, Manchester Center, VT 05255. Tel: 802/362-4565 or 800/743-4565.
16 rooms.

¶¶ Chanticleer $$$
Route 7A, East Dorset, VT (north of Manchester). Tel: 802/362-1616. *Classy Swiss-inspired cooking.*

¶¶ Little Rooster Café $–$$
Route 7A, Manchester Center, VT. Tel: 802/362-1779. *Inventive breakfasts, sandwiches.*

WESTON
¶¶ Inn at Weston $$–$$$
Route 100, Weston, VT 05161. Tel: 802/824-5804. *International cuisine.*

CHESTER
🏨 Fullerton Inn $$–$$$
40 The Common, Chester, VT 05143. Tel: 802/875-2444.
21 rooms.

🏨 Stone Hearth Inn $$–$$$
698 Route 11 West, Chester, VT 05143. Tel: 802/875-2525.
10 rooms.

GRAFTON
🏨 ¶¶ Old Tavern at Grafton $$$$
Routes 35 and 121, Grafton, VT 05146. Tel: 802/843-2231.
46 rooms.

NEWFANE
🏨 ¶¶ Four Columns Inn $$$
21 West Street, Newfane, VT 05345. Tel: 802/365-7713 or 800/787-6633. *Award-winning gourmet food. Distinctive blend of New American, Asian and French cuisine.*
15 rooms.

BRATTLEBORO
🏨 ¶¶ Colonial Motel and Spa $–$$
889 Putney Road, Brattleboro, VT 05301. Tel: 802/257-7733.
73 rooms.

¶¶ Backside Café $–$$
24 High Street, Brattleboro, VT. Tel: 802/257-5056. *A good local breakfast and lunch spot.*

TOUR 16
RUTLAND
🏨 The Inn at Rutland $$–$$$$
70 North Main Street, Rutland, VT 05701. Tel: 802/773-0575.
8 rooms.

¶¶ Little Harry's $$
121 West Street, Rutland, VT. Tel: 802/747-4848. *Global cuisines, from steak to Thai.*

MENDON
🏨 ¶¶ Red Clover Inn $$$
7 Woodward Road, Mendon, VT 05701. Tel: 802/775-2290. *Modern American cuisine. Open for dinner Thu–Sun.*
14 rooms.

QUECHEE
🏨 Quechee Inn $$–$$$$
Mashland Farm, Main Street, Quechee, VT 05059. Tel: 1-800/235-3133.
25 rooms.

¶¶ Simon Pearce Restaurant $$$
At the Mill, Quechee, VT. Tel: 802/295-1470. *Contemporary New England with international twist.*

WOODSTOCK
🏨 ¶¶ Jackson House Inn $$$$
114 Senior Lane, Woodstock, VT 05091. Tel: 802/457-2065.
15 rooms.

⌂ **Shire Riverview Motel $$–$$$**
46 Pleasant Street, Woodstock,
VT. Tel: 802/457-2211.
42 rooms.

⌂ ¶¶ **Woodstock Inn $$$$**
14 The Green, Woodstock,
VT 05091. Tel: 802/457-1100
or 800/448-7900.
142 rooms.

¶¶ **Bentleys Restaurant $$**
3 Elm Street, Woodstock, VT.
Tel: 802/457-3232.
Contemporary cuisine.

**TOUR 17
BURLINGTON**
⌂ ¶¶ **Inn at Essex $$$–$$$$**
70 Essex Way, Essex Junction,
VT 05452. Tel: 802/878-1100 or
800/727-4295.
119 rooms.

¶¶ **Daily Planet $–$$**
15 Center Street, Burlington,
VT. Tel: 802/862-9647.
Imaginative pub food.

VERGENNES
⌂ ¶¶ **Basin Harbor Club $$$$**
Basin Harbor Road, Vergennes,
VT 05491. Tel: 802/475-2311.
115 rooms.

MIDDLEBURY
Swift House Inn $$$–$$$$
25 Stewart Lane, Middlebury,
VT 05753. Tel: 802/388-9925.
21 rooms.

⌂ ¶¶ **Old English Carvery
$–$$**
Middlebury Inn, 14 Court
House Square, Middlebury, VT.
Tel: 802/388-4961. *Roasts/grills.*
75 rooms.

¶¶ **Storm Café $$**
3 Mill Street, Frog Hollow,
Middlebury, VT. Tel: 802/388-
1063. *Chef-owned café with a
wide-ranging menu.*

EAST MIDDLEBURY
⌂ ¶¶ **Waybury Inn $$$–$$$$**
457 East Main Street, East
Middlebury, VT. Tel: 802/
388-4015.
14 rooms.

WARREN
¶¶ **The Common Man $$–$$$**
3209 German Flats Road,
Sugarbush, Warren, VT. Tel:
802/583-2800. *Vermont produce is
given a European touch.*

WAITSFIELD
⌂ ¶¶ **Inn at the Mad River
Barn $$–$$$**
Route 17, 2849 Mill Brook
Road, Waitsfield, VT. Tel:
802/496-3310.
15 rooms.

WATERBURY
⌂ ¶¶ **Old Stagecoach Inn
$$–$$$**
18 North Main Street,
Waterbury, VT 05676.
Tel: 802/244-5056.
11 rooms.

STOWE
⌂ ¶¶ **Stoweflake Mountain
Resort and Spa $$$$**
1746 Mountain Road, Stowe,
VT 05672. Tel: 802/253-7355
or 800/253-2232.
170 rooms.

⌂ ¶¶ **Whip Bar and Grill $–$$**
Green Mountain Inn, 18 Main
Street, Stowe, VT. Tel: 802/253-
7301. *Stylish tavern fare.*
105 rooms.

**TOUR 18
PORTSMOUTH**
⌂ **Inn at Strawbery Banke
$$$**
314 Court Street, Portsmouth,
NH 03801. Tel: 603/436-7242
or 800/428-3933.
7 rooms.

⌂ **The Sise Inn $$$–$$$$**
40 Court Street, Portsmouth,
NH 03801. Tel: 603/433-1200.
34 rooms.

¶¶ **Portsmouth Brewery $–$$**
56 Market Street, Portsmouth,
NH. Tel: 603/431-1115. *Casual;
hamburgers and more.*

¶¶ **Rosa Restaurant $–$$**
80 State Street, Portsmouth,
NH. Tel: 603/436-9715.
*Traditional Italian cuisine in an
historic setting.*

**TOUR 19
FRANCONIA**
⌂ ¶¶ **Franconia Inn $$$–$$$$**
1300 Easton Road, Franconia,
NH 03580. Tel: 603/823-5542.
32 rooms.

BETHLEHEM
¶¶ **Tim-bir Alley at the Adair
Country Inn $$$**
80 Guider Lane, Bethlehem,
NH. Tel: 603/444-6142. *Modern
American cuisine, tempting desserts.*

BRETTON WOODS
⌂ **Bretton Arms Country Inn
$$$–$$$$**
US Route 302, Bretton Woods,
NH 03575. Tel: 603/278-3000.
34 rooms.

JACKSON
⌂ ¶¶ **Inn at Thorn Hill
$$$–$$$$**
Thorn Hill Road, Jackson,
NH 03846. Tel: 603/383-4242
or 800/289-8990. *Rates include
breakfast, high tea, and gourmet
dinner.*
25 rooms.

NORTH CONWAY
Briarcliff Motel $–$$
⌂ Route 16, North Conway,
NH. Tel: 603/356-5584.
30 rooms.

¶¶ **1785 Inn Restaurant $$**
3582 White Mountain Highway,
North Conway, NH 03860.
Tel: 603/356-9025 or 800/421-
1785. *Traditional fine dining.*

¶¶ **Horsefeathers $**
Center of village, North
Conway, NH. Tel: 603/356-
2687. *Pasta and burgers.*

LINCOLN
⌂ ¶¶ **Mountain Club on Loon
$$–$$$**
90 Loon Mountain Road, Route
112, Lincoln, NH. Tel: 603/
745-2244.
234 Rooms.

¶¶ **Clement Room Grille/
Woodstock Station $$**
Route 3, Main Street, North
Woodstock, NH. Tel: 603/745-
3951. *Fine dining in the Grille;
pub fare in Woodstock Station.*

TOUR 20
HOLDERNESS
🏨 ¶¶The Manor on Golden
Pond $$$$
Shepard Hill Road, Holderness,
NH 03245. Tel: 603/968-3348.
25 rooms.

¶¶Walters Basin $$
By the bridge, Holderness, NH.
Tel: 603/968-4412. *Cajun cuisine.*

CENTER SANDWICH
¶¶ Corner House Inn $–$$
Main Street, Center Sandwich,
NH 03227. Tel: 603/284-6219.
New England country dining.

WOLFEBORO
¶¶Wolfboro Inn $–$$
90 North Main Street,
Wolfeboro, NH. Tel: 603/569-
3016. *Pub known for seafood
and steaks.*
44 rooms

MEREDITH
🏨 Inn at Mill Falls $$$
312 Daniel Webster Highway,
Meredith, NH 03253.
Tel: 603/279-7006.
158 rooms.

TOUR 21
FREEPORT
🏨 Kendall Tavern $$–$$$
213 Main Street, Freeport,
ME 04032. Tel: 207/865-1338.
7 rooms.

🏨 Maine Idyll Motor Court
$–$$
1411 US Route 1, Freeport,
ME 04032. Tel: 207/865-4201.
20 rooms.

🏨 ¶¶ Harraseeket Inn $$$$
162 Main Street, Freeport,
ME 04032. Tel: 207/865-9377.
84 rooms.

¶¶ Jameson Tavern $$–$$$
115 Main Street, Freeport,
ME. Tel: 207/865-4196. *Mainly
seafood classics.*

BRUNSWICK
¶¶ Star Fish Grill $$
100 Pleasant Brunswick, ME.
Tel: 207/725-7828. *Fresh local
seafood.*

BATH
🏨 Galen C Moses House
$$–$$$
1009 Washington Street, Bath,
ME. Tel: 207/442-8771.
5 rooms.

WISCASSET
¶¶ Sarah's Café $
Main Street, Wiscasset, ME.
Tel: 207/882-7504. *Pizzas,
pastas, calzones.*

ROCKLAND
🏨 Lime Rock Inn $$$
96 Lime Rock Street, Rockland,
ME 04841. Tel: 207/594-2257.
8 rooms.

¶¶ Café Miranda $$
15 Oak Street, Rockland, ME.
Tel: 207/594-2034. *Fun bistro.*

ROCKPORT
🏨 Samoset Resort $$$–$$$$
220 Warrenton Street, Rockport,
ME 04856. Tel: 207/594-2511 or
800/341-1650.
250 rooms.

CAMDEN
🏨 Camden Windward House
$$–$$$$
6 High Street, Camden,
ME 04843. Tel: 207/236-9656.
8 rooms.

🏨 Maine Stay $$$–$$$$
22 High Street, Camden,
ME 04843. Tel: 207/236-9636.
8 rooms.

¶¶Atlantica $
1 Bayview Landing, Camden,
ME. Tel: 207/236-6011. *Modern
American.*

TOUR 22
PORTLAND
🏨 The Danforth $$–$$$
163 Danforth Street, Portland,
ME 04102. Tel: 207/879-8755
or 800/991-6557.
9 rooms.

🏨 ¶¶ Portland Regency Hotel
$$$$
20 Milk Street, Portland,
ME 04101. Tel: 207/774-4200
or 800/727-3436.
95 rooms.

¶¶ Back Bay Grill $$
65 Portland Street, Portland,
ME. Tel: 207/772-8833. *Modern
New England cuisine; innovative
appetizers; extensive wine list.*

¶¶ Fore Street Restaurant $$
288 Fore Street, Portland, ME.
Tel: 207/775-2717. *Modern
American cuisine.*

TOUR 23
BETHEL
🏨 ¶¶ Bethel Inn and Country
Club $$$–$$$$
On the Common, Bethel, ME
04217. Tel: 207/824-2175 or
800/654-0125.
40 rooms.

🏨 L'Auberge Country Inn
$$–$$$$
15 L'Auberge Lane, Bethel,
ME 04217. Tel: 207/824-2774.
Also has excellent bistro.
7 rooms.

¶¶ Sunday River Brewing
Company $–$$
Route 2 at Sunday River Road,
Bethel, ME. Tel: 207/824-4253.
Informal brew-pub fare.

RANGELEY
🏨 Rangeley Inn $$–$$$
2443 Main Street, Rangeley,
ME 04970. Tel: 207/864-3341
or 800/666-3687.
50 rooms.

¶¶The Red Onion $
Main Street, Rangeley, ME.
Tel: 207/864-5022. *Pizzas, steaks;
informal.*

KINGFIELD
¶¶ Longfellow's Restaurant
$–$$
Main Street, Kingfield, ME.
Tel: 207/265-4394. *Casual dining
in a tavern overlooking the
Carrabassett River.*

FARMINGTON
¶¶ Homestead Bakery $
186 Broadway Street,
Farmington, ME. Tel: 207/778-
6162. *Down-home dishes.*

Practical Information

The addresses, telephone numbers, websites and opening times of the attractions and Tourist Information Offices mentioned in the tours, are listed below tour by tour.

TOUR I

[i] Cambridge Visitor Information Booth, Harvard Square, Cambridge, MA 02138. Tel: 617/441-2884; www.cambridge-usa.org

[i] Lexington Visitor Center, 1875 Massachusetts Avenue, Lexington, MA 02420. Tel: 781/862-1450; www.lexingtonchamber.org

[i] Minute Man Visitor Center, Route 2A, Lexington, MA 02420. Tel: 978/369-6993; www.nps.gov/mima

[i] Concord Visitor Center, 58 Main Street, Concord, MA 01742. Tel: 978/369-3120; www.concordchamberof commerce.org

[i] North Bridge Visitor Center, 174 Liberty Street, Concord, MA 01742. Tel: 978/369-6993; www.nps.gov/mima

❶ National Heritage Museum
33 Marrett Road (Route 2A), Lexington. Tel: 781/861-6559; www.national heritagemuseum.org. Open Mon–Sat 10–5, Sun noon–5.

❷ Munroe Tavern
1332 Massachusetts Avenue. Lexington. Tel: 781/862-1703; www.lexingtonhistory.org. Open Apr–Jun weekends, Jul–Oct daily 1.30–3.

❸ Lexington
Buckman Tavern
1 Bedford Street. Tel: 781/862-1703; www.lexington-history.org. Open Apr–Oct daily 10–4.

Hancock-Clarke House
36 Hancock Street. Tel: 781/861-0928; www.lexingtonhistory.org. Open Apr–Jun weekends; Jul–Oct daily 11–2.

❹ Minute Man National Historical Park
Route 2A, Lexington. Tel: 978/369-6993; www.nps.gov.mima

❺ Concord
The Wayside
455 Lexington Road. Tel: 978/318-7862; www.nps.gov/mima/ wayside. Open May–Oct.

Orchard House
399 Lexington Road. Tel: 978/369-4118; www.louisamayalcott.org. Open Mon–Sat 10–4.30, Sun 1–4.30; shorter hours on winter weekdays. Closed first 2 weeks Jan.

Concord Museum
200 Lexington Road. Tel: 978/369-9763; www.concordmuseum.org. Open Mon–Sat 9–5, Sun noon–5. Shorter hours in winter.

Ralph Waldo Emerson House
28 Cambridge Turnpike. Tel: 978/369-2236. Open mid-Apr to mid-Oct, Thu–Sat 10–4.30, Sun 1–4.30.

Sleepy Hollow Cemetery
Bedford Street, Concord. Tel: 978/318-3233.

Old Manse
269 Monument Street. Tel: 978/369-3909; www.old manse.org. Open mid-Apr to Oct, 10–5. Sun noon–5.

❻ Walden Pond
Walden Pond State Reservation, Route 126 Walden Street. Tel: 978/369-3254.

❼ Gropius House
68 Baker Bridge Road, Lincoln. Tel: 781/259-8098; www.historicnewengland. org. Open Jun to mid-Oct, Wed–Sun. Weekends in winter. Phone for hours.

❽ DeCordova Museum
51 Sandy Pond Road,

Lincoln. Tel: 781/259-8355; www.decordova.org. Open Tue–Sun 11–5. Park open to 10pm in summer.

Recommended trips
South Bridge Boathouse
496 Main Street, Concord. Tel: 978/369-9438. Open Apr–Oct daily.

TOUR 2

[i] Boston Common Visitor Information Center, 147 Tremont Street. Tel: 617/536-4100; www.bostonusa.com

[i] Marblehead Information Booth, Pleasant and Spring streets, Marblehead, MA 01945. Tel: 781/631-2868; www.marbleheadchamber.org

[i] National Park Service Regional Visitor Service, New Liberty and Essex streets, Salem, MA 01970. Tel: 978/740-1650; www.nps.gov/sama

[i] Stage Fort Park Information Center, Hough Avenue, Gloucester, MA 01930. Tel: 978/281-8865 (seasonal); 33 Commercial Street. Tel: 978/283-1601; www.gloucesterma.com

[i] Rockport Chamber of Commerce, 3 Whistlestop Mall, Rockport, MA 01966. Tel: 978/546-6575; www.rockportusa.com

❷ Marblehead
Jeremiah Lee Mansion
161 Washington Street. Tel: 781/631-1768; www.marbleheadmuseum.org. Open Jun–Oct, Tue–Sat 10–4.

Marblehead Museum and Historical Society
170 Washington Street. Tel: 781/631-1768. www.marbleheadmuseum.org. Open Tue–Sat 10–4. Closed Fri Nov–May.

❸ Salem
Salem Witch Museum
Washington Square North. Tel: 978/744-1692; www.salemwitchmuseum.com. Open daily 10–5 (till 7pm Jul, Aug).

Salem Witch Village
282 Rear of Derby Street. Tel: 978/740-9229; www.salemwitchvillage.net. Open Apr–Oct, daily 10–6 (extended hours Jul, Aug, Oct). Nov–Mar 11–4.

Witch House
310½ Essex Street. Tel: 978/744-8815; www.salemweb.com/witchhouse. Open May–Nov 10–5 (extended hours in Oct).

Peabody Essex Museum
East India Square. Tel: 978/745-9500; www.pem.org. Open daily 10–5.

Salem Maritime National Historic Site
193 Derby Street. Tel: 978/740-1660; www.nps.gov/sama. Open daily 9–5.

❻ Hammond Castle Museum
80 Hesperus Avenue, Gloucester. Tel: 978/283-2080/7673; www.hammondcastle.org. Open. Mon–Fri 10–4. Seasonal.

❼ Gloucester
Cape Ann Historical Museum
27 Pleasant Street. Tel: 978/283-0455; www.cape annhistoricalmuseum.org. Open Tue–Sat 10–5, Sun 1–4. Closed Feb.

Gloucester Maritime Heritage Center
23 Harbor Leap. Tel: 978/281-0470; www.gloucester maritimecenter.org. Open end May–early Sep daily 10–5.30. Off-season weekends 10–5.30.

❽ Rocky Neck and Beauport
Sleeper-McCann House Museum
75 Eastern Point Boulevard, Beauport, Gloucester. Tel: 978/283-0800; www.historicnewengland.org. Open Jun to mid-Sep Mon–Fri 10–4; daily to mid-Oct.

❾ Rockport
Rockport Art Association Gallery
12 Main Street. Tel: 978/546-6604; www.rock portartassn.org

Practical Information

⑩ Pigeon Cove
Paper House
52 Pigeon Hill Street. Tel:
978/546-2629; www.
paperhouserockport.com.
Open daily Apr–Oct, 9–6.

⑪ Essex
Shipbuilding Museum
28 Main Street. Tel: 978/
768-7541; www.essexship
buildingmuseum.org. Open
Jun to mid-Oct Wed–Sun
10–5; rest of year weekends.

⑫ Ipswich
Whipple House Museum
Route 1A, 1 South Village
Green. Tel: 978/356-2811;
www.ipswichmuseum.org.
Open May–Oct, Wed–Sat
10–4, Sun 1–4 (last tour 3).

Heard House Museum
Route 1A, 54 South Main
Street. Tel: 978/356-2811;
www.ipswichmuseum.org.
Open May–Oct, Wed–Sat
10–4, Sun 1–4 (last tour 3).

Castle Hill/Crane's Beach
290 Argilla Road. Tel: 978/
356-4351 (beach 4354);
www.thetrustees.org

**⑬ Plum Island and the
Parker River National
Wildlife Refuge**
Plum Island Turnpike,
Newburyport. Tel: 978/
465-5753; www.fws.gov/
northeast/parkerriver

⑭ Newburyport
Custom House Maritime
Museum
25 Water Street. Tel: 978/
462-8681; www.the
maritimesociety.org.
Mar–Dec, Tue–Sun 11–4.

Cushing House Museum
98 High Street. Tel: 978/
462-2681; www.newbury
hist.com. Open May–Oct,
Tue–Fri 10–4, Sat noon–4.

For history buffs
Abbot Hall
188 Washington Street.
Tel: 781/631-0000; www.
marblehead.org. Open
May–Oct Fri–Sun; Nov–Apr
Mon–Fri. Phone for hours.

Special to…
The House of the Seven
Gables
115 Derby Street. Tel: 978/
744-0991; www.7gables.

org. Open daily 10–5 (to 7,
Jul–Oct).

Woodmans of Essex
121 Main Street, Essex. Tel:
978/768-6451 or 800/649-
1773; www.woodmans.
com. Open summer 11–10
(closes 8/9pm in winter).

Recommended walks
Halibut Point State Park
Off Route 127, Rockport.
Tel: 978/546-2997;
www.mass.gov/dcr

Back to nature
Wolf Hollow
144 Essex Road, Ipswich.
Tel: 978/356-0216; www.
wolfhollowipswich.org

TOUR 3

ⓘ Cape Cod Chamber of
Commerce, Hyannis, MA
02601. Tel: 508/362-3225;
www.capecodchamber.org

ⓘ Cape Cod Canal
Chamber of Commerce,
70 Main Street, Buzzards
Bay, MA 02532.
Tel: 508/759-6000; www.
capecodcanalchamber.org

ⓘ Yarmouth Area
Chamber of Commerce,
424 Route 28, West
Yarmouth, MA 02673. Tel:
508/778-1008; www.
yarmouthcapecod.com

ⓘ Dennis Chamber of
Commerce, Routes 134/28,
West Dennis, MA 02760.
Tel: 508/398-3568;
www.dennischamber.com

ⓘ Brewster Chamber of
Commerce, Brewster
Town Hall, 2198 Main
Street, Brewster, MA
02631. Tel: 508/896-3500;
www.brewstercapecod.org

ⓘ Eastham Tourist
Information Booth, Route
6 at Governor Prence
Road, Eastham, MA 02642.
Tel: 508/255-3444; www.
easthamchamber.com
(seasonal).

ⓘ Wellfleet Chamber of
Commerce Information
Booth, off Route 6, South
Wellfleet, MA 02667.
Tel: 508/349-2510; www.
wellfleetchamber.

ⓘ Provincetown
Chamber of Commerce,
307 Commercial Street,
Provincetown, MA 02657.
Tel: 508/487-3424; www
ptownchamber.com

ⓘ Chatham Chamber of
Commerce, 533 Main
Street, Chatham, MA
02633. Tel: 508/945-5199;
www.chathaminfo.com.
Also at 2377 Main Street
(same telephone number
as above).

② Sandwich
Thomas Dexter Grist Mill
Water Street. Tel: 508/888-
4910 (town hall). Open
mid-Jun to mid-Sep, daily
10–4.45.

Hoxie House
18 Water Street. Tel: 508/
888-4910. Open mid-Jun to
mid-Sep, daily 10–4.45.

Thornton W. Burgess
Museum
4 Water Street (Route
130). Tel: 508/888-4668;
www.thorntonburgess.org.
Open Apr–Oct, Mon–Sat
10–4.

③ Barnstable
Sturgis Library
Route 6A. Tel: 508/362-
6636; www.sturgislibrary.
org. Call for hours.

④ Yarmouth
Captain Bangs Hallet
House
11 Strawberry Lane. Tel:
508/362-3021; www.hsoy.
org. Open Jun to mid-Oct,
Thu–Sun.

Winslow-Crocker House
250 Route 6A. Tel: 617/
227-3957, ext. 256; www.
historicnewengland.org.
Open Jun–Oct.

⑤ Dennis
Josiah Dennis Manse
Museum
Nobscusset Road and
Whig Street, Dennis. Tel:
508/385-2232; www.
dennishistsoc.org. Open
Jul–Aug. Phone for times.

Cape Playhouse
820 Main Street, Dennis.
Tel: 508/385-3838; www.
capeplayhouse.com. Open

summer Mon–Sat evenings,
matinees Wed, Thu. Children's
Theater Thu and Fri am.

Cape Cod Museum of Art
Route 6A, Dennis. Tel: 508/
385-4477; www.ccmoa.
org. Open May–Oct Tue–Sat
10–5, Sun noon–5.

⑥ Brewster
Brewster Historical
Society Museum
Route 6A, 3171 Main St.
Tel: 508/896-9521; www.
brewsterhistoricalsociety.
org. Open Thu–Sat 1–4.

New England Fire and
History Museum
1439 Main Street, Route
6A. Tel: 508/896-5711.
Open Jun to mid-Oct.

⑧ Eastham
Cape Cod National
Seashore
Salt Pond Visitor Center,
Route 6. Tel: 508/255-3421;
www.nps.gov/caco. Open
daily 9–5 (4.30 off season).

Oldest Windmill
Opposite Town Hall.
www.easthamhistorical.org.
Open Jul–Aug Mon–Sat
10–5, Sun 1–5.

⑫ Provincetown
Pilgrim Monument and
Provincetown Museum
High Pole Hill. Tel: 508/487-
1310; www.pilgrim-monu
ment.org. Open mid-Apr to
Oct daily 9–5 (later Jul and
Aug). Nov weekends.

⑬ Chatham
Chatham Lighthouse
Chatham Harbor.
Tel: 508/430-0628;
www.lighthouse.cc/
chatham. Call for details..

Special to…
Sandwich Glass Museum
129 Main Street. Tel: 508/
888-0251; www.sandwich
glassmuseum.org. Open
Feb–Mar, Wed–Sun 9.30–4;
Apr–Oct, daily 9.30–5.

For children
Heritage Museums and
Gardens
67 Grove Street. Tel: 508/
888-3300; www.heritage
museumsandgardens.org.
Open Apr–Dec daily 10–5.

i Tourist Information Office
12 Number on tour

Green Briar Nature Center & Jam Kitchen
6 Discovery Hill Road, East Sandwich. Tel: 508/888-6870; www.thornton burgess.org. *Open Jan–Mar, Tue–Sat 10–4; Apr–Dec, Mon–Sat 10–4, Sun 1–4.*

Cape Cod Museum of Natural History
Route 6A, Brewster. Tel: 508/896-3867; www.ccmnh.org. *Open Jun–Sep daily 9.30–4; Oct–May Wed–Sun 11–3 or 4.*

Scenic route
Cape Cod Central Railroad
252 Main Street, Hyannis. Tel: 508/771-3800; www.capetrain.com. *Scenic excursions daily May–Oct; also lunch and dinner trains.*

TOUR 4

i Greater Springfield CVB, 1441 Main Street, Springfield, MA 01103. Tel: 413/787-1548; www.valleyvisitor.com

i Riverfront Park Information Center, 1200 West Columbus Avenue, Springfield, MA 01115. Tel: 413/750-2980.

i Stockbridge Information Booth, Main Street, Stockbridge, MA 01262; www.stockbridgechamber.org

i Lenox Chamber of Commerce, 5 Walker Street, Lenox, MA 01240. Tel: 413/637-3646; www.lenox.org

i Pittsfield Visitor Information Center, 111 South Street, Pittsfield, MA 01201. Tel: 413/395-0105; www.berkshires.com

i Williamstown Information Booth, Routes 2 and 7.

i Williamstown Chamber of Commerce, 70 Denison Park Drive, Williamstown, MA 01267. Tel: 413/458-9077; www.williamstownchamber.com

i Shelburne Falls Village Information Center, 75 Bridge Street, Shelburne Falls, MA 01370. Tel: 413/625-2544; www.shelburnefalls.com

i Upper Pioneer Valley Visitors Center, 18 Miner Street (exit 26, I–91), Greenfield, MA 01301. Tel: 413/773-9393; www.mohawktrail.com

i Northampton Area Visitors Center, 99 Pleasant Street, Northampton, MA 01060. Tel: 413/584-1900; www.northampton uncommon.com

5 Stockbridge
Red Lion Inn
30 Main Street. Tel: 413/298-5545; www.redlioninn.com

Norman Rockwell Museum
Route 183. Tel: 413/298-4100; www.nrm.org. *Open daily 10–5 (4 on weekdays Nov–Apr).*

Chesterwood
Off Route 183. Tel: 413/298-3579; www.chesterwood.org. *Open May–Oct, daily 10–5.*

Naumkeag
Prospect Hill Road. Tel: 413/298-3239; www.thetrustees.org. *Open end May to mid-Oct, daily 10–5.*

Berkshire Botanical Garden
Junction Routes 183 and 102. Tel: 413/298-3926; www.berkshirebotanical.org. *Open May–Oct, daily 10–5.*

7 Lenox
The Mount–Edith Wharton Home
2 Plunkett Street. Tel: 413/637-1899; www.edithwharton.org. *Open late May–Oct, daily 9–5.*

8 Arrowhead
780 Holmes Road, Pittsfield. Tel: 413/442-1793; www.mobydick.org. *Open May–Oct. daily 9.30–5 or by appointment.*

9 Hancock Shaker Village
Junction Routes 20 and 41, Pittsfield. Tel: 413/443-0188; www.hancockshaker village.org. *Open end May to mid-Oct, daily 9.30–5; rest of year 10–4.*

10 Williamstown
Sterling and Francine Clark Art Institute
225 South Street. Tel: 413/458-2303; www.clarkart.edu. *Open Tue–Sun 10–5; also Mon Jul–Aug.*

Williams College Museum of Art
Main Street. Tel: 413/597-2429; www.wcma.org. *Open Tue–Sat 10–5, Sun 1–5.*

Williamstown Theatre Festival
Williams College. Tel: 413/597-3400; www.wtfestival.org. *Open Jul–Aug.*

11 North Adams
MASS MoCA
87 Marshall Street. Tel: 413/664-4481; www.massmoca.org. *Open Wed–Mon 11–5 (daily until 6 Jul–Aug).*

13 Deerfield
The Street. Tel: 413/774-5581; www.historic-deefield.org. *Open Apr–Dec daily 9.30–4.30.*

Emily Dickinson Museum
280 Main Street, Amherst. Tel: 413/542-8161; www.emilydickinsonmuseum.org

Special to...
Basketball Hall of Fame/Naismith Memorial
1000 West Columbus Avenue, Springfield. Tel: 413/781-6500; www.hoophall.com. *Open daily 10–5.*

For children
Six Flags New England
Route 159, Agawam. Tel: 413/786-9300; www.sixflags.com. *Open Jun–Oct, daily, hours vary.*

Magic Wings Butterfly Conservatory and Garden
Routes 5 and 10, South Deerfield. Tel: 413/665-2805; www.magicwings.com. *Open all year daily 9–5 (to 6 end May–early Sep).*

For history buffs
Col John Ashley House
Cooper Hill Road, Ashley Falls. Tel: 413/298-3239; *Open Jun to mid-Oct, Sat–Sun 10–5.*

Back to nature
Barthlomew's Cobble
Weatogue Road off Route 7A, Ashley Falls. Tel: 413/229-8600; www.thetrustees.org. *Open daily dawn–dusk, museum 9–4.30. Closed Sun, Mon Dec–Mar*

Pleasant Valley Wildlife Sanctuary
472 West Mountain Road. Tel: 413/637-0320; www.massaudbon.org. *Open Tue–Fri 9–5, Sat–Sun 10–4 (also Mon in summer).*

TOUR 5

i Boston Common Visitor Information Center, 147 Tremont Street. Tel: 617/536-4100; www.bostonusa.com, www.thefreedomtrail.org

i Boston National Historical Park Visitor Center, 15 State Street. Tel: 617/242-5642; www.nps.gov/bost

i Charlestown Navy Yard Visitor Center. Constitution Road, Charlestown. Tel: 617/242-5601; www.nps.gov/bost

2 State House
Beacon Street. Tel: 617/727-3676; www.sec.state.ma.us/trs. *Tours weekdays.*

9 Old South Meeting House
310 Washington Street. Tel: 617/482-6439; www.oldsouthmeeting house.org. *Open daily.*

10 Old State House
Corner of State and Washington streets. Tel: 617/720-1713; www.bostonhistory.org. *Museum open daily 9–5 (6 Jul–Aug).*

11 Faneuil Hall
Merchants Row. Tel: 617/242-5642; www.thefree domtrail.org. *Open daily 9–5.*

Practical Information

☞ Tourist Information Office
🔢 Number on tour

🔢 Paul Revere House
19 North Square. Tel:
617/523-2338; www.paul
reverehouse.org. Open
daily 9.30–4.15 (5.15 summer). Closed Mon, Jan–Mar.

🔢 USS Constitution
Pier 1, Charlestown Navy
Yard. Tel: 617/242-5670/
5671; www.oldironsides.
com. Open Tue–Sun
10–3.30 (Thu–Sun only
Nov–Mar). Museum daily
9–6 (10–5 in winter).

**🔢 Bunker Hill
Monument**
Monument Square,
Charlestown. Tel: 617/242-
5641; www.nps.gov/bost.
Open daily 9–5.

Special to…
Omni Parker House
60 School Street. Tel: 617/
227-8600; www.omni
hotels.com

TOUR 6

☞ Boston Common
Visitor Information Center,
147 Tremont Street.
Tel: 617/536-4100;
www.bostonusa.com

☞ Boston National
Historical Park Visitor
Center, 15 State Street.
Tel: 617/242-5642;
www.nps.gov/bost

**❶ New England
Aquarium**
Central Wharf. Tel: 617/
973-5200; www.neaq.org.
Open daily 9–5 (6 Sat–Sun).

❸ Faneuil Hall
See Tour 5.

**❻ Otis House
Museum**
141 Cambridge Street.
Tel: 617/227-3956; www.
historicnewengland.org.
Open Wed–Sun 11–4.30.

❼ Black Heritage Trail
Museum of Afro-American
History/Abiel Smith
School
46 Joy Street. Tel: 617/725-
0022; www.afroam
museum.org. Open daily
10–4. Closed Sun.

African Meeting House
8 Smith Court. Tel: 617/
725-0022; www.afroam
museum.org. Closed for
renovations until 2007.

**❽ Nichols House
Museum**
55 Mount Vernon Street.
Tel: 617/227-6993; www.
nicholshousemuseum.org.
Open Tue–Sat noon–4
(Thu–Sat only Nov–Apr).

Special to…
Durgin-Park
340 Faneuil Hall Market-
place. Tel: 617/227-2038;
www.durgin-park.com

Scenic routes
Boston Duck Tours
Prudential Center,
Huntington Avenue or
Museum of Science. Tel:
617/267-3825; www.
bostonducktours.com.
Apr–Nov.

TOUR 7

☞ Cambridge Visitor
Information Booth,
Harvard Square,
Cambridge, MA 02139.
Tel: 617/441-2884;
www.cambridge-usa.org

☞ Harvard Information
Center, Holyoke Center
Arcade, 1350
Massachusetts Avenue,
Cambridge, MA 02138.
Tel: 617/495-1573;
www.harvard.edu

**❼ Fogg and Busch-
Reisinger Art
Museums**
32 Quincy Street.
Tel: 617/495-9400. Open
Mon–Sat 10–5, Sun 1–5.

**❽ Arthur M. Sackler
Museum**
485 Broadway.
Tel: 617/495-9400. Open
Mon–Sat 10–5, Sun 1–5.

❾ Memorial Hall
45 Quincy Street for
Sanders Theater perfor-
mances. Tel: 617/496-2222.
Transept open weekdays.

**🔟 Museums of
Natural History**
26 Oxford Street. Tel: 617/
495-3045. Open daily 9–5.

🔢 Brattle Street
Cambridge Historical
Society
159 Brattle Street.
Tel: 617/547-4252;
www.cambridgehistory.org.
Open Tue, Thu 2–5.

🔢 Longfellow House
105 Brattle Street.
Tel: 617/876-4491;
www.nps.gov/long. Open
Tue–Sat 10–4.30

TOUR 8

☞ Hartford Civic Center,
1 Civic Center Plaza,
Hartford, CT 06103.
Tel: 860/249-6333;
www.enjoyhartford.com

❷ Old State House
800 Main Street. Tel: 860/
522-6766; www.ctosh.org.
Open Mon–Sat 10–4.

**❸ St Paul Travelers
Tower**
1 Tower Square Tel: 860/
277-4208. Tours mid-May to
Oct, Mon–Fri 10–2.30.

**❹ Wadsworth
Atheneum**
600 Main Street. Tel: 860/
278-2670; www.wads
worthatheneum.org.
Open Wed–Fri 11–5,
Sat–Sun 10–5.

**❼ Bushnell Park
Carousel**
Jewell Street. Tel: 860/585-
5411; www.thecarousel
museum.org. Open late
Apr–late Oct, Tue–Sun 11–5.

❽ State Capitol
210 Capitol Avenue. Tel:
860/240-0222; www.
cga.ct.gov/capitoltours.
Tours Mon–Fri 9.15–1.15
(2.15 Jul–Aug); also Sat
10.15–2.15 Apr–Oct.

**❾ Museum of
Connecticut History**
231 Capitol Avenue.
Tel: 860/617-6535; www.
cslib.org/museum. Open
Mon–Fri 9–5, Sat 9–2.

**🔟 Mark Twain House
and Museum**
351 Farmington Avenue.
Tel: 860/247-0998;
www.marktwainhouse.org.
Open Mon–Sat 9.30–5.30,

Sun noon–5.30. Closed Tue
Jan–Apr.

**🔢 Harriet Beecher
Stowe Center**
77 Forest Street. Tel: 860/
525-9258; www.harriet
beecherstowecenter.org.
Open Mon–Sat, 9.30–4.30,
Sun noon–4.30. Closed Mon
mid-Oct to Nov, Jan– May.

**🔢 Connecticut
Historical Society
Museum**
1 Elizabeth Street. Tel: 860/
236-5621; www.chs.org.
Open Tue–Sun, noon–5;
Library Tue–Sat 10–5.

**🔢 Noah Webster
House**
227 South Main Street,
West Hartford. Tel: 860/
521-5362; www.noah
websterhouse.org. Open
Thu–Mon 1–4.

Back to nature
Elizabeth Park Rose
Garden
Prospect Avenue. Tel: 860/
231-9443; www.elizabeth
park.org. Open daily.

For children
Science Center of
Connecticut
950 Trout Brook Drive,
West Hartford. Tel: 860/
231-2824; www.science
centerct.org. Open Tue–Sat
10–5, Sun noon–5. Also Mon
in summer.

TOUR 9

☞ Greater New Haven
Convention and Visitors
Bureau, 169 Orange Street,
New Haven, CT 06510.
Tel: 203/777-8550;
www.newhavencvb.org

☞ Info New Haven,
corner of College and
Chapel, New Haven, CT
06510. Tel: 203/774-9494.

☞ Yale University Visitor
Information Center, 149
Elm Street, New Haven, CT
06520. Tel: 203/432-2300;
www.yale.edu

**❺ Yale University Art
Gallery**
1111 Chapel Street at York

Practical Information

Street. Tel: 203/432-0600;
www.artgallery.yale.edu.
*Open Tue–Sat 10–5,
Sun 1–6.*

6 Yale Center for British Art

1080 Chapel Street. Tel:
203/432-2800; www.yale.
edu/ycba. *Open Tue–Sat
10–5, Sun noon–5.*

7 Yale Repertory Theatre

Corner of Chapel and York
streets. Tel: 203/432-1234;
www.yale.edu/yalerep.
Open Sep–May.

11 Beinecke Rare Book and Manuscript Library

121 Wall Street Tel: 203/
432-2977; www.library.
yale.edu/beinecke. *Open
Mon–Thu 8.30–8, Fri 8.30–
5, Sat 10–5. Closed Sun.*

TOUR 10

i Greater Hartford
Convention and Visitors
Center, 1 Civic Center
Plaza, Hartford, CT 06103.
Tel: 860/249-6333;
www.enjoyhartford.com

i Litchfield Hills
Information Booth, Route
202, On-the-Green,
Litchfield, CT 06759.
Tel: 860/567-4506;
www.litchfieldhills.com

1 Litchfield

Tapping Reeve House and Law School
Route 63 South, 82 South
Street. Tel: 860/567-4501;
www.litchfieldhistorical
society.org. *Open Apr–Nov,
Tue–Sat 11–5, Sun 1–5.*

Litchfield History Museum
7 South Street. Tel: 860/
567-4501 www.litchfield
historicalsociety.org. *Open
mid-Apr to mid-Nov, Tue–Sat
11–5, Sun 1–5.*

3 Lake Waramaug

Hopkins Vineyard
25 Hopkins Road, New
Preston. Tel: 860/868-7954;
www.hopkinsvineyard.com.
*Open May–Dec daily;
Jan–Feb Fri–Sun; Mar–Apr
Wed–Sun. Phone for times.*

4 Kent

Sloane-Stanley Museum and Kent Furnace
Route 7. Tel: 860/927-3849;
www.chc.state.ct.us/sloane
stanleymuseum. *Open
Jun–Oct, Wed–Sun 10–4.*

Connecticut Antique Machinery Association Museum
Route 7. Tel: 860/927-0050;
www.ctamachinery.com.
*Open May–Sep, Wed–Sun
10–4.*

8 Cornwall Bridge to West Cornwall

Clarke's Outdoors
163 Route 7, West Corn-
wall. Tel: 860/672-6365;
www.clarkeoutdoors.com.
Open mid-Mar to Dec.

9 Lime Rock Park

Routes 7 and 112, Lake-
ville. Tel: 860/435-5000;
www.limerock.com.
Regular meets Apr–Nov.

Special to…
White Flower Farm
Route 63. Tel: 860/567-
8789; www.whiteflower
farm.com. *Open daily
Apr–Oct, daily 9–5.30.*

The Silo
44 Upland Road, New
Milford. Tel: 860/355-0300;
www.hunthillfarmtrust.org.
Open Wed–Mon 10–5.

Cornwall Bridge Pottery
Route 7, between Routes
45 and 4. Tel: 860/672-
6545; www.cbpots.com.
*Open Mon–Fri noon–5,
Sat–Sun 10.30–5.30.*

Recommended walks
Kent Falls State Park
Route 7. Tel: 860/927-3238;
www.dep.state.ct.us.
Open daily 8am–dusk.

TOUR 11

i Greater New Haven
Convention and Visitors
Bureau, 169 Orange
Street, New Haven, CT
06511; www.newhaven
cvb.org. Tel: 203/777-8550.

i Info New Haven,
corner College and Chapel
streets. Tel: 203/774-9494.

1 Branford

Nathaniel Harrison House
124 Main Street. Tel: 203/
488-4828; www.branford-
history.org. *Phone for hours.*

3 Guilford

Henry Whitfield State Museum
248 Old Whitfield Street.
Tel: 203/453-2457; www.
whitfieldmuseum.com.
*Open Apr to mid-Dec,
Wed–Sun 10–4.30.*

Hyland House
84 Boston Street. Tel: 203/
453-9477; www.hyland
house.com. *Open Jun–Oct,
Tue–Sat 10–4.30, Sun
noon–4.30.*

Thomas Griswold House Museum
171 Boston Street. Tel:
203/453-3176; www.
thomasgriswoldhouse.com.
*Open Jun–Sep, Tue–Sun
11–4; Oct weekends.*

4 Madison

Hammonasset Beach State Park
Route 1. Tel: 203/245-2785;
www.dep.state.ct.us. *Open
daily 8–sunset.*

5 Old Saybrook

General William Hart House
350 Main Street. Tel: 860/
388-2622; www.old
saybrookhistoricalsociety.
com. *Open limited hours.*

6 Essex

Connecticut River Museum
67 Main Street, Steamboat
Dock. Tel: 860/767-8269;
www.ctrivermuseum.org.
Open Tue–Sun 10–5.

Pratt House Museum
19 West Avenue. Tel: 860/
767-1191; www.essexct.
com. *Open Jun–Sep,
Sat–Sun 1–4.*

7 East Haddam

Goodspeed Opera House
Route 82. Tel: 860/873-
8664; www.goodspeed.org.
Open Apr–Dec, Wed–Sun.

Nathan Hale Schoolhouse
Main Street. *Open end
May–early Sep, Sat–Sun
noon–4.*

8 Gillette Castle

Gillette Castle State Park
67 River Road. Tel: 860/
526-2336. *Open, castle: Jun
to mid-Oct, daily 10–5; park:
daily 8am–sunset..*

9 Old Lyme

Florence Griswold Museum
96 Lyme Street. Tel: 860/
434-5542; www.florence
griswoldmuseum.org. *Open
Tue–Sat 10–5, Sun, 1–5.*

Lyme Academy College of Fine Arts
84 Lyme Street. Tel: 860/
434-5232; www.lyme
academy.edu. *Open
Mon–Sat 10–4.*

10 New London

Hempsted Houses
11 Hempsted Street.
Tel: 860/443-7949 or
860/247-8996;
www.hartnet.org/als. *Open
mid-May to mid-Oct,
Thu–Sun noon–4.*

US Eagle (when in port)
US Coast Guard Academy,
Mohegan Avenue. Tel: 860/
444-8270; www.uscga.edu/
eagle. *Open Fri–Sun 1–5.
Museum daily 9–5.*

Lyman-Allyn Art Museum
625 Williams Street.
Tel: 860/443-2545;
www.lymanallyn.org.
*Open Tue–Sat 10–5,
Sun 1–5.*

Monte Cristo Cottage
325 Pequot Avenue. Tel:
860/443-0051 or 860/443-
5378; www.theoneill.org.
*Open end May–early Sep,
Tue–Sun 10–5; early Sep to
mid-Oct, Thu–Sun 1–5.*

Eugene O'Neill Theater Center
305 Great Neck Road,
Waterford. Tel: 860/443-
5378; www.theoneill.org

11 USS Nautilus

Naval Submarine Base, 1
Crystal Lake Road, Groton.
Tel: 860/694-3174; www.
ussnautilus.org. *Open daily
9–5, Tue 1–5; Nov to mid-
May 9–4, closed Tue.*

Practical Information

[i] Tourist Information Office
[12] Number on tour

[12] Noank
Abbott's Lobster-in-the-Rough
117 Pearl Street.
Tel: 860/536-7719; www.
abbotts-lobster.com. *Open Jun–Aug, daily; weekends in May and Sep to mid-Oct.*

[13] Mystic
Mystic Seaport
75 Greenmanville Avenue.
Tel: 860/572-5315; www.
mysticseaport.org. *Open daily 9–5, winter 10–4.*

Mystic Aquarium
55 Coogan Boulevard. Tel:
860/572-5955; www.mystic
aquarium.org. *Open daily 9–6 (10–5 Mon–Fri winter).*

[14] Stonington
Old Lighthouse Museum
7 Water Street. Tel: 860/
535-1440; www.
stoningtonhistory.org. *Open May–Oct, daily 10–5.*

Scenic routes
The Essex Steam Train
and Riverboat Ride
Valley Railroad, 1 Railroad
Avenue (off Route 9). Tel:
860/767-0103; www.essex
steamtrain.com. *Open May–Dec.*

Special to…
Mashantucket Pequot
Museum and Research
Center
110 Pequot Trail, Mashan-
tucket. Tel: 800/411-9671;
www.pequotmuseum.org.
Open daily 10–4.

For history buffs
Fort Griswold Battlefield
State Park
57 Fort Street, Groton. Tel:
860/449-6877 (seasonal);
www.dep.state.ct.us. *Open daily, 8am–sunset.*

For children
Denison Pequotsepos
Nature Center
109 Pequotsepos Road.
Tel: 860/536-1216;
www.dpnc.org. *Open Mon–Sat 9–5, Sun 10–4.*

Ocean Beach Park
1225 Ocean Avenue, New
London. Tel: 860/447-3031;
www.ocean-beach-park.
com. *Open late May–early Sep, daily 9am–11pm.*

TOUR 12

[i] Providence and
Warwick Convention and
Visitors Bureau, 1 West
Exchange Street,
Providence, RI 02903. Tel:
401/274-1636 or 800/233-
1636; www.pwcvb.com

**[3] Rhode Island School
of Design**
Museum of Art
224 Benefit Street. Tel:
401/454-6500; www.risd.
edu. *Open Tue–Sun 10–5.*

**[4] Providence
Athenaeum**
251 Benefit Street.
Tel: 401/421-6970; www.
providenceathenaeum.org.
Open Mon–Thu 9–7, Fri–Sat 9–5, Sun 1–4 (Jun–Aug, Sat 9–1, closed Sun).

**[5] David Winton Bell
Gallery**
64 College Street. Tel: 401/
863-2932; www.brown.
edu/Facilities/David_Winton
_Bell_Gallery. *Open Mon–
Fri 11–4, Sat and Sun 1–4.*

[6] Libraries
John Hay Library
Prospect and College
streets. Tel: 401/863-2146.
Open Mon–Fri 9–5.

[7] Brown University
45 Prospect Street,
College Hill. Tel: 401/863-
1000; www.brown.edu.
Tours Mon–Fri, some Sats.

[8] Benefit Street
Governor Stephen
Hopkins House
Benefit/Hopkins streets.
Tel: 401/421-0694. *Open Apr–Dec, Wed and Sat 1–4.*

**[10] John Brown House
Museum**
52 Power Street. Tel: 401/
273-7507; www.rihs.org.
Open Apr–Dec, Tue–Sat 10–4; Jan–Mar, Fri–Sat 10.30–4.30.

TOUR 13

[i] Gateway Information
Center, 23 America's Cup
Avenue, Newport, RI
02840. Tel: 401/845-9123;
www.gonewport.com

**[1] Museum of
Newport History**
Thames Street/Washington
Square. Tel: 401/841-8770;
www.newporthistorical.
org. *Open mid-Apr to mid-Dec, Thu–Sat 10–4, Sun 1–4 (daily 10–4 summer).*

**[4] Wanton-Lyman-
Hazard House**
17 Broadway. Tel: 401/846-
0813; www.newport
historical.org. *Open by tour only; phone for information.*

[5] Touro Synagogue
85 Touro Street. Tel: 401/
847-4794; www.touro
synagogue.org. *Open for tours May–Jun, early Sep–Oct Mon–Fri 1–3, Sun 11–3; Jul–early Sep Mon–Fri, Sun 10–5; Nov–Feb limited.*

**[6] The Newport
Historical Society**
82 Touro Street. Tel: 401/
846-0813; www.newport
historical.org. *Open Mon–Fri 9.30–4.30, Sat am only.*

**[10] The Redwood
Library**
50 Bellevue Avenue.
Tel: 401/847-0292; www.
redwoodlibrary.org. *Open Tue–Thu 9.30–8; Mon, Fri, Sat 9.30–5.30, Sun 1–5.*

**[11] Newport Art
Museum**
76 Bellevue Avenue. Tel:
401/848-8200; www.new
portartmuseum.com. *Open Mon–Sat 10–5, Sun noon–5 (4 early Sep–end May).*

**[12] Newport Casino
and the International
Tennis Hall of Fame**
194 Bellevue Avenue.
Tel: 401/849-3990;
www.tennisfame.com.
Open daily 9.30–5. Call during tournaments.

[13] Kingscote Mansion
Bellevue Avenue. Tel: 401/
847-1000; www.newport
mansions.org. *Open end May to mid-Oct, daily 10–5.*

[14] The Elms
Bellevue Avenue. Tel: 401/
847-1000; www.newport
mansions.org. *Open early Apr–Dec daily 10–5.*

Chepstow
Narragansett Avenue.
Tel: 401/847-1000. *Open in season, by reservation only.*

[15] Château-sur-Mer
Bellevue Avenue. Tel: 401/
847-1000; www.newport
mansions.org. *Open early Apr to mid-Oct daily 10–5; Jan–early Apr limited.*

[16] Vernon Court
National Museum of
American Illustration
Bellevue Avenue. Tel: 401/
851-8949; www.american
illustration.org. *Open by reservation only.*

[17] The Breakers
Ochre Point Avenue. Tel:
401/847-1000; www.new
portmansions.org. *Open daily 9–5 (10–4 Jan–Apr).*

[18] Rosecliff
Bellevue Avenue.
Tel: 401/847-1000; www.
newportmansions.org.
Open early Apr to mid-Nov, daily 10–5; Jan–early Apr, limited opening.

[19] Astors' Beechwood
580 Bellevue Avenue.
Tel: 401/846-3772; www.
astorsbeechwood.com.
Open daily 10–4. May close early for special events.

[20] Marble House
Bellevue Avenue. Tel: 401/
847-1000; www.newport
mansions.org. *Open mid-Apr to Dec, daily 10–5.*

[21] Belcourt Castle
657 Bellevue Avenue. Tel:
401/846-0669; www.bel
courtcastle.com. *Open most of year, call for info.*

[22] Rough Point
Bellevue Avenue. Tel: 401/
849-7300; www.newport
restoration.org. *Open mid-Apr–early Nov. Call for times.*

Special to…
Fort Adams State Park
Ocean Drive. Tel: 401/847-
2400; www.riparks.com.
Open daily dawn–dusk.

Museum of Yachting
Tel: 401/847-1018; www.
museumofyachting.org.
Open mid-May to Oct, daily.

Scenic Routes

Cliff Walk
Memorial Bouelvard. Tel:
401/849-8048; www.new
portcliffwalk.com. *All year.*

[i] Route 7, Bennington,
VT 05201.
Tel: 802/447-3311;
www.bennington.com

❶ The Bennington Museum
West Main Street. Tel: 802/
447-1571; www.
benningtonmuseum.org.
Open Thu–Tue 10–5.

❷ Bennington Center for the Arts
44 Gypsy Lane. Tel: 802/
442-7158; www.benning
toncenterforthearts.org.
Open Tue–Sun 10–5.

❹ Bennington Battle Monument
Monument Circle, Old
Bennington, off Route 9.
Tel: 802/447-0550; www.
historicvermont.org. *Open
mid-Apr to Oct, daily 9–5.*

❺ Hemmings Sunoco Station
216 Main Street.
Tel: 802/447-9652;
www.hemmings.com.
Open daily 7am–9pm.

❽ Potters' Yard
324 County Street.
Tel: 802/447-7531; www.
benningtonpotters.com

❿ Park-McCullough House
Park and West streets,
North Bennington. Tel:
802/442-5441; www.park
mccullogh.org. *Open for
tours mid-May to mid-Oct,
daily 10–3. Grounds open
most of year.*

[i] Route 7, Bennington,
VT 05201. Tel: 802/447-
3311; www.bennington.
com

[i] The Green, Chester,
VT 05143.
Tel: 802/875-2939;
www.okemovalleyvt.org

❶ Arlington
Norman Rockwell
Exhibition
Route 7A. Tel: 802/375-
6423; www.vmga.org.
*Open May–Oct, daily 9–5;
Nov–Apr, daily 10–4.*

❷ Mt Equinox
Skyline Drive
Toll Road, Route 7A. Tel:
802/362-1114; www.equi
noxmountain.com. *Open
May–Oct 9am–10pm.*

American Museum of Fly Fishing
Route 7A, 4104 Main
Street, Manchester.
Tel: 802/362-3300; www.
amff.com. *Open daily 10–4.*

❸ Hildene
Robert Todd Lincoln's
Hildene
Route 7A, Manchester. Tel:
802/362-1788; www.hil
dene.org. *Open daily 9.30–
4.30 (11–3 Nov–May).*

❻ Bromley Mountain Ski Area
Bromley Mountain, Route
11. Tel: 802/824-5522;
www.bromley.com

❽ Weston
Vermont Country Store
Route 100. Tel: 802/824-
3184; www.vermont
countrystore.com. *Open
daily 9–5.30.*

Weston Playhouse
On the Green. Tel: 802/
824-5288; www.weston
playhouse.org. *Open late
Jun to mid-Oct.*

❾ Ludlow
Okemo Mountain Resort
77 Okemo Ridge Road.
Tel: 802/228-4041;
www.okemo.com

❿ Chester
Green Mountain Railroad
54 Depot Street, Bellows
Falls. Tel: 800/707-3530;
www.rails-vt.com. *Open
late Jun to mid-Oct, daily.*

⓫ Grafton
Grafton Village Cheese
Company
533 Townshend Road.
Tel: 800/843-2221; www.
graftonvillagecheese.com.

*Open Mon–Fri 8–4, Sat–Sun
10–4.*

❷ Newfane
Historical Society Museum
of Windham County
Tel: 802/365-4148; www.
newfane.com/historical.
*Open late May to mid-Oct,
Wed–Sun noon–5.*

❸ Brattleboro
Museum and Art Center
10 Vernon Street. Tel: 802/
257-0124; www.brattle
boromuseum.org. *Open
Apr–Feb, Wed–Mon 11–5.*

[i] Rutland Chamber of
Commerce, Routes 4 and
7 (seasonal) and 256
North Main Street,
Rutland, VT 05701.
Tel: 802/773-2747;
www.rutlandvermont.com

❶ Norman Rockwell Museum of Vermont
Route 4E. Tel: 802/773-
6095; www.norman
rockwellvt.com. *Open daily
9–5 (4 in winter).*

❷ Bethel
White River National
Fish Hatchery
Route 107, 2086 River
Street. Tel: 802/234-5400;
www.fws.gov. *Open daily
8–3.*

❸ Quechee and Quechee Gorge
Simon Pearce Glass
Main Street. Tel: 802/295-
2711; www.simonpearce.
com. *Open daily 9–9.*

❹ Woodstock
Marsh-Billings-Rockefeller
National Historic Park
Route 12. Tel: 802/457-
3368; www.nps.gov/mabi.
*Open late May–Oct, daily
10–5.*

Billings Farm and Museum
Route 12. Tel: 802/457-
2355; www.billingsfarm.
org. *Open Apr–Oct, daily
10–5; Nov, Dec weekends.*

❺ Bridgewater
Long Trail Brewing
Company
Junction Route 4 and
100A, Bridgewater

Corners. Tel: 802/672-
5011; www.longtrail.com

❻ Plymouth
President Calvin Coolidge
State Historic Site
Tel: 802/672-3773;
www.historicvermont.org.
*Open end May to mid-Oct
daily 9.30–5.*

Frog City Cheese
106 Messer Hill Road.
Tel: 802/672-3650;
www.frogcitycheese.com.
Open daily 9.30–5.

Green Mountain Sugar House
820 Route 100 North,
Ludlow. Tel: 800/643-9338;
www.gmsh.com. *Open daily
9–6.*

Special to...
Crowley Cheese
Healdville. Tel: 802/259-
2340; www.crowley
cheese.com. *Shop open
daily; factory open Mon–Fri.*

Recommended walks
Green Mountain Club
Route 100 between Stowe
and Waterbury. Tel: 802/
244-7037; www.green
mountainclub.org. *Open
Mon–Fri (daily in summer).*

For history buffs
Joseph Smith Birthplace
Memorial
Dairy Hill Road. Tel: 802/
763-7742. *Open daily May–
Oct 9–7; Nov–Apr 9–5.*

[i] Lake Champlain
Regional Chamber of
Commerce, 60 Main
Street, Burlington, VT
05401. Tel: 802/863-3489;
www.vermont.org

[i] Addison County
Chamber of Commerce, 2
Court Street, Middlebury,
VT 05753. Tel: 802/388-
7951 or 800/733-8376;
www.midvermont.com

[i] Stowe Area
Association, Main Street,
Stowe, VT 05672.
Tel: 802/253-7321 or
877/GO STOWE;
www.gotostowe.com

Practical information

[i] Tourist Information Office
[12] Tour Number

❶ Shelburne

Shelburne Farms
1611 Harbor Road. Tel:
802/985-8686; www.shel
burnefarms.org. *Open mid-May to mid-Oct, daily 10–5.*

Shelburne Museum
Route 7. Tel: 802/985-3346;
www.shelburnemuseum.
org. *Open May–Oct 10–5.*

Vermont Teddy Bear Company
Route 7. Tel: 802/985-3001;
www.vermontteddybear.
com. *Tours daily 9.30–5
(10–4 Nov–Apr).*

❷ Charlotte

Vermont Wildflower Farm
3488 Ethan Allen Highway.
Tel: 802/425-3641; www.
vermontwildflowerfarm.
com. *Open Apr–Oct, daily
10–5; Nov–Dec, weekends.*

❸ Ferrisburgh

Rokeby Museum
4334 Route 7. Tel: 802/
877-3406; www.rokeby.
org. *Open mid-May to
mid-Oct, Thu–Sun.*

❹ Vergennes

Lake Champlain Maritime Museum
4472 Basin Harbor Road.
Tel: 802/475-2022; www.
lcmm.org. *Open mid-Jun to
mid-Oct, Wed–Sun 11–6.*

❺ Middlebury

Henry Sheldon Museum of Vermont History
1 Park Street. Tel: 802/388-
2117; www.henrysheldon
museum.org. *Open daily
10–5. Closed Sun, Mon
Sep–Jun.*

Vermont State Craft Center at Frog Hollow
1 Mill Street, Frog Hollow.
Tel: 802/388-3177; www.
froghollow.org. *Open Mon–
Sat 10–5.30, Sun noon–5.*

❾ Waitsfield

Vermont Icelandic Horse Farm
3061 North Fayston Road,
Fayston. Tel: 802/496-7141;
www.icelandichorses.com.
*Open daily. Call ahead for
trail ride reservations.*

❿ Waterbury

Ben and Jerry's Ice Cream Factory
Route 100, Waterbury.
Tel: 802/882-1240;
www.benjerry.com. *Open
daily, June 9–6, Jul–Aug 9–9,
Sep–late Oct 9–7, late
Oct–May 10–6.*

Lake Champlain Chocolates
Route 100, Waterbury
Center. Tel: 802/241-4150;
www.lakechamplainchoco
lates.com. *Open daily 9–6.*

Cold Hollow Cider Mill
Route 100. Tel: 802/244-
8771 or 800/327-7537;
www.coldhollow.com.
Open daily 8–6 (7 Jul–Oct).

⓫ Stowe

Stowe Mountain Resort
5781 Mountain Road.
Tel: 802/253-3000;
www.stowe.com

For children

Spirit of Ethan Allen III
Departs from Burlington
Boathouse, College Street,
Burlington. Tel: 802/862-
8300; www.soea.com. *Boat
trips mid-May to mid-Oct.*

Waterfront Boat Rentals
Burlington. Tel: 802/864-
4858; www.waterfront
boatrentals.com

Special to…

University of Vermont Morgan Horse Farm
74 Battell Drive, Weybridge,
off Route 23. Tel: 802/388-
2011. *Open May–Oct, daily
9–4.*

TOUR 18

[i] 500 Market Street,
Portsmouth, NH 03802.
Tel: 603/436-1118; www.
portsmouthchamber.org

❸ John Paul Jones House

43 Middle Street (corner
of State Street). Tel: 603/
436-8420; www.ports
mouthhistory.org. *Open
end May to mid-Oct, daily
11–5.*

❺ Rundlet-May House

364 Middle Street. Tel: 603/
436-3205; www.historic
newengland.org. *Open
Jun–Oct, 1st Sat of month,
11–4.*

❼ Governor Langdon House

143 Pleasant Street. Tel:
603/436-3205; www.
historicnewengland.org.
*Open Jun to mid-Oct,
Fri–Sun 11–4.*

❿ Wentworth Gardner House

50 Mechanic Street.
Tel: 603/436-4406; www.
wentworthgardner
andlear.org. *Open mid-Jun
to mid-Oct, Tue–Sun 1–4.*

⓬ Strawbery Banke

Marcy Street, On the
Waterfront. Tel: 603/433-
1106; www.strawbery
banke.org. *Open May–Oct,
Mon–Sat 10–5, Sun noon–5;
Nov–Apr Sat 10–2, Sun
noon–2.*

⓭ Warner House

150 Daniel Street. Tel: 603/
436-5909; www.warner
house.org. *Open Jun–Oct,
Mon–Sat 11–4, Sun noon–4.*

⓯ Moffatt-Ladd House

154 Market Street. Tel: 603/
436-8221; www.moffatt
ladd.org. *Open mid-Jun to
mid-Oct, Mon–Sat 11–5,
Sun 1–5.*

Recommended trip

**Vaughn Cottage Memorial/
Celia Thaxter Museum**
Star Island. Tel: 603/430-
6272. *Open mid-Jun to
mid-Sep, museum daily 1–3.*

For children

USS *Albacore*
Albacore Park, 600 Market
Street. Tel: 603/436-3680;
www.ussalbacore.org.
*Open end May to mid-Oct,
daily 9.30–5; mid-Oct to end
May Thu–Mon 9.30–4.30.*

TOUR 19

[i] Chamber of
Commerce booth, exit 28,
off I-93. Tel: 603/726-3804,
800/237-2307; www.
watervillevalleyregion.com

[i] Visitor Center, North
Woodstock, NH 03262,
exit 32 off I-93. Tel:
603/745-8720 or 800/346-
3687; www.visitwhite-
mountains.com

❶ North Woodstock

Clark's Trading Post
Route 3, Lincoln. Tel: 603/
745-8913; www.clarks
tradingpost.com. *Open late
Jun to mid-Oct daily; weekends spring and fall.*

❷ Franconia Notch

Franconia Notch State Park
Tel: 603/823-8800; www.
franconianotchstatepark.
com

The Flume Visitor Center
Route 3. Tel: 603/745-8391;
www.flumegorge.com.
*Open mid-May to Oct
(weather permitting) daily
9–5 (5.30 Jul–Aug).*

Cannon Mountain Aerial Tramway
I-93. Tel: 603/823-8800;
www.cannonmt.com.
Open mid-May to Oct daily.

❸ Franconia

Robert Frost Place
Ridge Road, Franconia.
Tel: 603/823-5510;
www.frostplace.org. *Open
Jun weekends, Jul–mid-Oct,
Wed–Mon 1–5. Closed Tue.*

❻ Mount Washington

Mount Washington Auto Road at Great Glen
Route 16, Gorham.
Tel: 603/466-3988;
www.mt-washington.com.
*Open mid-May–late Oct
(weather permitting).*

Great Glen Trails
Tel: 603/466-2333;
www.greatglentrails.com

Mount Washington State Park
Tel: 603/466-3347;
www.nhstateparks.org.
*Open daily May–Oct, 8–8
(weather permitting).*

Mount Washington Observatory
Tel: 603/356-2137; www.
mountwashington.org.
Open daily 8–6.

❽ Glen

Story Land
Route 16. Tel: 603/383-
4293; www.storylandnh.
com. *Open early Jun, early
Sep to mid-Oct weekends
9–5; mid-Jun to early Sep
daily 9–6.*

9 North Conway
Conway Scenic Railroad
Route 16. Tel: 603/356-
5251; www.conwayscenic.
com. *Open end Apr–Oct.*

Weather Discovery Center
2779 Main Street, Route
16. Tel: 603/356-2137.
*Open end May–Oct daily
10–5. Some weekends rest
of year.*

11 Lincoln
Whale's Tale
Route 3. Tel: 603/745-8810;
www.whalestalewaterpark.
net. *Open early Jun–Sep,
daily 10–6.*

Hobo Railroad
Main Street. Tel: 603/745-
2135; www.hoborr.com.
*Open late Jun to mid-Oct,
daily; weekends mid-May to
mid-Jun.*

For history buffs
New England Ski Museum
Franconia Notch Parkway,
exit 34B. Tel: 603/823-
7177, or 800/639-4181;
www.skimuseum.org. *Open
Jun–Mar, daily 10–5.*

Scenic routes
Mount Washington Cog
Railway
Off Route 302, Bretton
Woods. Tel: 603/278-5404;
www.thecog.com. *Open
year-round.*

For children
Six Gun City
Route 2, Jefferson. Tel: 603/
586-4592; www.sixguncity.
com. *Open end May–early
Sep daily 10–5 (9–6
Jul–Aug).*

i Lakes Region
Association, Exit 23 off
I-93. Tel: 603/744-8664;
www.lakesregion.org

1 Ashland
Pauline Glidden Toy
Museum
49 Main Street. Tel: 603/
968-7289 or 7023. *Open
Jul–Aug Wed–Sat 1–4.*

4 Moultenborough
Castle in the Clouds
Route 171. Tel: 603/476-

2352; www.castleinthe
clouds.org. *Open Sat, Sun in
spring; daily Jun to mid-Oct.*

Loon Center and Markus
Wildlife Sanctuary
Lees Mill Road. Tel:
603/476-5666;
www.loon.org. *Open daily
Jul to mid-Oct; rest of year,
Mon–Sat 9–5.*

5 Wolfeboro
Libby Museum
Route 109. Tel: 603/569-
1035. *Open Jun–Oct daily.*

Wentworth State Park
Route 109. Tel: 603/569-
3699; www.nhstateparks.
org

Wright Museum
77 Center Street. Tel: 603/
569-1212; www.wright
museum.org. *Open
May–Oct, Mon–Sat 10–4,
Sun noon–4; Apr, early Nov
weekends.*

6 Alton Bay
Ellacoya State Park
Route 11, Gilford.
Tel: 603/293-7821;
www.nhstateparks.org.
Open Jun–Aug, 9–dusk.

8 Meredith
Annalee Doll Museum
44 Reservoir Road, off
Route 104. Tel: 603/279-
6542; www.annalee.com.
*Open end May to mid-Oct.
Phone for hours.*

Back to nature
Squam Lakes Natural
Science Center
23 Science Center Road,
Route 113, Holderness.
Tel: 603/968-7194;
www.nhnature.org. *Open
May–Oct daily.*

Scenic Rides
Mount Washington Cruises
Weirs Beach. Tel: 603/366-
5531; www.cuisenh.com.
*Cruises late May–late Oct.
Phone for times.*

Winnipesaukee Railroad
Tel: 603/279-5253;
www.hoborr.com. *Open
late May to mid-Jun week-
ends; mid-Jun to mid-Oct.
daily. Phone to check
timetables.*

i Convention and
Visitors Bureau of Greater
Portland, 245 Commercial
Street, Portland, ME 04101.
Tel: 207/772-5800;
www.visitportland.com

i Southern Midcoast
Maine Chamber of
Commerce, 59 Pleasant
Street, Brunswick, ME
04011. Tel: 207/725-8797;
www.midcoastmaine.com

i Damariscotta Region
Chamber of Commerce,
2 Courtyard Street,
Damariscotta, ME 04543.
Tel: 207/563-8340; www.
damariscottaregion.com

i 2 Park Drive, Rockland,
ME 04841. Tel: 207/596-
0376;
www.therealmaine.com

i Public Landing,
Camden, ME 04843.
Tel: 207/236-4404;
www.camdenme.org

i Main Street, Belfast, ME
04915. Tel: 207/338-5900;
www.belfastmaine.org

1 Brunswick
Peary-MacMillan Arctic
Museum
Hubbard Hall, Bowdoin
Campus. Tel: 207/725-
3416; www.bowdoin.edu.
*Open Tue–Sat 10–5, Sun
2–5.*

Bowdoin College
Museum of Art
Upper Park Row, Walker
Art Building. Tel: 207/725-
3275; www.bowdoin.edu.
*Closed for renovation. Due
to reopen spring 2007.*

2 Bath
Maine Maritime Museum
243 Washington Street.
Tel: 207/443-1316;
www.bathmaine.com.
Open daily 9.30–5.

3 Wiscasset
Musical Wonder House
18 High Street.
Tel: 207/882-7163; www.
musicalwonderhouse.com.
Open Jun–Oct daily 10–5.

Castle Tucker
Lee Street at High Street.
Tel: 207/882-7169;
www.historicnewengland.
org. *Open Jun to mid-Oct.
Tours hourly Fri–Sun 11–4.*

Nickels-Sortwell House
121 Main Street. Tel
207/882-6218;
www.historicnewengland.
org. *Open Jun to mid-Oct,
Fri–Sun, tours hourly 11–4.*

Lincoln County Museum
and Old Jail
Federal Street. Tel: 207/
882-6817; www.lincoln
countyhistory.org. *Open
Jul–Aug, Tue–Sat 10–4;
Jun, Sep Sat 10–4.*

4 Damariscotta
Chapman-Hall House
Main Street. *Open mid-Jun
to mid-Sep, 1–5. Closed
Mon.*

**5 Colonial Pemaquid/
Fort William Henry**
Off Route 130.
Tel: 207/677-2423;
www.friendsofcolonial
pemaquid.org. *Open late
May–early Sep, daily 9–5.*

**6 Pemaquid Light and
Fisherman's Museum**
End of Route 130.
Tel: 207/677-2494;
www.pemaquidlight
house.com. *Open Jun to
mid-Oct, daily 9–5.*

8 Thomaston
General Henry Knox
Museum
Montpelier, junction
Routes 1/131. Tel: 207/354-
8062; www.knox
museum.org. *Open late
May–early Oct, Tue–Sat
10–4, last tour leaves at 3.*

9 Rockland
Farnsworth Art Museum
and Wyeth Centre
16 Museum Street. Tel:
207/596-6457; www.
farnsworthmuseum.org.
*Open daily 10–5 (closed
Mon mid-Oct to May).*

Maine Discovery Center
1 Park Drive. Tel: 207/594-
3301; www.mainelight
housemuseum.com. *Open
Mon–Fri 9–4.30, Sat–Sun
10–4. Closed Sun in winter.*

Practical information

[i] Tourist Information Office

[12] Tour Number

[10] Rockport
Opera House
6 Central Street.
Tel: 207/236-2514;
http://town.rockport.me.
us/operahouse.

Maine Photographic Workshop
Central Street.
Tel: 207/236-8581
www.theworkshops.com

Center for Maine Contemporary Art
162 Russell Avenue.
Tel: 207/236-2875;
www.artsmaine.org. *Open Tue–Sat 10–5, Sun 1–5.*

[11] Camden
Conway Homestead
Tel: 207/236-2257;
www.crmuseum.org. *Open Jul–Aug, Tue–Fri 10–4.*

[13] Pownalborough Courthouse
Lincoln County Historical Association, Route 128, off Route 27. Tel: 207/882-6817; www.lincolncounty history.org. *Open Jul–Aug, Tue–Sat 10–4; Jun, Sep, Sat 10–4.*

Special to…
L. L. Bean
95 Main Street, Freeport.
Tel: 207/865-4761;
www.llbean.com

Fat Boy Drive-In
111 Bath Road, Brunswick.
Tel: 207/729-9431.

Moody's Diner
Route 1, Waldoboro.
Tel: 207/832-7785;
www.moodysdiner.com

Olson House
Hathorn Point Road, Cushing. Tel: 207/596-6457;
www.farnsworth museum.org. *Open Jun–mid-Oct, daily 11–4.*

Recommended trips
Monhegan Island
Monhegan Boat Line, Port Clyde. Tel: 207/372-8848;
www.monheganboat.com

For children
Owl's Head Transportation Museum
Next to Knox County Airport, off Route 73.
Tel: 207/594-4418;

www.ohtm.org. *Open daily 10–5 (4 Nov–Mar).*

Fort Knox State Historic Site
Route 174, off US Route 1, Stockton Springs, near Belfast. Tel: 207/469-7719 (seasonal);
www.maine.gov/doc/parks.
Open May–Oct.

TOUR 22

[i] Convention and Visitors Bureau, 245 Commercial Street, Portland, ME 04101.
Tel: 207/772-5800;
www.visitportland.com

[2] Portland Museum Of Art
7 Congress Square.
Tel: 207/775-6148;
www.portlandmuseum.
org. *Open daily 10–5 (Fri till 9). Closed Mon mid-Oct to late May.*

[3] Children's Museum of Maine
142 Free Street. Tel: 207/828-1234;
www.kitetails.com. *Open Mon–Sat 10–5, Sun noon–5. Closed Mon early Sep–May.*

[4] Maine College Of Art
522 Congress Street.
Tel: 207/775-3052;
www.meca.edu

[6] Wadsworth-Longfellow House
487 Congress Street.
Tel: 207/774-1822;
www.mainhistory.org.
Open May–Oct Mon–Sat 10–5, Sun noon–5.

Maine Historical Society Museum
489 Congress Street.
Tel: 207/774-1822. *Open Mon–Sat 10–5, Sun noon–5. Closed Sun in winter.*

[9] First Parish Church
425 Congress Street.
Tel: 207/773-5747;
www.firstparishportland.
org. *Open by appointment.*

[10] City Hall
389 Congress Street.
Tel: 207/879-0300;
www.portlandmaine.gov.
Open weekdays 8–4.30.

Portland Symphony
Tel: 207/842-0800 (box office); www.portland symphony.com

[14] Milk Street Armory
Portland Regency Hotel, 20 Milk Street.
Tel: 207/774-4200;
www.theregency.com

Special to…
Gritty McDuff's
396 Fore Street.
Tel: 207/772-2739;
www.grittys.com

Portland Observatory
138 Congress Street. Tel: 207/774-5561; www.port-landlandmarks.org. *Open late May to mid-Oct, 10–5.*

TOUR 23

[i] Convention and Visitors Bureau, 245 Commercial Street, Portland, ME 04101. Tel: 207/772-5800; www.visit-portland.com

[i] Bethel Area Chamber of Commerce, 8 Station Place, Bethel Train Station, Bethel, ME 04217.
Tel: 207/824-2282 or 800/442-5826;
www.bethelmaine.com

[i] Rangeley Lakes Region Chamber of Commerce, 6 Park Road, Rangeley, ME 04970. Tel: 207/864-5364; www.rangeleymaine.com

[i] Franklin County Chamber of Commerce, 407 Wilton Road, Farmington, ME 04938.
Tel: 207/778-4215;
www.franklincountycham-berofcommerce.org

[1] Sabbathday Lake
Sabbathday Lake Village
Route 26, New Gloucester.
Tel: 207/926-4597;
www.shaker.lib.me.us. *Open late May to mid-Oct, Mon–Sat 10–4.30.*

[2] Poland Spring
State of Maine Building
Tel: 207/998-4142;
www.polandspringps.org.
Open May–Oct Tue–Sat 9–4, Sun 9–noon.

[4] Trap Corner
Perham's of West Paris
194 Bethel Road, Routes 26 and 219. Tel: 207/674-2341. *Open daily 9–5; closed Mon, Tue, Jan–Apr.*

[8] Rangeley
Rangeley Historical Society Museum
Main Street. Tel: 207/864-5647. *Limited opening hours; phone ahead for information.*

Wilhelm Reich Museum
Dodge Pond Road, off Route 4/16. Tel: 207/864-3443; www.wilhelmreich museum.org. *Open Jul–Aug, Wed–Sun 1–5; Sep, Sun 1–5.*

[9] Kingfield
Stanley Museum
School Street. Tel: 207/265-2729; www.stanley-museum.org. *Open Tue–Sun 1–4 (Tue–Fri 10–4, Nov–May).*

[10] Farmington
Nordica Memorial Homestead
Holley Road. Tel: 207/778-2042. *Open Jun–early Sep, Tue–Sat 10–noon, 1–5, Sun 1–5.*

[11] Washburn-Norlands Living History Center
290 Norlands Road, Livermore Falls. Tel: 207/897-4366;
www.norlands.org. *Phone ahead to confirm opening times.*

Back to Nature
Maine Wildlife Park
Route 26. Tel: 207/657-4977; www.maine.gov/ifw.
Open mid-Apr to mid-Nov, 9.30–4.30.

INDEX

177

Index

Index & Acknowledgments

The Automobile Association
wishes to thank the following libraries and photographers for their assistance in the preparation of this book.

ALAMY 79 (Jon Arnold Images); 105 (Mike Briner); 146 (Cosmo Condina); 74/5 (Florida Images); 108/9 (Dennis Hallinan); 138 (Robert Harding Picture Library Ltd); 34, 37, 62b, 63, 72, 91, 150/1 (Andre Jenny); 72/3 (Photofusion Picture Library); 139a (Miro Vrlik Photography); MARY EVANS PICTURE LIBRARY 8a, 8b, 56a, 56/7; TOM MACKIE 59, 83, 92, 94/5, 95, 118/9, 120/1, 142, 143, 144/5, 153, 154/5, 154b, 157, 165; MAINE OFFICE OF TOURISM 148, 149; PICTURES COLOUR LIBRARY 9; RHODE ISLAND ECONOMIC DEVELOPMENT CORPORATION 84, 85; SPECTRUM COLOUR LIBRARY 6, 11, 44, 82/3, 97; TANGLE-WOOD (BOSTON SYMPHONY ORCHESTRA)/STEVE LISS 33; STOCK MARKET 26/7 (Jean Miele MCMXCII); YALE UNIVERSITY 68, 70.

All remaining pictures are held in the Association's own library (AA World Travel Library) with contributions from the following photographers:
C COE 31, 32/3, 38, 81, 86, 86/7, 103, 111, 126, 136/7, 137; R HOLMES 2, 14/5, 18, 29b, 30, 34/5, 36, 39b, 40, 41, 43, 45, 47, 50a, 53, 54, 55, 60, 61, 62a, 66, 76, 78/9, 122, 123b, 124, 125, 130/1, 132/3, 140; J LYNCH 12, 13, 19a, 19b, 20; M LYNCH 4, 5, 7, 23, 25, 27, 28, 29a, 39a, 50b, 52, 58, 64, 65, 67, 70, 80, 88, 89, 92/3, 96, 98, 99, 100, 101, 102/3, 104, 106, 106/7 110, 112/3, 113, 114, 115, 117, 120. 123a. 127, 129, 131, 132, 135, 139b, 145, 147, 154a; T LYNCH 116; C SAWYER 10, 17, 42, 51; J WILLIAMS 57.

Contributors
Copy editors: Larry Dunmire, Karen Bird   **Indexer:** Marie Lorimer
Thanks also to **Kathy Arnold** and **Paul Wade** for their updating work on this book.

Atlas

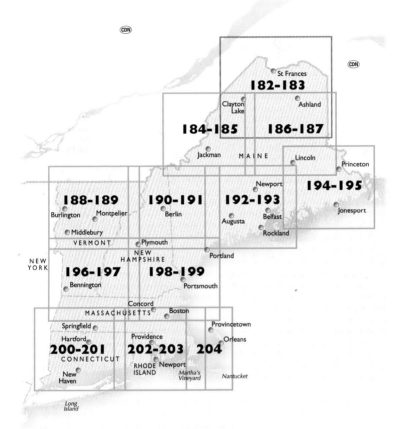

CDN

St Frances
182-183

Clayton
Lake

Ashland

CDN

184-185

186-187

Jackman

M A I N E

Lincoln

Princeton

Newport

192-193

194-195

188-189

190-191

Jonesport

Burlington

Montpelier

Berlin

Augusta

Belfast

Middlebury

VERMONT

Plymouth

Rockland

NEW
YORK

NEW
HAMPSHIRE

Portland

196-197

198-199

Bennington

Portsmouth

Concord

MASSACHUSETTS

Boston

Provincetown

Springfield

Providence

Orleans

Hartford

200-201

202-203

204

CONNECTICUT

New
Haven

RHODE
ISLAND

Newport

Martha's
Vineyard

Nantucket

Long
Island

Toll-free motorway	5 101 134 Road numbers	Built-up area
Toll motorway	International boundary	National park
Highway	State boundary	● Town / Attraction
Main road	Admin boundary	
Secondary road	✈ International airport	

182-183 0 10 20 30 km / 0 10 20 miles

184-204 0 10 20 30 km / 0 10 20 miles

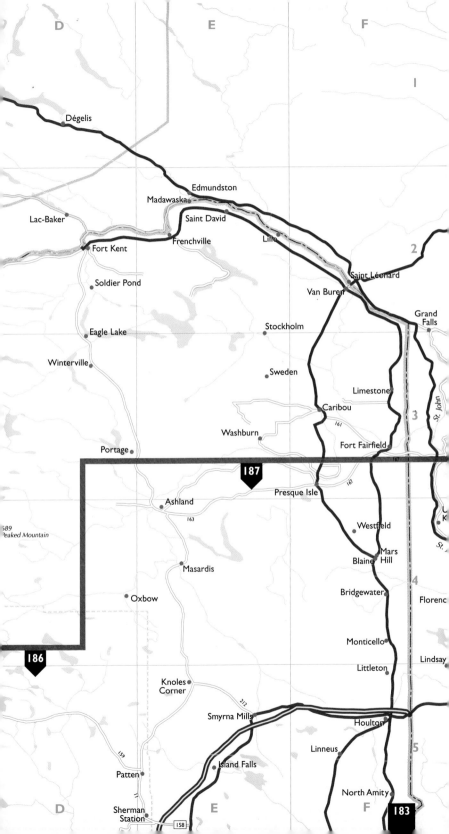

Saint-Henri

Saint-Philémon

Scott

Frampton

Sainte-Justine

QUEBEC

Saint-Joseph-
de-Beauce

Saint-Prosper

Saint-Georges

Courcelles

Lambton

Saint-Sébastien

Jackma

Mégantic

Lowelltown

Woburn

Eustis

A

191

B

C

Stratton

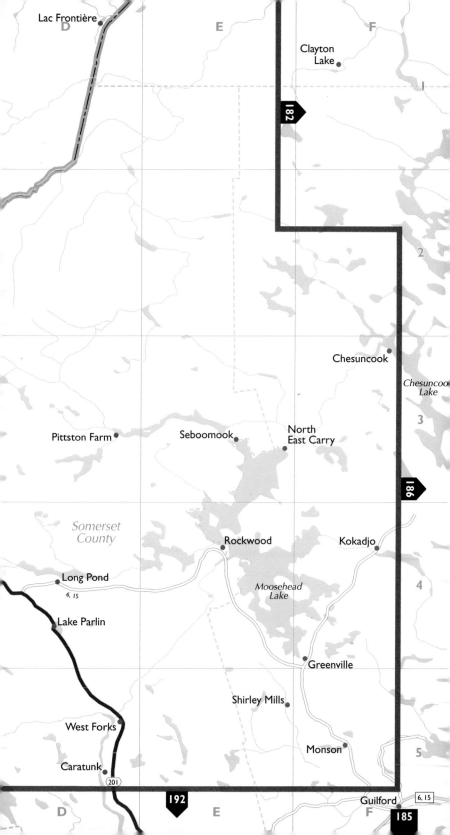

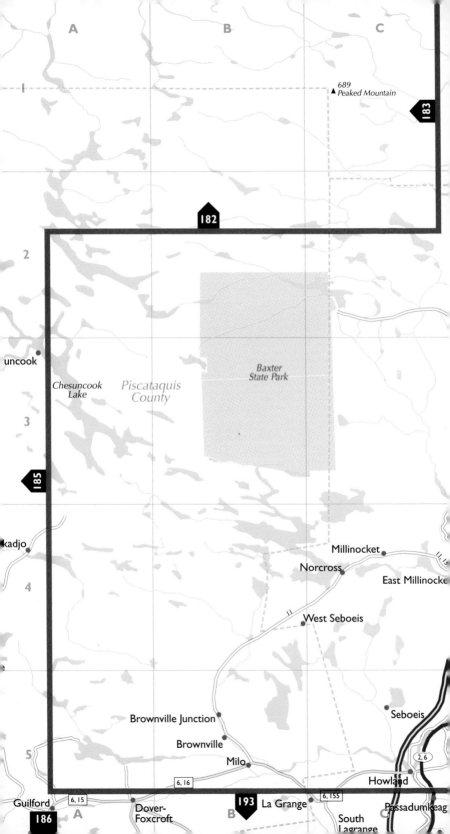

A   **B**   **C**

183

689
▲ *Peaked Mountain*

182

2

Baxter
State Park

uncook

*Chesuncook
Lake*

*Piscataquis
County*

3

185

kadjo

Millinocket
11, 15

Norcross

East Millinocke

4

11

West Seboeis

Seboeis

Brownville Junction

Brownville

5   Milo

2, 6

Howland

6, 16

Guilford   A   6, 15   B   **193**   La Grange   6, 155   C   Passadumkeag

186   Dover-
Foxcroft

South
Lagrange

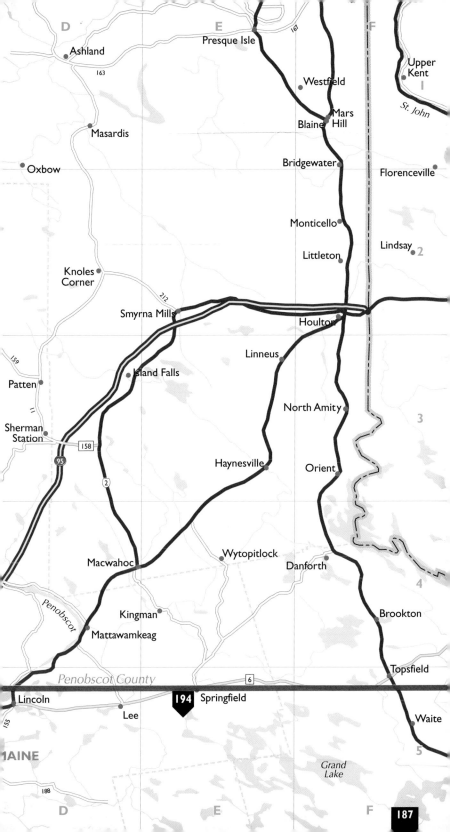

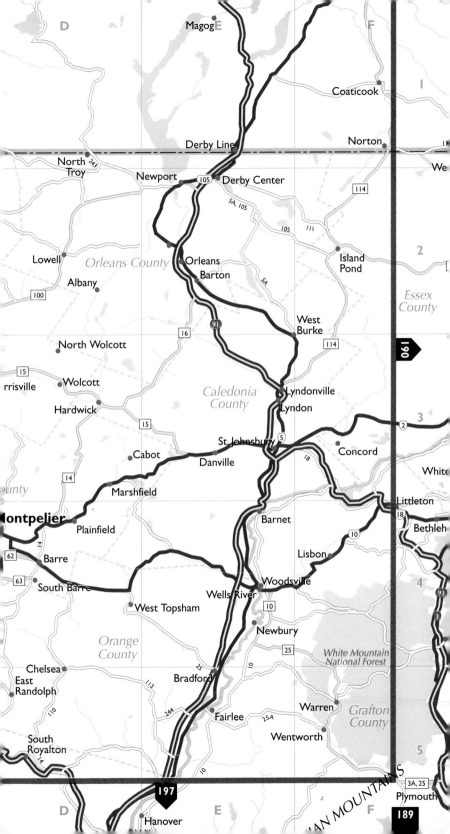

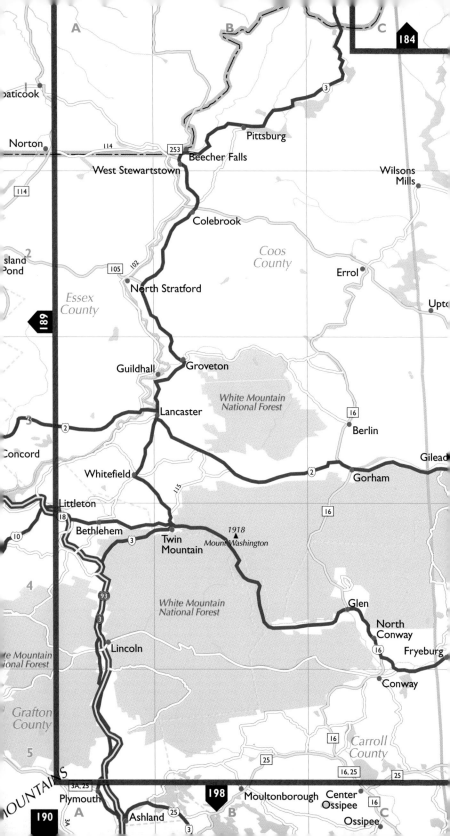

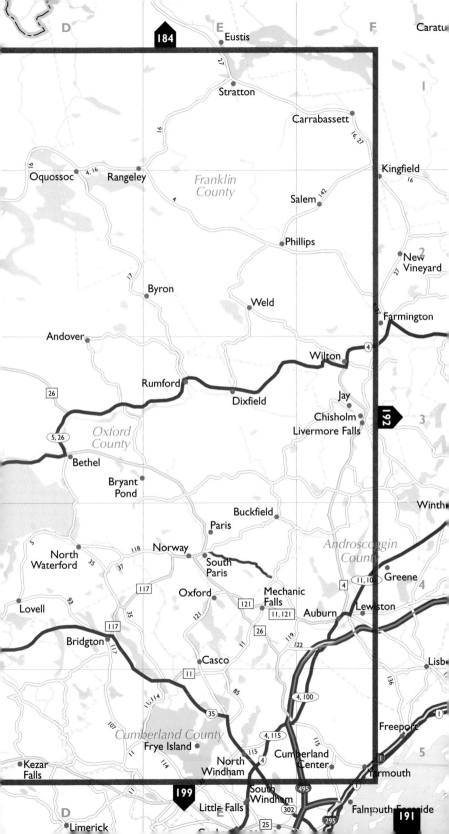

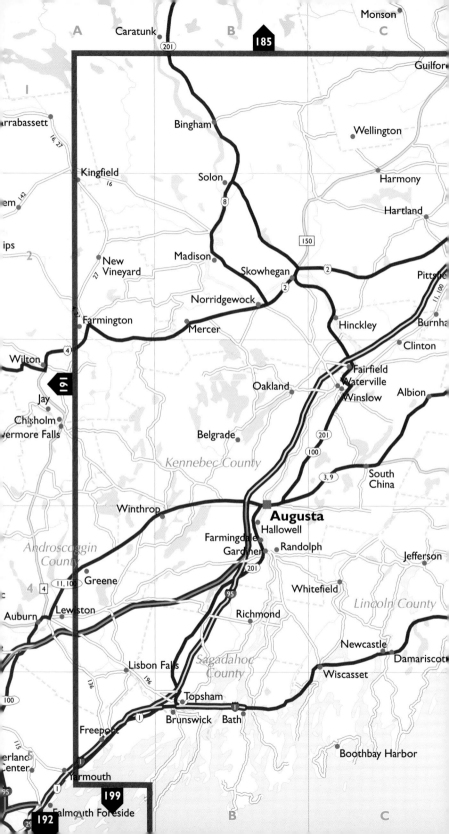

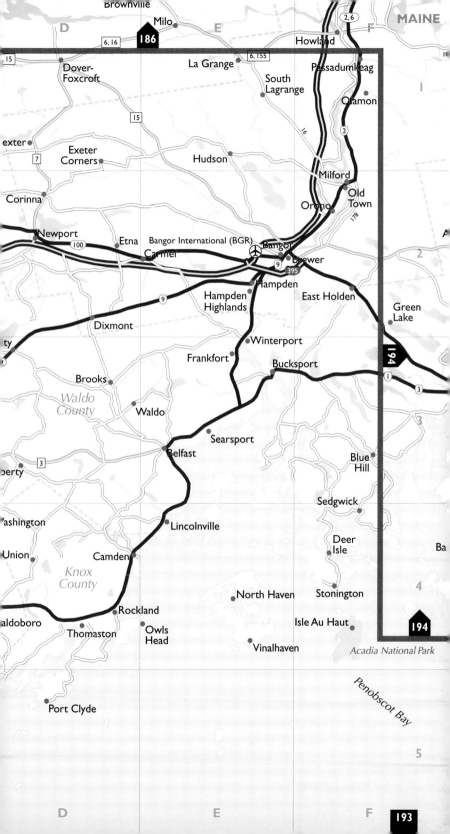

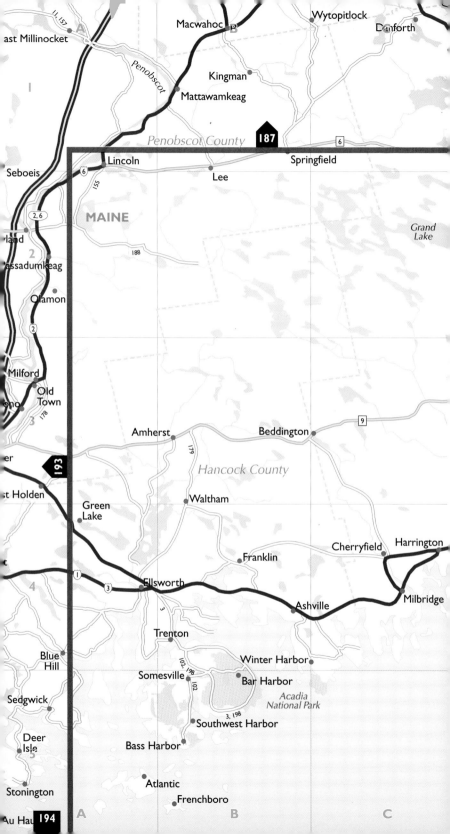

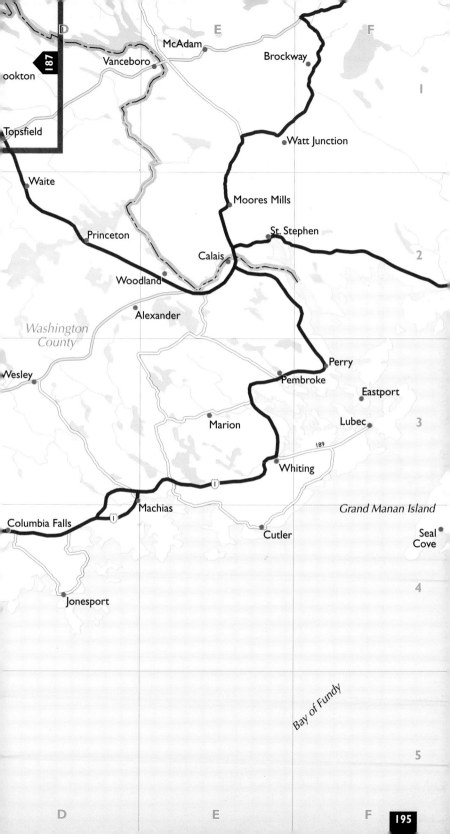

ookton

Topsfield

McAdam

Vanceboro

Brockway

Waite

Watt Junction

Princeton

Moores Mills

Woodland

St. Stephen

Calais

Alexander

*Washington
County*

Wesley

Pembroke

Perry

Eastport

Marion

Lubec

189

Whiting

Grand Manan Island

Machias

Columbia Falls

Cutler

Seal
Cove

Jonesport

Bay of Fundy

D

E

F

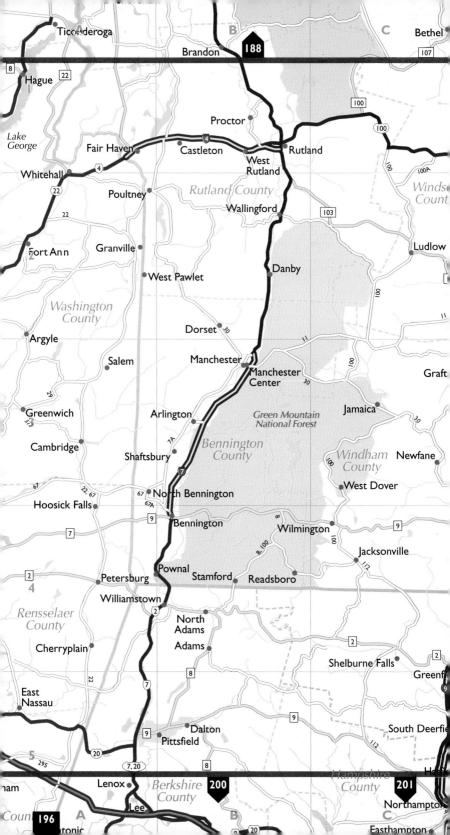

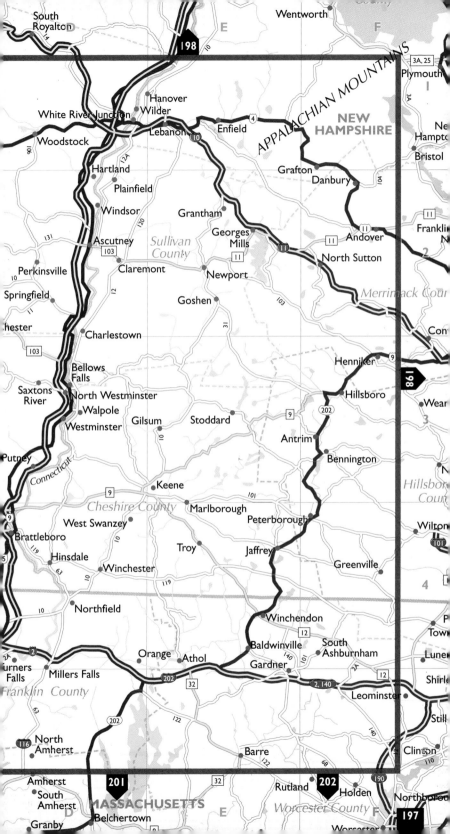

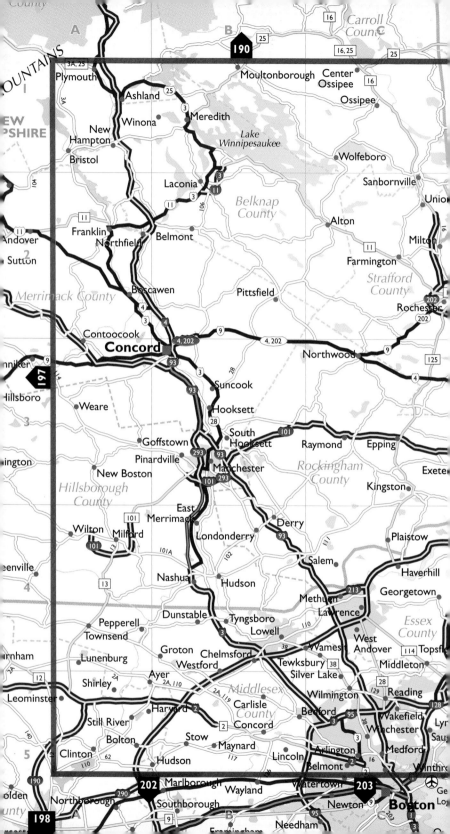

Cumberland County

Frye Island

Kezar
Falls

191

North
Windham

E

115

4, 115

Cumberland
Center

115

F

Freeport

Yarmouth

South
Windham

495

Little Falls

Falmouth Foreside

114

Limerick

Gorham

25

302

Westbrook

295

Portland

Bar
Mills

4

Portland International (PWM)

South Portland

Scarborough

Cape Elizabeth

York
County

202

I

Springvale

Alfred

111

Saco

Old Orchard Beach

2

Sanford

Biddeford

South Sanford

109

9

Kennebunk

11

North Berwick

9

Kennebunkport

Berwick

Rollinsford

Ogunquit

16

Dover

urham

Eliot

Cape Neddick

3

South Eliot

York Harbor

Newmarket

4

Kittery

101

Portsmouth

IA

Rye Beach

51

Hampton

Amesbury

Salisbury

110

Newburyport

113

IA

4

Rowley

Pigeon
Cove

Ipswich

Rockport

Hamilton

Essex

Wenham

128

Gloucester

Beverly

Manchester

Salem

Marblehead

Swampscott

Massachusetts
Bay

5

Edward Lawrence
ernational (BOS)

203

D

E

204

F

199

ull

North Cohasset

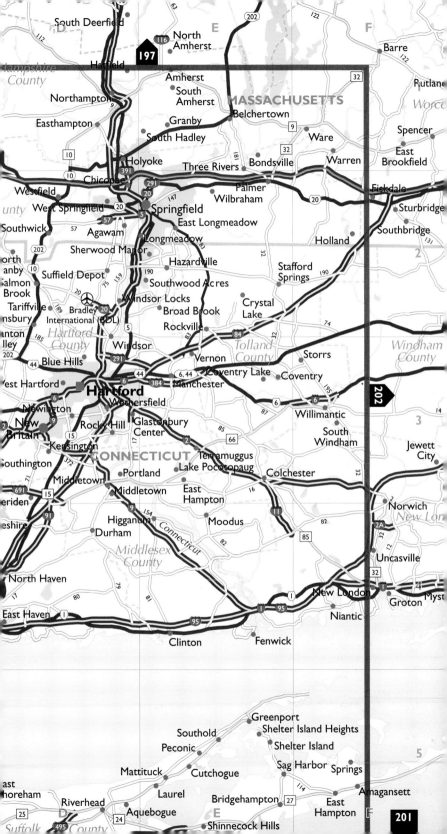

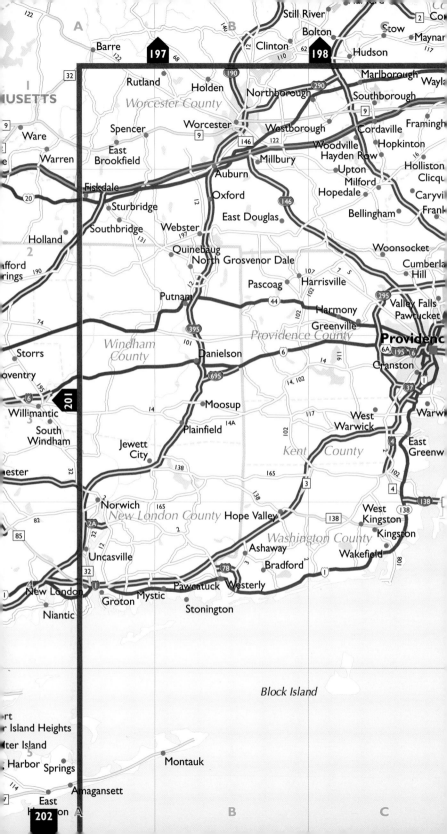

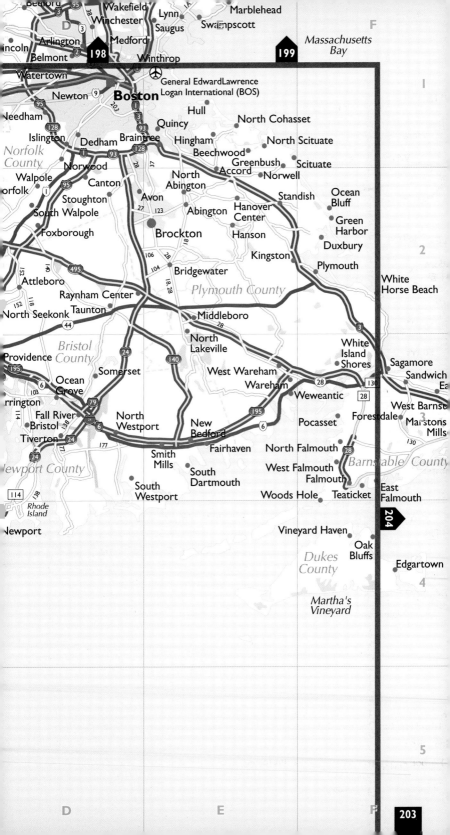

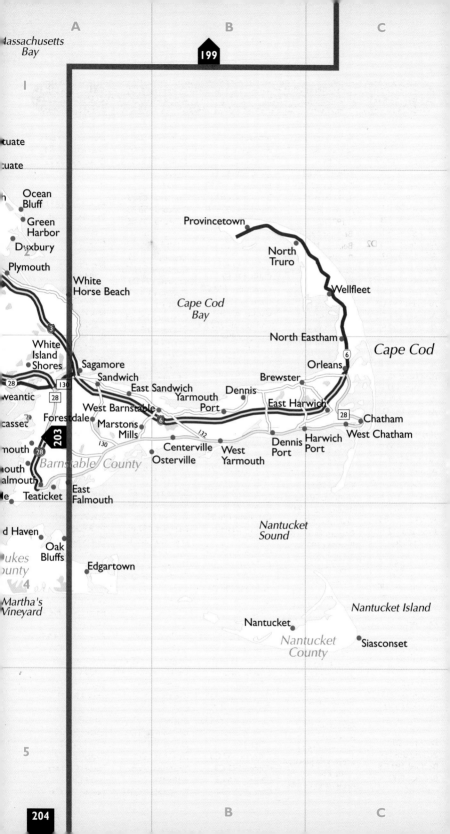

Massachusetts
Bay

I

cuate

cuate

Ocean
Bluff

Green
Harbor

Duxbury

Plymouth

White
Horse Beach

Cape Cod
Bay

Provincetown

North
Truro

Wellfleet

North Eastham

Cape Cod

Orleans

3

White
Island
Shores

Sagamore

Sandwich

Brewster

Dennis

28

weantic

28

East Sandwich

Yarmouth
Port

East Harwich

Forestdale

West Barnstable

6

28

Chatham

203

Marstons
Mills

132

Dennis
Port

Harwich
Port

West Chatham

mouth

28

130

Centerville

West
Yarmouth

Barnstable County

Osterville

mouth
almouth

Teaticket

East
Falmouth

Nantucket
Sound

d Haven

Oak
Bluffs

ukes
ounty

4

Edgartown

*Martha's
Vineyard*

Nantucket Island

Nantucket

Siasconset

*Nantucket
County*

5

Atlas Index